A NORTHWOODS COMPANION

Spring and Summer

by John Bates

Illustrated by April Lehman

Manitowish River Press, Mercer, Wisconsin

A NORTHWOODS COMPANION
Spring and Summer

II

Printed in the United States on 50% recycled paper.

Editor: Greg Linder
Illustrations: April Lehman
Cover photography: Jeff Richter
Book design: Jerry Lehman
Cover design: Katie Miller

Publisher's Cataloging in Publication Data
Bates, John, 1951-
    A northwoods companion: spring and summer /
    written by John Bates; illustrated by April Lehman.
    Includes bibliographical references and index.
    ISBN 0-9656763-0-7 (softcover)
    1. Natural History
    2. Seasons
    3. Nature Study
Library of Congress Catalog Card Number: 97-70781
09876543
Third Printing 2003

Published by: Manitowish River Press
                4245N Hwy. 47
                Mercer, WI 54547
                Phone: 715-476-2828
                Fax: 715-476-2818
                E-mail: manitowish@centurytel.net
                Website: manitowish.com

For Mary, Eowyn, and Callie.

THANKS to:

Greg Linder for his editing prowess and his willingness to answer endless publishing questions, Jeff Richter for his superb photography and work on the cover design, April Lehman for her wonderfully creative illustrations and kind spirit, Jerry Lehman for taking over the design process and giving the book the right look, Katie Miller for her cover design creativity, Chad McGrath for advice and counsel, Tom Joseph for believing in the project, Nancy VanBeest for her poetic input, the Lakeland Times for publishing "A Northwoods Almanac," and a host of DNR personnel who have tried to answer all the questions I've had over the years.

Thanks must also be given to the many people who have hiked, canoed, and explored with me over the years. They have contributed to my continuing education, and it is their wisdom that I try to reflect back in these pages. And thanks go to all the people who have phoned or written me with their sightings. Without them, I would have much less a sense of what really transpires in this place we call the northwoods.

Special thanks go to my wife Mary who still has the contagious enthusiasm of a child, and the eyes and heart of a wonderful naturalist.

Grateful acknowledgment is made to the following for permission to reprint previously published material:

Abbey, Edward. From *A VOICE CRYING IN THE WILDERNESS* by Edward Abbey. Copyright © 1989 by Edward Abbey. Reprinted by permission of St. Martin's Press Incorporated.

Adams, Richard. Reprinted with the premission of Scribner, a Division of Simon and Schuster from *WATERSHIP DOWN* by Richard Adams. Copyright © 1972 by Rex Collings Ltd.

Berry, Wendell. Excerpt from "The One-Inch Journey" from *THE UN-FORSEEN WILDERNESS* by Wendell Berry. Copyright © 1991 by Wendell Berry. Reprinted by permission of North Point Press, a Division of Farrar, Straus & Giroux, Inc.

Borland, Hal. From *BOOK OF DAYS* by Hal Borland. Copyright © 1976 by Random House, Inc. Reprinted by permission of Random House, Inc.

Carrighar, Sally. From *HOME TO THE WILDERNESS*. Copyright © renewed 1973 by I.C.E. Ltd. Reprinted by permission of Houghton Mifflin Co. All rights reserved.

Carson, Rachel. From *THE SENSE OF WONDER* by Rachel Carson. Copyright © 1956 by Rachel L. Carson. Copyright © renewed 1984 by Roger Christie. Reprinted by permission of HarperCollins Publisher, Inc.

Dillard, Annie. From *A PILGRIM AT TINKER CREEK* by Annie Dillard. Copyright © 1974. Used by permission of HarperCollins Publishers.

Hubbel, Sue. From *BROADSIDES FROM THE OTHER ORDERS* by Sue Hubbel. Copyright © 1993. Used by permission of Random House, Inc.

Isherwood, Justin. From "Of River, Time and Steerage," *Wisconsin Natural Resources Magazine*, (March, 1982), by Justin Isherwood. Used by permission of Justin Isherwood.

Kappel-Smith, Diana. From *WINTERING*. Copyright © 1979, 1980, 1982, 1983, 1984 by Diana Kappel-Smith. Reprinted by permission of McIntosh and Otis, Inc.

Leopold, Aldo. From *A SAND COUNTY ALMANAC: AND SKETCHES HERE AND THERE SPECIAL COMMEMORATIVE EDITION* by Aldo Leopold. Copyright © 1949. Used by permission of Oxford University Press.

Pielou, E.C. From *THE WORLD OF NORTHERN EVERGREENS*. Copyright © 1988. Permission gratefully acknowledged from Cornell University Press.

Stegner, Wallace. From *THE SOUND OF MOUNTAIN WATER* by Wallace Stegner. Copyright © 1969 by Wallace Stegner. Used by permission of Doubleday, a division of Bantam Doubleday Dell Publishing Group, Inc.

Steinhart, Peter. From "Eavesdropping in the Wilds," *Audubon Magazine* (November, 1989), and "Tough Times," *Audubon Magazine* (July, 1981), by Peter Steinhart. Used by permission of Peter Steinhart.

Welsch, Roger. From "Why God Put Mosquitoes on This Earth." With permission from *Natural History* (July, 1991). Copyright © the American Museum of Natural History.

Contents

7 June 1-15

Sex in the Pines; Yellowing Pines; Ephemeral Wildflowers; Lilacs in Bloom; Cotton in the North Country; Naming Flowers; Highbush Cranberry; Northwoods Tomatoes and Black Ash Leaves; Migratory Stopovers; Breeding Ducks; Not-So-Common Terns; Whip-poor-wills; Sandhill Cranes; Killdeer; The Man in Red and the Value of Baths; A Hummingbird's Appetite; Loon Hatchings; Surveying Frogs; Gray Tree Frogs; Dragonfly Metamorphosis; The Mosquito Army; Zap Your Bug Zapper; Life's Tough for a Turtle; Black Terns and Yellow-headed Blackbirds; Caprice; Fish Spawning Draws Eagles; Of Fawns and Adult Deer; A Big Appetite; The Long Lake Monster; Northern Lights; Aroundthebenditis; An Answer to How We Can Tolerate Long Winters; Sightings; Final Notes on Ice-out

8 June 16-30

Summer Solstice; Important Mosquitoes in History; Sexing Mosquitoes; Deerfly Strategy; Clean Water Isn't Always a Good Thing; Spittlebugs; Northwoods Tigers; Duped by a Duck; Big or Little Families?; Pleased to Meet You; Common Warblers; Yellow-Bellied Sapsuckers; Robins Nesting; Summer Bird Feeding; The Turtle River; Black Bear Mating; Swimming Red Squirrels; Bracken Ferns; Grasslands; Swamps, Bogs, Marshes, and Shrub-Carr; Breathing Underwater; Lupines; Phenology; Clear Water: Why Here and Not There?; The Cold Summer of 1992; Mercury; Hope Versus Assurance; Moon Deception; Hiking with Children; Sightings

9 July 1-15

July 4th; We're Cool; Discrimination: The Good Kind; Osprey Development; Grouse Gizzards; Canada Geese; July Flowers: Bog Orchids; Pitcher Plants: Bog Carnivores; Columbines; Old-growth Pines; Bryozoans; Blue Flag Iris; Night Fires; Glowworms; Mayfly Madness; Dragonfly Eyes and X-Rated Behavior; Moose; Endangered Species in Wisconsin; Floods and Trees

Introduction

To everything there is a season, and a time for every season under heaven.

A Northwoods Companion is the edited compilation of over seven years of biweekly columns that I have written for the *Lakeland Times* in Minocqua, Wisconsin. The column, called "A Northwoods Almanac," has tried to capture the phenology of the Northwoods. The study of phenology, or the orderly timing and progression of natural events, produces an awareness of the cycles of life around us. Observing over the years that wild strawberries almost always come ripe around June 20, or that the first male red-winged blackbird can be expected to return right around March 20, provides a sense of orderliness to the natural world and a feeling of very pleasurable expectancy.

Observing and noting the dates of bloomings, birthings, fruitings, and fledgings is the first step in gaining an understanding of our flora and fauna. The second step is to try to discover why the timing of the event occurs when it does, and what factors influence the timing to vary annually. No natural event I know of occurs on the same day every year. That exactness exists only in the world of clocks. The natural world is no more static than we humans are, though it can be predictable within certain ranges. How each event ties together with other processes and events can be a fascinating dance to try to comprehend. Expect the unexpected, never say never, and never say always, are three rules to take to heart in observing this world.

This book tries to bracket natural events in the Northwoods into two-week periods when it is reasonable to expect the events may occur. Money-back guarantees are not part of the deal though. The

Northwoods covers a lot of territory, from Minnesota to Maine, with an infinite array of variables like soil types, temperature, rain, and historical disturbance to take into account. Wildlife in particular are seriously challenged in their reading skills, so they frequently act independently of books and science (plants are much more accommodating, but still independent). So while the two-week periods are generally accurate parameters, they are no more set in stone than humans having babies exactly after a nine month pregnancy. The odds are higher, but they are odds after all, and not absolutes.

A Northwoods Companion is written as an informational jump-starter. Only a few sections are in-depth explorations of a species or an ecological process. My intent is to excite you with the possibilities of what can be experienced, and to generate your willing participation in the most wonderful of pastimes - exploring. I'm good at "poking around," a skill that is usually drummed out of us at an early age, and one that doesn't tend to generate much income as an adult. If I had to encourage readers of this book to learn one thing, it would be to learn to poke around. Take your time. Go slow. Get down on your hands and knees and dig around. Sit in one place for an hour at a time and let the world come to you.

Going slow is hard for an active society hellbent on collecting experiences. We're inundated with the "been there, done that" approach to life, and we nearly always confuse quantity of experiences with quality of experience. While I'm sure I would greatly enjoy traveling and "seeing the world," I've discovered more than enough universe near my doorstep in which to travel.

This almanac tells you some of what takes place in the Northwoods at any given time, but it doesn't come with a front row ticket to the play. The actors on this stage wish for anonymity. It is up to you to discover the theater, and then to be a quiet spectator. The detective work is part Sherlock Holmes, part undercover cop, and more often than not for me, part Inspector Clouseau. That's why when the discoveries come, they are so rich and so greatly appreciated.

In my column, I've written about my family's explorations throughout the Northwoods, and I've acted as a bulletin board for the sightings and experiences of other watchers of the Northwoods, and reported their stories. This book is full of their observations and marvels, big and little, as well as my own. These moments are all part of the northern fabric, and together they begin to represent how the whole cloth may be stitched together.

Will you find everything in this book that you should know regarding any time period in the Northwoods? Not even remotely so. I learned a while back that the more knowledge you gain, the more knowledge you realize is out there to be gained. If you bring humility to the woods with you, you will see and hear more and more, but the canvas upon which you are gazing will only grow larger and more intricately drawn. There's a lifetime and more of exploring to be done in the Northwoods. I hope this book helps bring to you some clarity and pleasure in this process.

A companion fall and winter guide to the Northwoods is also available.

<u>XII</u>

The world cannot be discovered by a journey of miles, no matter how long, but only by a spiritual journey, a journey of one inch, very arduous and humbling and joyful, by which we arrive at the ground at our feet, and learn to be at home.

- Wendell Berry

MARCH

*T*he Ojibwe word for March is bobakwudagime'gizis, or "the broken-snowshoe month," in reference to March's usual ice-coated snow conditions that often abrade away snowshoe lacings and even the wooden frames. The typical crusted snow of March may wreak havoc on your snowshoes, but skate skiers dream of such conditions. The hard-packed snow of March offers easier access to more back country than is found at any other time of the year.

March is transition time in the northwoods, and many scenarios are possible. An early snow-melt can spell disaster for the white-furred snowshoe hares, whose winter camouflage can become an explosion of contrast against dark ground. An extended snow season can place great stress on mammals that need fresh greens and calorie-saving warm temperatures. An on-again, off-again winter/spring carousel ride can capture early arriving migrants in the grasp of a week of heavy snow and cold that kills.

Sometime in March, the snow deflates and compresses into a heavy mass, the physiological equivalent of the psyche of those who are now tired of winter's occupancy. As the month progresses, ice fractures and turns black with age. Water, with an ice sheet sandwiched between, often stands on top of water, as snows begin to melt on the uplands and drain into channels. Springtime often seems like it will never come, but with the breakup of the winter shell, it is commencing, however slowly.

MARCH 1-15

March 1 to March 15

Alice in Wonderland

March is a month of optimistic promises and charming gestures. The spring equinox occurs on March 21, so spring will certainly arrive by then, right? If you believe this, you probably expect to win the lottery tomorrow.

As the March hare in Alice in Wonderland said to Alice, "Have some wine."

Alice looked at the table. There was nothing on it but tea. "I don't see any wine," she remarked.

"There isn't any," replied the Hare.

The month of March leads us on like the March hare, playing to our dreams of the wine of spring—gardening, wearing shorts, swimming, and hiking. The mirage beckons, but the reality of winter persists.

We aren't the only ones fooled. More than a few birds have hastened up north, only to be literally buried in a spring snowstorm.

> ## March Musings
>
> *I don't want to miss spring this year. I want to be there on the spot the moment the grass turns green. I always miss this radical revolution; I see it the next day from a window, the yard so suddenly green and lush . . . This year I want to stick a net into time and say "now" . . . But it occurred to me that I could no more catch spring by the tip of the tail than I could untie the apparent knot in the snakeskin; there are no edges to grasp.*
>
> -Annie Dillard

The word "spring" comes from the Old High German *springan*, meaning "to jump," and from the Greek *sperchesthai*, meaning "to hasten." I wouldn't recommend following through on a literal interpretation of the terms.

Poets, too, get carried away by the illusion of March. Chaucer described March as "the month in which the world began, when God first made man."

Tennyson exulted: "All in the wild March morning, I heard the angels call."

It's important to note that neither of these guys lived in the northwoods.

Mary and I tend to get carried away with our enthusiasm, too, even though we clearly recall our lessons from previous Marches. We start to plan our canoe, biking, and backpacking trips; we talk about how we'll build this, where we'll visit, and God knows what else. The winter ice is weakening within us, but we need to keep things in perspective and proportion. Although March has toyed with us before, its song is hard to resist.

Reproduction: March Madness

We tend to think of March and April as transitional months of very little activity. That may be true for humans, but there's plenty going on in the animal world. Most mammals are either mating, gestating, or birthing during this period. Animals can't afford to wait to mate until the weather warms and the flowers are blooming, because their young would not be born until June or July—often too late for all the growing that must happen before the young of the year face their first winter.

Every animal has evolved a period for mating, a period of gestation, and a time for birth. In the squirrel family, gray squirrels have their first litter in March, while red squirrels mate in March and give birth in April. Northern flying squirrels mate in April and give birth in May. Within the dog family, red foxes give birth to their kits in late March and early April, while coyotes produce young in April. Timber wolves mate in March and birth in May.

In the weasel family, nearly all members use delayed implantation to govern their breeding cycle. Mink breed in early March and employ a short delayed implantation, giving birth in late April and early May. Striped skunks likewise breed in March, but give birth a little later in May than mink. Martens, ermines, and long-tailed weasels use an intermediate delay, breeding in July but giving birth in late April to early May. The longest cycle of delayed implantation belongs to fishers and river otters—a cycle that keeps the females perpetually pregnant. Both otters and fishers breed in April. Three hundred and fifty days or so later, the females give birth. Then they promptly breed once again.

March courtship displays are hard to catch, but they're magical when found. Ravens show off their flight skills in courtship loops and dives. Snowshoe hares mate, the males "thumping their hind feet on the crust, bouncing in circles, and even flipping and twisting high into the air," as Minnesota naturalist Denny Olson has written. Male grouse begin to drum out messages to females. Chipmunks emerge seeking a partner to court, the male singing at the den entrance to his chosen female in the hope she will like the song.

If the weather warms, male redwing blackbirds and robins will appear one morning, as if a wand had been waved across the land. Their songs will jolt human spirits into an expression of thanks for a winter that is losing ground—no matter how much we humans like to ski.

Saw-whet Owls
Perching near Porches

Doug Jardine, a friend from Cornucopia in Bayfield County, WI, called me one night on the last evening of February. Doug held out his phone and said, "Identify this bird." I could clearly hear a dinging sound, one of our most unusual bird calls, and a dead giveaway for identification purposes. It was a saw-whet owl, calling from just beyond Doug's porch. As we were talking, Doug mimicked the bell-like call. The owl flew right over his head, landing on a bare branch where he could watch it in his porch light. Some guys have all the luck. I've never seen one, though I've heard them many times, and here Doug stands on his porch, probably in his slippers, and sees one perch 15 feet away.

Saw-whets usually don't migrate back through our area until early March, so Doug's sighting was particularly unusual. Our mild, nearly snowless winter in 1994-95 may have encouraged this saw-whet to stay throughout the winter; or it may have returned a week or two earlier than usual.

Saw-whets nest from mid-March to late April, usually in deciduous tree cavities 25 to 50 feet up. They are found in considerable numbers here in Wisconsin's northern counties, but they are so secretive that documented records are hard to come by. Listen at night for their soft, monotonous, bell-like, toot-toot-toot-toot call. They actually have a variety of calls in their repertoire. One is a wail. Another, a "challenge call," is a soft, catlike whine or yelp. Saw-whets stop calling in May, once the breeding season is over.

Listening for Great Horned Owls

In early March, I often hear great horned owls hooting late at night. They are our earliest nesting bird, generally sitting on nests by mid-February. Their deep, resonant "woo hoo-hoo, hoo, hoo, hoo" is quite common throughout Wisconsin. Wisconsin wildlife biologist Frances Hammerstrom writes, "Unless you live deep in the city, there is probably at least one horned owl within two miles of your home." It's as good a call as any to hang your spring hat on. It means winter is losing the war, though it may yet win a number of battles.

Do Not Try This in Your Own Home

More so than at any other time during the winter, owls seem to be on the move in March. Maybe that's because we humans are outside more to see them as the weather slowly begins to warm. One March day I saw two owls—a great horned and a barred owl. The barred owl was kind enough to sit tight in an old yellow birch, allowing me to observe it for a long time. Its body faced away from me, yet its head faced toward me, as if its head were on backward. Owls can swivel their heads 245°; this one turned its head that full range several times— a humorous and remarkable phenomenon to watch.

Short-eared Owls Flocking

Joan Elias, an excellent birder who lives near Gurney, told me about an area in southern Door County where 70 short-eared owls were seen during the last few months of winter in 1994-95. Joan visited the site in late February, and saw about 25 in one day. Short-eareds are the only Wisconsin owl that "flocks," although the term is actually inaccurate. Rather, these owls hunt together in areas that are rich in rodents, so it only appears that they are flocking. Otherwise, they're solitary birds. Dawn and dusk are considered the best times to see short-eareds, but they will hunt throughout the day in warm, calm conditions.

Ideal hunting grounds for short-eareds are large, weedy fields, meadows, and prairies that harbor meadow mice. They fly low like a northern harrier, and often share winter hunting sites with harriers. Their flight is buoyant, often referred to as "moth-like."

Short-eareds usually winter in southern Wisconsin and farther south. However, if the snow cover in the north is thin, they may move northward to take advantage of rodent-rich, open country. Once found, they can be watched from a nonintrusive distance over the course of many afternoons, because they often stay put in an area for months.

$\underline{7}$

Starlings, the First Songbirds

A couple from Sayner spotted a pair of starlings at their suet feeder one February 25th, the earliest sighting I've heard of in this area. A late February thaw with warm and strong southerly winds must have blown the starlings in, a migration they undoubtedly regretted when winter returned for its usual six weeks after that. In the spring, starlings are usually our first "songbird," though I hate to dignify them with such a title.

Most commonly, starlings appear in the second week of March. One sighting on March 4, 1992, when the Manitowish River opened up below our house, was atypical. This was the earliest sighting of starlings we have experienced during our years of keeping records. The ice-out was accompanied that night by the first incongruous thunderstorm of the year. A number of starlings visited our feeder the next day, and crows returned as well, though both species could have used common sense and waited for a few weeks. On March 15, the temperature dropped to -10°F, a bit nippy for these early migrants.

Starlings are seldom greeted with enthusiasm, even when they are the harbinger of spring. Introduced in 1890 by a man who wanted to bring all the birds mentioned in Shakespeare's writings to America, the starlings' first North American nest was built under the eaves of the American Museum of Natural History, near Central Park in New York City. They gradually spread to Milwaukee by 1923, filtered north to Ashland, WI, by 1936, and made it to California by 1942. The number of winter roosts in Milwaukee in 1981 exceeded 200,000.

Here in the northwoods, we don't feel the enormous impact of starlings as much as southern areas do, because starlings prefer open areas and shun deep forests. However, the starling ranks third in abundance in Wisconsin behind the red-winged blackbird and the house sparrow, another introduced species. Their abundance is indicative of how much of the state is no longer forested; in fact, their remarkable population growth resembles the success of another generalist species, Homo sapiens.

The name starling means "little star," apparently due to the speckled, starry spots on the bird's otherwise dark feathers. In spring, the starling's bill turns yellow, and the body is a shiny black. Bluebirds, flickers, purple martins, and great crested flycatchers would undoubtedly rather see this star go nova, because the starling is highly aggressive and often successful in competing for nesting holes.

Geese Returning

Look for Canada geese to return to the northwoods from March 10 onward. The earliest I've ever heard one was on March 13, when a goose flew over our house one morning, honking continually as if it was leading a band.

Wintering Robins

Our first robin should return around March 20, depending on the weather and the bird's state of sobriety. One winter I saw a newspaper clipping from Cleveland, OH. The writer was having difficulty understanding where all the robins had gone that generally over-winter in Ohio. Their Christmas Bird Count totaled 21,000 birds, but the tally included very few robins—quite unusual for the area. The absentee robins serve to illustrate the infidelity of winter birds to particular areas, and they're an equally good example of how geographically dependent the word "common" is when bird species are involved.

9

Courting Ravens and Returning Crows

At this time of year, ravens are in the midst of their courtship flights. The male flies with his wingtip touching the female's, and the birds often dive to earth like falcons or tumble over and over in the air. The result of such acrobatics is a mate for life.

Crows usually return in the first few weeks of March. To tell ravens and crows apart, look at their comparative size. Ravens are much larger than crows. Another quick way to tell the difference is to look at the tail. The crow's tail is nearly squared off, while the raven's is long and wedge-shaped. Since I can never remember this distinction, my wife Mary came up with the memory trick I need for recalling which bird is which. Remember that a squared tail equals "squarecrow," as in scarecrow.

Members of the crow family, which includes ravens and jays, are reputedly the most intelligent among birds. Crows have been known to count up to three or four, solve puzzles, perform feats of memory, and quickly learn to associate noises and symbols with food. They even appear to have a language of their own that includes 23 different calls, each with a distinct meaning. Crows are also known as good mimics. They can whine like a dog, squawk like a hen, cry like a child, and laugh like an adult human. Birds are the only animals, excepting humans, able to make sounds they were not born to make.

Courting Eagles and Talon Clasping

Eagles return to their nests to begin courtship flights in March. It's all a well-timed reproductive race, formulated and practiced over thousands of years, aimed at pushing the edges of survivability and ensuring reproductive success. The eaglets need 75 days after hatching before undertaking their first flight, followed by several months of flight time during which they learn the hunting skills required of an independent youth. Until the lakes open up, the breeding adult eagles scavenge carrion or fish the open waters around dams and along the few open streams.

10

Courtship displays and territorial encounters often involve spectacular talon clasping and tumbling through the air. The Northwoods Wildlife Center in Minocqua received a call one spring from the manager of a cranberry bog in the Manitowish Waters area. Two eagles had locked talons in an aerial duel, tumbling into a maple tree. By the time the call was forwarded to Jackie and Dave DeBauche and they were able to reach the site, two hours had passed. The eagles were still there. One eagle hung below the other and held its wings wide open, while the eagle on top had closed its wings. In Jackie's words, both looked "pretty silly." Dave rapped on the tree with the end of his net and, rather anti-climactically, the eagles split apart. Both then flew away, apparently no worse for the wear.

Talon clasping occurs with some frequency and seems to be the eagle equivalent of arm wrestling for territorial rights. Linda Thomas, an avid birder from Plum Lake, watched a pair lock together one spring and tumble groundward, only to separate 100 feet above the ground, almost as if they were playing a form of "chicken."

Hugh Seeley, who owns a cabin on the Manitowish River near Boulder Lake, wrote to describe a remarkable talon-clasping scene he witnessed. Hugh heard a nonstop cry of eagles coming from down on the ice. Upon investigating, he saw three eagles, one immature and two adults. The two adults were lying side by side on the ice with their wings somehow interlocked, and in Hugh's words, they were "constantly talking to each other." The immature eagle flew immediately upon seeing Hugh, but he watched the adults through his binoculars for over an hour, until it became too dark to see them. They were gone the next morning.

Most likely their talons were locked in a territorial dispute, though courtship is another possibility. An eagle may attack another eagle from above. The one below will flip over and flash its talons at the attacker. The talons occasionally interlock, and the birds may tumble through the air. These two eagles were probably engaged in a fight that neither was willing to concede. Ron Eckstein, an eagle bander and wildlife manager from Rhinelander, found two adult eagles dead one spring—one on St. Germain Lake and one on Trout Lake. Both had received injuries consistent with territorial battles. As eagles continue to increase in numbers, territories become more condensed, fostering potentially deadly disputes.

Merlin Nests

Department of Natural Resources personnel put up several merlin nests on the Flambeau Flowage in early March of 1991. Merlins don't build their own nests, but commonly use an abandoned crow's nest. The DNR's system involves "borrowing" an old crow's nest and placing it in the highest fork of a pine tree along a shoreline. One merlin pair nested in such a construction along the flowage in the summer of 1990, fledging two young. Unfortunately, the DNR later received a tag from one of the two immatures, which had been shot in Alabama during the winter. Unlike males of most bird species, the male merlin maintains nest fidelity, so the same male was expected back on the flowage nest with a new female mate. He never returned either.

The merlin is a small, fast falcon common to the boreal forests of Canada, but it only occasionally nests into northern Wisconsin. These birds seem to be on the increase in our area, but perhaps we are simply paying more attention to their presence and "discovering" nest sites that have been here all along. Merlins aren't the least bit secretive around their nests. They often scatter tiny carcasses of numerous songbirds below the nest site, testimony to the merlins' exceptional hunting abilities. Because they dine on songbirds, their presence is usually regarded as a mixed blessing.

11

Shrieking Shrikes

Northern shrikes inhabit this area during the winter, and we often spot them at our feeder into March. The birds breed in the northern parts of Canada and Alaska, generally moving as far south in winter as the northern tier states of the U.S. During invasion years, they may be recorded well south of here. No pattern has yet been detected in their invasions, so no one can predict years in which the shrikes may be numerous.

Research on radio-tagged northern shrikes indicates that they occupy very large territories, averaging 530 acres. They inhabit their territories for about three months each year. Because the territories are so large, shrikes are often hard to relocate; thus we often assume they have left an area in which they've been seen. Northern shrikes seem to prefer brushy, woody habitats in winter, shunning agricultural areas and open fields due to the lack of prey. As our spring migrants begin moving in for their mating and nesting periods, the shrikes likewise begin moving north to their breeding areas.

The cries of a shrike may be heard when a hawk circles overhead. Linnaeus thought that the cries might be a warning to small birds, but I'm baffled as to why a small bird would listen to a shrieking shrike when the shrike will eat it just as readily as the hawk. Shrikes aren't called the "watchful butchers" without reason.

I'm hoping one day to see a shrike take a bird. I've watched them give chase, but I've never seen one close the deal. They are said to be exceptionally good at darting through thick brush to capture large insects and birds. Naturalist John Muir wrote of their ability to kill gophers by striking them on the back of the head.

12

Turkeys and Pheasants
in the Northwoods?

Jack Bull from the Winchester area called one winter to report that he had seen a cock pheasant and some turkeys. Al Wisniewski from the Boulder Junction area had also spotted some turkeys (avian types) during the same winter. How can this be? Their official range barely reaches into central Wisconsin.

Turkeys and pheasants have not suddenly evolved into winter lovers; nor is there evidence to indicate that they are breeding in our area. The sighted birds were probably escapees or "liberated" individuals. There are apparently a few people who believe that the northwoods should be stocked with turkeys and pheasants. If the DNR won't do it, they will. It reminds me of the old "Free Huey Newton" movement, but with an avian twist. However, the birds are best adapted to the climate of central and southern Wisconsin. So if you see a turkey or pheasant, put it on the next bus south.

13

A Peppering of Snow Fleas

Lennert Bakken, who has lived on the Manitowish River chain since 1918, wrote asking about snow fleas. He says he has seen them in the snow around wooden posts, or even in his tracks on mild, sunny March days. What are these little specks, he wanted to know?

Snow fleas belong to an order of insects called springtails, which have springing organs that hurl them into the air, allowing them to sail for a few inches before they land. Generally much less than one-fifth of an inch in length, each snow flea resembles little more than a black dot on the snow surface. When hundreds creep up onto the snow, the base of a tree may look like someone has shaken pepper around it. In this case, though, the pepper jumps around. This natural seasoning may include up to 10 million individuals per acre, and densities of 500 to 50,000 snow fleas per square meter are common. Springtails are particularly abundant in acidic soils, which are common in our area.

Springtails eat mostly decaying plant material, performing an important role in the decomposition food web along with the unsung hosts of mites, spiders, bacteria, fungi, ants, beetles, isopods, milli-pedes, earthworms, snails, and others who convert 90 percent of the dry matter dropped by forest plants over the year into soil. Like other cold-blooded animals, snow fleas prefer sunny locations near dark bodies that absorb heat. That's why you'll find them in the microcli-mates that surround trees and posts.

The Sweet Tooths
of Red Squirrels and Porcupines

14

Bill Laut, a retired DNR warden near Minocqua, has often watched red squirrels in March lick and chew at maple sap that they have "tapped" from sugar maples. The red squirrels and flying squirrels at Bill's place also visit sapsucker holes in maples and birches, in order to drink the oozing sap. He has also witnessed red squirrels chewing on the pitch of young white pines, most often those trees infected with white pine blister rust. Neither of us have a good hypothesis to explain why squirrels chew infected pitch.

Bill has watched the red squirrels go to the same sugar maple trees (among many other sugar maples) every year. They seem to know the difference between red maples and sugar maples, and they can ap-parently locate sugar maples with high sugar concentration. Their pow-erful sense of smell may allow them to "grade" the sap quality, but who knows?

More interesting yet, Bill noted that porcupines sometimes wander into his area and eat the bark of the very same maples. What is it about these maples that is so attractive? How do the porkies know these are the prime maples? Porcupines do have a highly developed sense of smell. Because one of their main food sources is inner bark, perhaps it's not so surprising that they can determine the sweetest maple trees.

Otter Screams

Roy and Cora Mollen of St. Germain wrote to describe an encounter with an otter on the Big St. Germain River, which flows behind their home. The river stays open in all but the coldest winter weather, and the Mollens frequently watch otters and muskrat feed and frolic. One morning though, they listened to an otter that sat on the shoreland ice, calling or "singing" for nearly a half an hour. "The call was high-pitched, almost like a shrill whistle," they wrote. "It was loud enough to hear it in the house 150 feet away, on top of a hill. We first thought of it as a painful call, but perhaps it was a mating call."

The literature on otters says these animals emit a high-pitched scream during a fight or mating, but whether this particular otter was seeking love or battle only it can say.

Otters commonly give birth to their young in March. The litter size is usually two to four, and the cubs are tiny, about eight inches long. Otter dens are most often located along the bank of a stream or lake, with the main entrance underwater, below the ice line.

15

Implants

Female badgers usually "self-impregnate" in March. No, they're not the animal equivalent of the Virgin Mary. They mated back in September, but the embryo doesn't implant until early March, in order to ensure that the young will be born between late April and early June. Black bears, fishers, otters, and others also use delayed implantation to optimize the survival of their young.

March Snowshoeing

In mid-March of 1991, after what had been a nearly snowless winter, we went 'cross river on our first snowshoe hike of the year. "'Cross river" means a trek into the Manitowish River Wilderness Area, 6,200 acres of wild lands. Two-thirds of the wilderness is wetlands not too hospitable to the human foot. There are some big pines on the sandy uplands along the river, though the term "uplands" must be understood in the context of the Manitowish area. Uplands around here often rise little more than a few feet above the wetlands, but that's all it takes for shallow-rooted species like pines to obtain a good foothold.

That day our most interesting sighting was the dried flowerhead of a pitcher plant, chock-full of seeds. I rather foolishly brought some of the seeds home, but how would I simulate a bog habitat in my sandy garden? I don't think the rhubarb and strawberries would appreciate the change.

We walked on top of a beaver lodge and wondered what it must be like in there after four months of close cohabitation. We decided we didn't want to know. Beaver mate in February, so our rooftop hiking probably didn't interrupt the one major event of their winter. Later, walking in a small forest on the other side of the lake, we saw a number of small red maples that were the obvious victims of these beaver last fall.

The only downside of snowshoeing in our pine woods is the omni-presence of hazel shrub. Invariably I get whipped across the face by their supple stems; or lose my hat to their clutches; or get my snow-shoe impaled on a stem and sprawl forward on my face. It's the typi-cal predicament of any woodsperson. You can't look all directions at once, and the inquisitive hiker looking up and all around is bound to take a few missteps.

The upside of snowshoeing is the ability to travel anywhere, uncon-fined by ski or snowmobile trails, through country often inaccessible in the summer. With snowshoes it's nearly impossible to get lost, thanks to those large footprints that remain behind wherever you go. And it's gloriously quiet.

Exploring the Virtues of Inaction

One of the joys of living in the northwoods is looking at maps and realizing how much public land there is to explore. Mary and I are famous (among ourselves, that is) for becoming nearly paralyzed by the task of deciding where to go. One weekend, after our usual lengthy consideration, we settled on snowshoeing across Tucker Lake to the Round Lake wilderness area in the Chequamegon National Forest. A remnant 40-acre, old growth hemlock/yellow birch stand was our goal, and we found it—a victory in itself because we don't always find what is on the map. A cross-country ski trail also passes through the stand and follows most of the perimeter of Round Lake.

We also had the opportunity that weekend to ski in the Sylvania Wilderness Area in Michigan's Upper Peninsula. Sylvania consists of 17,000 acres of old growth timber, some of it up to 375 years old.

Both of these stands remind me of a talk given years ago by Freeman Tilden, an author and naturalist, to the Association of Interpretive Naturalists. He discussed his principle of "the constructive aspect of inaction," or "the virtue of not doing something." Tilden observed that our lives are "directed as much by what we have not done as by what we have done." Occasionally, he said, we are "providentially protected by our inaction." In the realm of natural resources, he applied his philosophy by noting that we preserve resources mainly through inaction. Tilden was quick to acknowledge the reasonable fear that a world of inaction would lead to stagnation. Not to worry, according to Tilden. Humans "crave to be doing something—usually something unwise." There are multitudes of people who "want to do something about something—so there will be no atrophy."

Sylvania and the old growth stand at Round Lake were providentially protected by constructive inaction. By not doing something to these forests, the previous owners took a wonderful action. Tilden said the state of non-doing is a state of doing. He offered a few slides in his talk: Examples of a pristine lake where a road and lakeside homes were not built; of a mountainside where a ski lift had not been installed; of a waterfall where a dam had not been built; and all because of constructive inaction.

One slide depicted an organizational chart for the hypothetical agency Tilden wished to form—The Agency of Planned Inaction, headed by an executive "with a talent for not doing things, as a way of life. A man, you might say, never weary of not doing." The Agency would have two branches: the Branch of Tentative Negation, which would include two offices, one of definite postponement, and the other of indefinite postponement; and the Computer Branch, with enough ab-

17

sent parameters to guarantee coming to no conclusions about any-thing.

I quote Tilden to point out how lucky we are to have left some old growth in the north country. Much of what is left is due to those who had the wisdom to preserve. For the northwoods, I think Tilden's principles mean we need to look hard at our pace of growth and decide whether action or inaction would be the most constructive. As writer and wilderness proponent Edward Abbey observed, "Growth for the sake of growth is the ideology of the cancer cell."

Exploring Bogs

The bogs and wetlands of the North are often best explored in March, while they are still frozen and much of the snow cover is gone. Travel on snowshoes or, if you're lucky and the snow is way down, in your winter boots. One of the trees you should examine closely is the tamarack, our only deciduous conifer. Actually, all of our conifers are deciduous, but on a longer time scale. All conifers lose their needles over the course of several years. Tamarack takes a quicker course, dropping all of its needles in one fell swoop in late October.

Dominant bog dwellers like tamaracks and black spruce have some-how developed a liking for the cold, acid, nutrient-poor conditions offered by a bog. Life in the sphagnum moss mat of the bog is tough, with all sorts of conditions that make mere survival quite difficult. For example, tree roots can only penetrate a short distance into the spongelike moss, making the possibility of being toppled by the wind very real. Another difficulty emerges as the peat mat builds up on top of itself. Decay organisms are unable to do their job in such an acidic, cold environment. Tamarack has adapted by producing new roots from the main trunk, which are above the earlier roots.

Tamaracks need full sun to survive and won't grow in their own shade. A bog, with its extremely poor tree growth, is a good place to find plenty of sun. Those trees that do survive usually grow very slowly. Cut a small sapling in an area with good reproduction sometime—you might discover that a six-foot tree is 80 years old. Tamaracks can grow on upland sites, and in better conditions they will grow much more quickly.

Enjoy the bogs now. They're nearly impassable from spring through fall.

Ashes to Dirt

Mary and I have been lugging ashes from our woodstoves onto our compost pile for as many winter seasons as we've had a garden. We do this as much to cover up the "fresh goodies" from our kitchen as to improve the soil. I figure we haul a full bucket every week or two, each bucket weighing about eight pounds; this means we add about 80 pounds to our compost pile every winter. The question is, are the ashes doing our soil any good?

On the N-P-K scale, wood ashes come in at 0-1-7, which means they have no nitrogen, a little phosphorous, and a good dose of potassium (potash). Although this indicates that ashes are an unbalanced fertilizer, it doesn't mean they are not beneficial. Potassium aids in photosynthesis; it helps increase plant hardiness against cold and disease; and it strengthens stem and root systems. Wood ash also contains trace minerals like copper, zinc, and magnesium, which play useful roles in the garden dramas enacted every summer.

19

Ashes help break down organic matter, making them an important addition to the grapefruit halves and banana peels in the compost heap. The ashes also raise the pH of soil, like lime does. Because much of the Lakeland area has acidic, sandy soils that pines and blueberries tend to enjoy, a higher pH is often desirable. One gardening source advocates adding about three pounds of ashes per 100 square feet of garden if the pH is less than 6.0. Adding too much ash puts into play the old adage of "too much of a good thing is a bad thing." Soil that is too alkaline can be just as problematic as soil that is too acidic. So be sparing.

Plants vary in their pH desires, so selective application of ashes is the wisest approach. Check a good gardening book for plant specifications.

As for using ashes as a pesticide, many gardeners claim ashes repel cabbage root maggots, cutworms, and snails and slugs.

Arctic Owls

Jeff Richter, a friend and photographer from the Mercer area, traveled west on March 12, 1996, to St. Croix County, where he photographed four great gray owls. The owls he saw were just a few of the many that had moved south in February and early March, apparently in response to the deep, crusted snow that made hunting for rodents in the snowpack nearly impossible. There were great gray reports from northern counties like Pierce, Burnett, Taylor, and Forest counties, but the reports from Wood, Green Lake, Manitowoc, and Milwaukee counties were real surprises. Iowa even recorded its second record of a great gray.

Like just about every other animal that March, owls experienced very difficult feeding conditions. A good indicator was the arrival of barred owls at backyard bird feeders. Mark Pflieger from Harshaw called while he was watching a barred owl eating suet from his feeder. The owl had spent over two weeks hanging around his feeder, perched on a red pine branch only 25 feet from his window. One afternoon, Mark watched a gray squirrel run up the tree and sit within inches of the owl without provoking more than a blink of the owl's eye. Mark had hung deer ribs up all winter for the birds. The barred owl also hung and fed from the ribs.

Reports of owls dead from starvation came from Park Falls and Vilas and Oneida counties. Six boreal owls were found that winter in Wisconsin, all but one of them dead. One boreal was seen at a bird feeder in Mellen, but was found dead the next day. Vole numbers were apparently down, and in any case the owls couldn't get to a vole in three feet of crusted snow.

Blue Jay Courting

Roy Mollen of St. Germain wrote with this observation of blue jays. "One day I observed a jay in a nearby tree and another gathering seeds from the ground. The 'gatherer' brought a seed to the one perched in the tree. The one in the tree proceeded to crack open the seed. The gatherer soon returned with another seed. Then the perched jay gave the gatherer the bare seed and received another in return to crack open. The jay in the tree was apparently an observer of predators or a mate, but was duly rewarded."

Roy was possibly watching the male feed the female in a process known as courtship feeding, though it seemed early for the jays to be courting. The male jay commonly feeds the female throughout the day during courtship. The female may fluff her feathers out when she receives the food, or simply call. The male usually hops toward the female, touching his bill to hers, then transferring the seed and hopping off. Researchers believe that courtship feeding not only serves a pair-bonding function, but also provides the female with an important nutritional benefit. The female may stop hunting for food, possibly because she is getting too heavy with eggs to hunt efficiently. Or, as one writer says, the male may be "increasing his own chances of reproductive success by keeping her fat and healthy."

One study included an observation of several jays that were feeding and guarding an old, worn, and partly blind jay. The healthy birds also led the enfeebled jay to water. Many species of birds help one another. One researcher has counted 130 species worldwide that help members of their own kind.

21

March Musings

The happiest life has the greatest number of points of contact with the world, and it has the deepest feeling and sympathy with everything that is.

-Liberty Hyde Bailey

March 16 to March 31

Spring Equinox

The first day of spring arrives every year between March 20 and March 22, which means we should theoretically experience equal periods of day and night. In northern Wisconsin, though, conditions are not quite so equal. The sun will actually rise near 6:01 a.m. and set near 6:10 p.m., granting us nine extra minutes of daylight. Given the usual continuation of cold weather well into April, I doubt that anyone complains.

On the equinox, the sun rises precisely in the east and sets precisely in the west. Ancient cultures used these dates to determine absolute directions,

and to align monuments to the sun. The Egyptian pyramids at Giza, the massive stones at Stonehenge, Mayan temples in Guatemala, and American Plains Indians medicine wheels are all thought to have been celestially aligned in reverential praise of the sun.

The problem with the spring equinox is that the weather gods of the northwoods seldom listen to the official demarcations of any seasonal beginning or ending. Late March temperatures can rise into the 50s, ushering in the first round of mud. Or we can get buried in another foot of snow.

From this day until the summer solstice, the sun rapidly gains staying power—over three minutes a day. By March 27, we will enjoy 12 hours and 32 minutes of daylight; by April 5, 13 hours of daylight; by April 24, 14 hours of daylight.

River Steam

Steam rises every cold March morning from open lakes and rivers, in repeat performances from the fall, when the air is also colder than the water but working hard to form ice. The rime frost on the alder and willow in the marshes, backlit through the curling steam by a rising sun, makes early morning awakenings worth savoring.

Hopkins Law

How soon will spring occur in the northwoods compared to southern Wisconsin? We can accurately predict the date of the first bloom of our spring flowers based on Hopkins Law, which says that phenological events vary at the rate of one day for each 15 minutes of latitude and one day for each 100 feet of altitude. (Phenology is the study of the seasonal march of observable biological events—when the first robin returns, when the first trillium blooms, etc.) If we compare biological events in Madison to those in Manitowish, there should be a 21-day interval between the two areas, given their distance apart (about 250 miles) and differences in elevation.

How did I come up with that figure? One degree of latitude is about 69 miles, and since 15 minutes is one-fourth of a degree, we can say spring moves north at a rate of about 17 miles per day. It should therefore take spring about 15 days to reach me from Madison (250 divided by 17). But because Manitowish is in the Northern Highlands region, higher in altitude (1,600 feet) than areas in the south (about 1,000 feet), we have to add an additional six days to the total. Thus, it takes about 21 days for spring to reach us, marching at an average rate of nearly 12 miles per day.

The long and short of this is: If a friend in Madison calls to say she saw her first robin, I can expect to see my first robin in about three weeks. I offer no money-back guarantees on this formula, but several studies have shown it to be quite accurate. Variations do occur along the Great Lakes, where the weather is moderated by cool waters. The figures are also considered valid only up to June 1, when other factors take control, like available sunlight, soil conditions, and rainfall.

Facing South

South-facing slopes are usually snow-free in late March, while north slopes may still hold several feet of snow. The microclimates of each of these slopes is significantly different. The south slopes receive the most solar energy, contributing to a 50 percent higher evaporation rate, higher soil and air temperatures, lower soil moisture, and greater extremes of temperature and moisture. Studies indicate that temperatures may be 60°F higher on south slopes. The extra heat gives these slopes a head start in snow melting and spring growing, but it creates less favorable growing conditions for plants in summer.

25

One Crust That Won't Ease Starvation

By late March, deer trails in the northwoods often take on the look of a highway; buds are rare commodities on browsable shrubs and saplings. If the snow is crusted, it can support lighter-weight mammals. But if the deer leave their well-worn trails, they often break through the crust, cutting their ankles and then often struggling in the snow. Getting off the trails into unbrowsed areas may be essential for their survival, so deer often face a no-win situation at this time of year.

Wild Creeks

Many creeks are open by late March, or they may have just a crust of ice over free-flowing water. My wife Mary found this to be true even in January, when one morning at -30°F, she broke through the ice while crossing what appeared to be a frozen creek. "You just can't trust creeks," she has concluded. Maybe that's part of their attraction. I tend to forget just how interesting creeks can be. They aren't named after states or famous people or generals or chiefs, and they aren't found in travel brochures or recreational magazines. Most folks don't know whether to call them streams, brooks, or creeks. Canoes are seldom launched down them. In this area, even their names seem to be afterthoughts: Swamp Creek, Lost Creek, Beaver Creek, Four Mile Creek, Hay Creek. Hardly sufficient to ignite thoughts of romance and adventure.

We are fortunate in the north country, because we still have pristine creeks to follow. In developed areas, creeks are often considered impositions, convenient waste carriers, or a threatening source of 50-year floods. Since creeks aren't covered by legislation that protects wild and scenic rivers, who is out there protecting them?

Get a good topo map of most any northwoods area. Creeks are veining just about everywhere. Author Peter Steinhart wrote, "A creek may pluck one's imagination and bear it away like a drifting leaf. And helpless, we may trundle along after it, delighted by its liquid babble, dazzled by the leap and sparkle of sunlight on water. Creeks lead one on, like perfume on the wind."

I hope my canoe is soon drifting down a series of little creeks I have always wondered about on the maps. The water is usually high in March, the vegetation is low, and spring is in the wind. It's time to set out.

March Mountain Biking

Late March is a good time of the year for exploring snowmobile trails on mountain bikes. Mary and I go out on the trails once they've turned back to frozen dirt. It's fun to bike through alder swamps and tamarack bogs. We headed out briefly one weekend in 1991 and met a snowmobiler who just didn't want to accept the fact that the snow was gone. He did a triple take as he went by. I guess bikers weren't on his list of expected sights. A snowmobiler blasting through frozen mud wasn't on our list, either.

A Bird in the Hand

Mary and I both went out to our bird feeder in late March of 1991 and fed the chickadees out of our hands. The previous year I had six pine siskens going after seed in my hand at one time. Chickadees are a bit more circumspect. They sit there and study you for a while before they come in. I like the feel of their little claws holding onto my fingers. I momentarily indulge myself in the delusion that the chickadee and I have crossed the boundaries of speciation and are somehow communicating.

Nest Thieves

Mary and our youngest daughter Callie, guided by our friend Jeff Wilson, skied one late March on the Flambeau Flowage to an abandoned eagle's nest. Surprise of surprises—a great horned owl had taken up residence, flying from the nest when they caused a little commotion nearby.

Studies of great horned owl nests have shown that they rarely if ever build their own nests. They prefer to commandeer the previously owned nests of red-tailed hawks, crows, and great blue herons, sometimes even nesting amid the heron rookeries. This probably reduces the sleep comfort level of the heron community, because great horned owls eat virtually everything known, including major predators like hawks and other owls.

Gray Jay Saliva

Gray jays seldom seem to frequent feeders, but we have had them at our feeder during late March. Most gray jay pairs have built their nests by mid-March, and are sitting on two to five eggs. Hatching is possible by the end of March. Much like woodpeckers, gray jays have abnormally large salivary glands that secrete a mucouslike fluid. The secretion coats the tongue, so food will adhere to it when the jay probes into crevices and conifer cones. More remarkably, gray jays use the sticky substance to mold food particles together into a ball. In what amounts to an innovation unique to the gray jay, the food balls can then be adhered to a surface like a twig or a needle, making the hiding of food an easier proposition.

Look for nesting gray jays in northern cedar swamps, and less frequently in spruce and balsam trees.

Pishing

This is a good time of year to "pish" for birds. I pished in a little spruce bog, and within 30 seconds a flock of redpolls and chickadees flew in, landing in nearby trees. Pishing involves slurring the word "pish" over and over again. Many birds are attracted to the sound and will fly in to check you out.

Loon Scouts

If the weather stays mild in late March (the chances of this are nil, but we can dream), and if the lake ice begins to give a bit, watch the skies for loon "scouts." Loons usually show up within hours of ice-out on their nesting lakes, and biologists believe that they fly back and forth daily to check out the ice conditions. Their uncanny ability to appear on a lake so soon after ice-out can only be explained by their daily scouting.

How to Find Rare or Unusual Birds

If you're at all like me, you may get out to do some birding now and again, but you don't go out every day. Nor do you have the time to thoroughly tramp one area (much less several) to assess what birdlife is there. Lastly, unless you belong to an active birder's group, you may have little idea what remarkable sightings are taking place elsewhere in the state. There is a solution to the last part of the problem. The Wisconsin Society for Ornithology (WSO) offers a Rare Bird Alert Hot Line, which is updated every few weeks to bring the most current sighting information to birders around the state. The number to call is (414) 352-3857. Call it to report rare sightings yourself, so that others may benefit. Or contact their World Wide Web site at (http://www.uwgb.edu/~richter/wbba.html).

First Birds of Spring

First bird sightings of the spring are always exciting. The same robin that a person wouldn't look twice at in July often receives overwhelming appreciation in March. Every morning Mary and I search our feeder areas for new arrivals, and our vigilance is often rewarded when a new species appears out of the blue. Although records of first sightings vary from year to year, here are a few sightings from 1995 in the greater metropolitan Manitowish area (population 29): robin, 3/14; red-winged blackbird, 3/14; European starling, 3/15; dark-eyed junco, 3/16; common grackle, 3/17; American tree sparrow, 3/25.

Another year, 1993, varied substantially as follows: starlings, 3/22; house finches, 3/25 (the first time we have ever seen house finches around our home); saw-whet owl, 3/26; and robins, 3/28.

In 1991, Mary spotted our first robin on March 18. Boulder Junction resident Paul Brenner has kept records for the last 40 years in his area. He wrote to tell me his earliest robin sighting occurred on March 14, 1973; his latest happened on April 12, 1975. His 40-year average for robin sightings fell on March 30.

Joining these recent migrants at the feeders are numerous winter residents wise enough to hang around here until the weather clearly improves—American goldfinches, pine siskins, evening grosbeaks, black-capped chickadees, red-breasted nuthatches, purple finches, blue jays, hairy and downy woodpeckers, and pine grosbeaks. It's a regular army of freeloaders, and we go through seed at an incredible clip. But in spring, who would have it any other way?

Trumpeter swans return by mid-March, too. Five swans—two adults, one two-year-old, and two cygnets—returned to the Turtle River near Mercer on March 16, 1995. Only 10 pairs of trumpeters nested in Wisconsin in 1994; eight of these pairs raised a total of 24 young to flight stage, so their return to our area has great significance beyond the beauty they bless us with.

Snow geese usually stop off briefly in mid-March on their way north. Mallards, goldeneye, hooded mergansers, and common mergansers come back as soon as the water first opens.

The spring of 1995 seemed to come early, but bird arrival dates were similar to dates from the previous four years. As for the Manitowish River below our house, it opened on the following dates: March 30, 1986; March 7, 1987; March 20, 1991; March 4, 1992; March 26, 1993; March 14, 1994; March 15, 1995. Was the spring of 1995 an "early" spring? It would be hard to judge without longer-term data.

Cattail Bedding

One late March Bob Kovar, who has a bald eagle pair nesting on his property, watched the eagles swoop low through cattails on his lake, yank them up, then carry them back to the nest, using them to line the nest's interior.

Top 10 Birds

The Wisconsin Society for Ornithology (WSO) and the Whitefish Point Bird Observatory (WPBO) in Michigan both surveyed members in 1994 to determine their membership's 10 favorite birds. The results:

WSO	WPBO
1. Common loon	Black-capped chickadee
2. Sandhill crane	Northern cardinal
3. Bald eagle	Red-breasted nuthatch
4. Eastern bluebird	Blackburnian warbler
5. Black-capped chickadee	Eastern bluebird
6. Great blue heron	Scarlet tanager
7. Scarlet tanager	Cedar waxwing
8. Red-tailed hawk	American kestrel
9. Winter wren	Great gray owl
10. White-throated sparrow	Northern saw-whet owl

In the meantime, I made up my own list, though often my favorite bird is the one I happen to be observing at the time. I didn't include birds that I seldom see, like the hawk owl, which I've seen only once.

1. Black-capped chickadee
2. Veery
3. Common loon
4. Hermit thrush
5. Common snipe
6. Sandhill crane
7. Black tern
8. American woodcock
9. White-throated sparrow
10. Black-throated green warbler

My runners-up include the American bittern, pied-billed grebe, northern harrier, hooded merganser, and northern oriole.

Not wishing to be outdone by the professional birding groups, I asked readers in the Lakeland area to send me lists of their 10 favorite birds. Here are the results:

1. Black-capped chickadee
2. Common loon
3. Ruby-throated hummingbird
4. Nuthatch (both species lumped together)
5. Pileated woodpecker
6. Bald eagle
7. American goldfinch
8. Great blue heron
9. Northern oriole
10. Evening grosbeak

31

Sixty-eight species were represented on the lists I received, demonstrating the diversity of birding interests in our area.

Mammals Mating, Gestating, Birthing

Here's a mammal phenology chart for the northwoods. We have some 53 mammals whose breeding range occurs in our area, but I've only included those most often asked about (for instance, I seldom get questions on the mating habits of our five species of shrews). Delayed implantation in a species is designated as "(DI)."

SPECIES	BREEDING	GESTATION	BIRTH	LITTER
Eastern Cottontail	March	30 days	April	3 to 6
Snowshoe Hare	Mar/Apr	36 days	Apr/May	3 to 4
Least Chipmunk	April	30 days	May	4 to 7
Eastern Chipmunk	Mar/Apr	31 days	Apr/May	2 to 7
Woodchuck	April	30 days	May	4 to 6
Gray Squirrel	February	40 days	Mar/Apr	2 to 5*
Red Squirrel	March	38 days	Apr/May	2 to 7**

Species	Breeding	Gestation	Birth	Litter
Northern Flying Squirrel	Apr/May	40 days	May/June	2 to 3
Beaver	Jan/Feb	120 days	May	1 to 8
Muskrat	Mar/Apr	30 days	Apr/May	4 to 8
Porcupine	Oct/Nov	210 days	Apr/May	1
Coyote	Feb	60 days	April	4 to 8
Gray Wolf	Feb/Mar	63 days	Apr/May	4 to 10
Red Fox	Jan/Feb	53 days	Mar/Apr	2 to 9
Gray Fox	Feb/Mar	51 days	Apr/May	3 to 5
Black Bear (DI)	June/July	225 days	Jan/Feb	2 to 3
Raccoon	Feb/Mar	64 days	Apr/May	3 to 5
Marten (DI)	July	270 days	Apr/May	2 to 4
Fisher (DI)	April	352 days	April	2 to 3
Ermine (DI)	July/Aug	255 day	Apr/May	4 to 8
Long-tailed Weasel (DI)	July/Aug	279 days	Apr/May	6 to 8
Mink (short DI)	Feb/Mar	51 days	Apr/May	3 to 6
Badger (DI)	Aug/Sept	240 days	Apr/May	2 to 3
Striped Skunk	Feb/Mar	63 days	May/June	6 to 7
River Otter (DI)	Mar/Apr	1 year	Apr/May	2 to 4
Lynx	Feb/March	63 days	Apr/May	2 to 3
Bobcat	Feb/March	62 days	Apr/May	1 to 4
White-tailed Deer	November	200 days	late May	1 to 2
Moose	Sept/Oct	240 days	late May	1 to 2

*May have second litter in August.
**May have second litter in late August or September.

32

Hare Courtship

Mary and I skied along an old woods road one late March day, coming into a clearing sprinkled liberally with the droppings and bloody urine of what we think were snowshoe hares. The breeding season begins in March, and we guessed that the blood was an indication of females in estrus. I've never observed the pre-mating behaviors of snowshoes, but apparently the male and female jump alternately over each other, in no special order, urinating on the prospective mate beneath in order to set the "romantic mood." After mating, gestation takes about 35 days, so we should see young hares by mid-April.

The snowshoes had browsed the buds of most low, woody shrubs in the area, and had worked over numerous blackberry canes. Somehow they had tolerated the very sharp thorns.

Furry Snakes with Legs

A Woodruff couple called to share a video they had made in mid-March. The film showed a short-tailed weasel (ermine) visiting their bird feeder and hauling away scraps of fat. The white pelage and black-tipped tail of the animal, along with its long, thin body, made it easy to identify. If the ermine had been stretched taut, it would likely have been 10 inches long, indicating that it was probably a female. One writer has described an ermine as "a furry snake with legs." Females are 30 percent shorter and 50 percent lighter than males. The short-tailed female measures from nine to 10 inches and weighs two to three ounces; the male stretches 11 to 13 inches long and weighs three to six ounces.

While their tiny tracks barely imprint on the snow (a width and length of three-quarters of an inch), ermines display more pound-for-pound fearlessness than virtually any other predator, taking on animals up to 30 times their weight. They are lightning quick, and lithe enough to squeeze into the burrows of most small mammals. Nearly 50 percent of the ermine's diet consists of mice; the balance is made up of rats, shrews, rabbits, and chipmunks, and a few birds, frogs, and snakes.

Ermines are highly curious. They can quickly acclimate to human

33

presence. Mid-March brings on their spring molt, which is usually completed by late April—in time to match the final snow melt.

Sightings

An eagle bander reported that an eagle pair had laid its eggs one spring on March 27. The bander looked into another nest tree the next day, checking for eggs, and instead found a porcupine sunning itself! I suppose a nest could be a regular penthouse suite for a porcupine, offering protection from the wind and comfy bedding without fear of falling out of the tree.

34

A northwoods couple wrote to tell of a wayward white-throated sparrow that had wintered over at their feeder. The sparrow apparently did not realize that members of its species migrate to southern Wisconsin and southward during the fall. Occasional records of wintering white-throateds in northern counties have cropped up over the years, but their winter presence is still a rarity. The clear, simple song of the white throat is as eagerly awaited by bird lovers as any spring bird song.

One late March, Erwin and Ada Karow of Lac du Flambeau watched a barred owl that was perched in a tree off the edge of their deck for nearly an hour. It was patiently hunting the area below the Karows' feeder for rodents, without success. At one point it suddenly flew directly at the window where Erwin and Ada were quietly observing it. The owl hit the window with such force that it landed on the ground, lying there for half an hour. It eventually wobbled up onto a post on the deck, then later flew into a nearby tree. It sat in the tree for another hour or more, probably trying to shake off the stunning blow it had absorbed. Meanwhile, Erwin and Ada enjoyed a magnificent, close-up view of an adult barred owl.

Ada wondered at first why the owl flew straight at them, realizing later that it was probably attracted by the silhouette of a kestrel on their window. They had put the silhouette there to discourage warblers from smacking into the glass. The kestrel hadn't worked that well in previous springs in preventing warbler headaches; it now seems clear that it doesn't dissuade barred owls, either.

Mona Wiechmann of Manitowish Waters may have reported the most unusual observation around these parts in recent late Marches.

On March 24, 1996, she spotted a bear on the Powell Marsh. I suspect the bear had heard the weather forecast, which was predicting a blizzard for the next day, and was heading south.

Transition on the Manitowish

When the Manitowish River opens, in comes a host of birds. Goldeneyes arrive with the river transition; eagles begin moving up and down the river; and red-winged blackbirds pull in within a few days.

The Manitowish River opened up one spring on March 26, and we canoed a stretch of the river two days later. The river was kind—we kicked up a semipalmated plover, mallards, hooded mergansers, red-breasted mergansers, and Canadian geese along the way, all first sightings of the year. We watched a mink and three muskrats. Two eagles soared together at low altitudes over the river, but we had been seeing eagles every day for many weeks. Here are the earliest sightings we have witnessed over the years in Manitowish:

35

Chipping sparrow	March 19	Hooded merganser	April 1
Canada goose	March 21	Northern harrier	April 1
Killdeer	March 21	Great blue heron	April 3
Broad-winged hawk	March 21	Ring-necked duck	April 3
Mallard	March 22	Common snipe	April 4
Osprey	March 23	Kingfisher	April 5
Junco	March 27	Wood duck	April 5
Kestrel	March 28	Pied-billed grebe	April 5
Red-tailed hawk	March 28	Flicker	April 7
Tree sparrow	March 30	Turkey vulture	April 9
Common merganser	March 31	Scaup	April 9
Tundra swan	March 31	Bittern	April 11
Woodcock	April 1	Bufflehead	April 11

I suspect my records are a bit late, because all sightings are based on being in the right place at the right time. Given the frequently nasty weather at this time of year, I don't spend inordinate amounts of time in the rain/snow and cold. I probably miss as much, if not more, than I see.

Growth, Progress, and Other Non Sequiturs

I attended a mining forum on a proposed open-pit zinc mine near the Willow Flowage. In witnessing the economic "progress" of the northwoods, I am reminded of the words of Aldo Leopold: "How like fish we are: Ready, nay eager, to seize upon whatever new thing some wind of circumstance shakes down upon the river of time! And how we rue our haste, finding the gilded morsel to contain a hook."

We need to be conducting annual community forums on our growth, to determine whether in our economic gain we are paying too large a price. Progress is a personal concept, one we should not assume rides on the back of the word "more."

Starlight, Star Bright

The Greek astronomer Hipparchus developed the system of classifying stars by their brightness, placing the brightest stars in the first category of brightness or magnitude, and the faintest stars visible to the eye in the sixth magnitude. Today each step of magnitude represents a factor of 2.5 times in brightness. An average first-magnitude star is thus 2.5 times brighter than an average second-magnitude star; six times brighter than a third-magnitude star; 16 times brighter than a fourth; 40 times brighter than a fifth; and 100 times brighter than a sixth. The largest telescope currently in use can detect stars of the 28th magnitude. To give you an idea of how dim such a star really is, a sixth-magnitude star is 585 million times brighter than a 28th-magnitude star. The sun, on the other hand, is rated at magnitude -26, six trillion times brighter than a sixth-magnitude star.

Pleiades is the brightest and most distinctive star cluster in the night sky. Binoculars help substantially in trying to see the individual stars within the Pleiades.

Redpolls and Winter Storms

We had upwards of 100 redpolls at our feeders in late March of 1996. Our blizzard on March 24 of that year must have excited them even less than it did the human populace. However, redpolls may be better than any other songbird at surviving cold temperatures. They have several physiological adaptations that help them get through the cold. Redpolls have a structure called an "esophageal diverticulum" about halfway down their necks. This essentially serves as a pocket in which to store seeds, particularly through the evening and during severe weather. The storage cupboard helps reduce the amount of time the redpolls must spend foraging, allowing them to eat while resting in a sheltered area.

37

Still, redpolls are always the first birds to show up at our feeders in the morning, and they're usually the last to leave. Laura Erickson, author of *For the Birds*, tells me this is because redpolls have more rods in their eyes than other songbirds, permitting them to feed in the dimmer light of dawn and dusk.

Late March

Are not flowers the stars of earth, and are not our stars the flowers of heaven?

-Anonymous

APRIL

The Ojibwe word for April is ickiganisigegizis, or "maple sugar-making month." Literally, the word means "boiling month."

In April, The Thaw begins. The frost is usually still hard in the ground, so the snow-melt has nowhere to go. The first few inches of soil in open areas may thaw; then the ground will sponge up the meltwater until it's fully saturated, creating a slick mudscape. Potholes magically spring up in roads heaved again and again by the capricious spring temperatures, and the dirt roads turn into slurries. Author Diana Kappel-Smith had this to say about April mud in New England: "Last year someone with a good nose for black comedy put up a sign on the brow of the hill: 'SiMULATed MOON SURFACe NeXT 2 MiLeS,' it said. After a week the sign disappeared. . . another sign promptly appeared in its place: 'NO FISHiNG iN POTHOLeS,' it said. It's April."

Mark Twain understood the vagaries of spring and the cabin fever that overwhelms the north country when he wrote, "The people of New England are by nature patient and forbearing, but there are some things which they will not stand. Every year they kill a lot of poets for writing about 'Beautiful Spring.' These are generally casual visitors, who bring their notions of spring from somewhere else, and cannot, of course, know how the natives feel about spring."

peen-t

APRIL 1-15

April 1 to April 15

There's Gold in Them Thar Trees

The maple sap should be running by April (sometimes the sap run is already over by now). One author refers to the annual spring sap run as "the arboreal equivalent of removing one's winter flannels and restringing the tennis racket." Pails are hung on the maples in anticipation of those fast and furious early runs, when the nights are subfreezing and the days are warm. The work to collect and boil the sap is excessive, and the cost per gallon reflects that effort, but I'm hard-pressed to find any product from the northwoods that I enjoy more. There's something wild in the taste of the first sap run. The condensing of clear, tasteless sap (though Mary insists it has a "pinprick of flavor") into the liquid gold of sweet syrup is much like the catharsis from winter into spring.

Maple sap contains about 2-1/2 percent sugar. An average-sized tree will produce a half gallon of syrup or four pounds of maple sugar, but a large tree in a good season may yield eight gallons of syrup. That doesn't sound like much until you consider that the syrup was distilled from over 300 gallons of sap.

We buy our usual three gallons of maple syrup in April. That gets us through just one year, illustrating our addiction to homemade waffles. One member of my family has even been known to drink maple syrup by the spoonful (name withheld to protect the guilty). The sap run usually begins in late March and continues as long as we get freezing nights and warm days.

American Indians were the first people to make syrup. Without an easy means of heating the sap, they dropped hot stones into birch bark containers to bring the liquid to a boil. Some Indians would allow it to freeze overnight. The sugary sap would settle to the bottom, and the water would rise to the top. In the morning the ice on top was thrown away—a clever practice that greatly reduced the amount of boiling that was needed.

42

The sap run often proceeds in fits and starts, because the weather does the same. Sugaring can last from a week to nearly a month, though the end of the season sap produces syrup the color of old coffee. Grade A syrup from the first run looks like ginger ale, a color known as "light amber."

The final product is 63 percent sugar and 35 percent water, an elixir sweet enough to erode the enamel on your teeth, but what a fine way to go. As the weather warms, the sap will change its chemical composition, and the syrup will become dark and bad-tasting. If you look up in the branches at this time, you'll find that the maple buds are bursting and new leaves are on their way.

In 1791 Benjamin Rush, a Philadelphia physician, wrote rather formally to Thomas Jefferson of his love for maple syrup: "In contemplating the present opening prospects in human affairs, I am led to expect that a material part of the general happiness which heaven seems to have prepared for mankind will be derived from the manufacture and general use of Maple Sugar."

Spring Arrival "On Time"

A gentleman wrote me one spring to say he had seen his first loon on a Madison area lake on March 28. His sighting provided a good opportunity to test Hopkins Law, which holds that spring moves north into the Northern Highlands at about 12 miles per day, thus taking about 21 days to reach the Manitowish area from Madison. Mary heard our first loon flying over the Manitowish River that spring on

April 18, exactly 21 days after the Madison sighting. In this case, at least, the theory held.

To Be a Fool in April

I have always wondered why we have April Fool's Day. I can think of no better reason than the absolutely foolish notion that spring arrives here by April 1. Still, as April begins to chart its course, the signs of spring are everywhere. If the return to our Manitowish home of Canada geese, red-winged blackbirds, robins, hooded mergansers, mallards, goldeneye, and mourning doves constitutes evidence, then spring's approach is in progress by April 1, contrary to the ongoing presence of snow in the woods and the continued below-freezing days.

The April transition period provides wonderful opportunities for hiking deep into areas that are inaccessible during most other periods of the year. The crusted snow, ideal for walking over bogs and other wetlands, is appreciated by foresters, who get more work done at this time of year than virtually any other season. For someone like myself who enjoys looking at topo maps and picking out new areas to explore, pre-spring provides freedom from mosquitoes, from deep snows requiring snowshoes, from wet feet and mud, and from being stopped by water bodies requiring a canoe. Most folks rue how long spring agonizes in its homecoming, but as with most unwanted offerings from the natural world, the less one resists, the better one enjoys.

First Paddle

As intriguing a sighting as any Mary and I have experienced while paddling on the Manitowish River was an early April observation of what may have been a species of Dobson fly. The flies appeared to be imbedded in the melting ice sheets, and were coming to life as the ice melted around them, crawling by the thousands on top of the shelves of ice splayed over the river. It was an observation that left us with many questions and no answers, but the natural world often serves up such mysteries.

The ice, too, amazed us. It hung over the river, defying gravity.

43

Along its edge, the ice crystals could be rubbed off in long, thin shards. Mary and I could adjust the temperature of our canoeing by either staying in the middle of the river, where it was warm in the sun, or by paddling near the ice, where it was decidedly cooler. Great whumps of ice sheared off into the river as we proceeded. The overhanging ledges were dripping meltwater all along the banks, and Mary observed that the cumulative sound was like that of a chorus of spring peepers. We've seen geese on the river hunker under the ice plates, making themselves nearly invisible.

In April the river is usually down, and the north wind, decidedly not a harbinger of spring, plays havoc with the bow of our canoe, trying to introduce us on an up-close and personal basis to many of the ice sheets.

What a pleasure it is to be back in the canoe on open water again, rounding curves and anticipating the surprises of spring.

Frog Hibernation

In the northwoods, amphibian emergence from hibernation usually happens in the first two weeks of April, triggered by a spring rain that occurs at the same time as frost-out. Emergence results in a migration after dark by early breeding frogs, like spring peepers, chorus frogs, leopard frogs, and wood frogs; and by salamanders like the blue spotted salamander. Often this migration occurs in just one night.

You can observe the nocturnal migration by driving roads adjacent to ponds, especially ponds that are across the road from an undisturbed woods, out of which these species may be emerging. We've never seen the full migration in one night, though we've seen the next day's carnage—major frog road kills. Watch the weather and see if you can catch one of the least-observed migrations in the northwoods.

Wood Frog Debauchery

If you step outside near a wetland during the first week of April, you will likely become aware that wood frogs are calling, quacking softly all around you. They are the first frogs to call in the spring; in two weeks they will be silent again. Using temporarily flooded areas for breeding, thereby reducing competition with other frogs that breed later in permanent waters, the wood frogs engage in a few days of "wild debauch," in which males clasp just about anything. Males have been found clasping other males, egg masses, female spring peepers, even lumps of mud and dead toads.

Wood frogs haven't studied at the Julliard School of Music. Their song is like a bunch of mallards talking at low volume. The quacking doesn't travel far, unlike the choruses of spring peepers that start soon after the wood frogs commence their crooning. But loud is seldom better. Listen for the wood frogs this April. They signal spring as surely as the return of any robin, and as beautifully as any "V" of geese.

45

Frog Breathing

Frogs amaze me. They breathe in more ways during their short life span than any other northwoods animal. Eggs exchange oxygen and wastes with the surrounding water through simple diffusion. Tadpoles use feathery gills to absorb oxygen. In frog "adolescence," the gills are reabsorbed and lungs develop to gulp air directly. Finally, in winter, adults can breathe directly through their skin while buried in soil or at the bottom of a lake. A frog can even absorb oxygen directly through membranes in its mouth while panting in the heat of summer.

Bats in the Fridge

One winter the Northwoods Wildlife Center in Minocqua cared for two little brown bats that were brought in during a brief February warming spell. Because bats hibernate through the winter, the Center kept them in butter containers in a refrigerator, in order to simulate hibernating conditions. The staff brought them out once a week to feed them waxworms, leaving them out for the rest of the day so they could digest their food before returning to the fridge. The bats were released in good shape in April, as soon as there was a good insect hatch.

Beaver Duplexes

My wife Mary, our daughters, and I were traipsing around a frozen wilderness lake one early April when we found two active beaver lodges side by side. A beaver duplex like this one sits on a wetland near our home, too. More than likely, one of the lodges is inhabited by an old bachelor, while the other serves a family unit of six or so.

Mystery Enfolds Knowledge

One could legitimately ask the birds, as Mary did one morning while the rain turned to snow and the early birds at our feeder looked forlorn, "What do you think you are doing?" A good question. Understanding spring migration may be as easy as comprehending the Milky Way on a clear night. Diana Kappel-Smith says about migrations: "I feel as though I were caught in the absurd and wonderful position of the blind man who is trying to describe sight to the equally sightless—I can only say what miracles there are."

The trigger for migration is the pituitary gland, which acts almost like a third eye, sensing the increase in day length and releasing hormones to push the birds skyward. Once aloft, birds navigate by using a combination of skills, piloting by the sun, by the stars, by magnetic fields, and by landmarks. Kappel-Smith compares the instinctual navigating abilities of birds to our ability as young children to acquire language. We are able to use complex language to meet many needs before we can even coordinate opening a door or wielding a spoon. Kappel-Smith reflects: "Perhaps the flocks of young swallows and song sparrows moving in the woods are learning these things; the syntax and vocabulary of darkness and light. Of magnetic dip and rise. Of stillness and motion."

When I see and hear the first birds return I am reminded of one philosopher's view of life: "Mystery enfolds knowledge, and is always more than our knowing." Feeling that mystery makes migrations all the more worth seeing.

Return of Trumpeter Swans

If March bows out like a lamb with a week of warm weather that sunburns many faces unaccustomed to such luxury, spring migration will heat up rapidly, too. The March return of trumpeter swans is of great significance because until the late 1980s, trumpeters had been seen just twice in Wisconsin during the 20th century. The first time swans were sighted was in 1904, when one individual in Waukesha County was observed and summarily shot. The carcass was then hung in a Chicago billiards parlor. The second sighting occurred in 1937, when four trumpeters landed briefly near Oconto as part of a larger flock of tundra swans on their way to far north nesting areas.

The Wisconsin DNR began a restoration program in 1987 that continues today. In 1989 one wandering, Minnesota-reared trumpeter swan pair nested in Wisconsin—the first since the 19th century. In the spring of 1992, the first Wisconsin-released swans paired and nested. Six pairs nested in 1993, five of which were Wisconsin-released. Four of the families successfully raised young.

On rare occasions, trumpeters have displayed highly aggressive territorial behaviors. One Wisconsin swan was killed by an individual who was threatened by these displays. On the Turtle River near our home, the protective male of a mated pair has attacked several people in separate incidents. One five-year-old girl was chased down on land and repeatedly bitten on her back. Another woman, fishing in an area that she and her husband have fished since 1954, was bitten and badly bruised while in her fishing boat.

Most trumpeters respond either shyly or in a friendly manner to human presence, but their personalities vary, just as ours do. Thus the DNR asks people not to feed the swans, in order to protect humans as well as the swans, which readily eat the usual offering of corn. The corn acts as a digestive grinder, effectively speeding up lead poisoning, which is the leading cause of death among trumpeters. The well-intentioned gesture of feeding trumpeters may amount to "loving them to death," so please don't.

A gentleman called me one spring on April 9 to discuss two trumpeter swans he had just seen. The birds had landed 25 feet from the caller and five others, who were ice fishing on Papoose Lake. The swans "played" on the ice near them for 45 minutes before flying off. The man got the numbers on the neck bands, and I phoned Jeff Wil-

47

son at the Mercer DNR. Jeff then phoned the Bureau of Endangered Species in Madison, where swan data is kept. As it turned out, the two trumpeters were taken as eggs from a nest in Alaska in 1989 and brought to the Milwaukee Zoo to be hatched. They were raised in Pewaukee, and released with another pair on a secret site in Vilas County the previous year.

We also have mute swans in the northwoods. To tell the two apart from a distance, simply look at the neck; the mutes hold their necks in a graceful curve and point their bills down, while trumpeters swim with straight necks and horizontal bills. While they are beautiful to observe, the non-native mutes are a wetland scourge, driving native species away and uprooting native wetland plants as they forage. Beauty can be deceptive. In the case of mute swans, our wetlands would be better off without their aesthetic presence.

Learning Bird Calls

April opens the seasonal gate to the reappearance of an amazing array of life, but nothing is more appreciated than the return of bird songs. Likewise, few things can be as frustrating as trying to learn all of their songs. Besides continual field experience, the best way I know is to purchase *Birding by Ear: Eastern/Central U.S.,* Volumes 1 and 2 by Richard Walton and Robert Lawson. Each volume is a three-tape set, and each is part of the Peterson Field Guide series. The first volume groups birds by acoustic similarity into 17 categories, such as "whistlers," "name-sayers," "mimics," and "chippers and trillers." The authors offer easily memorized phonetic sayings, like the well-known "who cooks for you," which approximates the barred owl call. If you're like me, and you have driven yourself crazy trying to memorize 200 bird calls from tapes before, then this is the recording for you.

The second tape, called *More Birding by Ear,* is more advanced, including 25 species of warblers among the 96 birds covered. The many suggested memory aids and the grouping by phonetic category help immensely.

48

Love of Land

Male red-wingeds return in late March; in April, they stake out their territories on the marsh below our house. Their "o-ka-lee" song, trilled over the still-frozen marsh, along with the display of their red epaulets, helps define the boundaries of their kingdoms as they antici-pate the females' return several weeks later. Once mated, the male appears to care more for his territory than for his mate. In one study of red-wingeds, the nest itself and the female were moved out of a male's territory to see what he would do. He responded by showing no further interest in them. But when a new nest belonging to a differ-ent female was moved into his territory, the male immediately ac-cepted it, protecting the nest and female. The males apparently agree with Ralph Waldo Emerson's thinking on land: "If a man owns land, the land owns him."

49

Buffaloed

In early April, buffleheads commonly stop and rest on northern lakes on their way to nesting grounds in Canada. I've always won-dered what inspired their name, and I finally looked it up. The name is derived from the Greek term *boukephalow*, meaning "buffalo-headed," an apparent reference to the large head of this little duck, though the comparison isn't remotely accurate in terms of actual size or color. If you've not seen a bufflehead, it is a very small duck, pre-dominantly white, with a black back and a dark head adorned by a large, white, bonnetlike patch. If there's a resemblance here to a buf-falo, I'm Roy Rogers.

Listening for Snipe

Whenever I mention to people that the snipe return in April, they look at me like I'm trying to trick them. I've never figured out how the practical joke of taking someone on a snipe hunt began but, honest, we have snipe nesting throughout the northwoods wherever good wetland habitat exists. Snipe are particularly worth noting in the spring because of the sound they make during their territorial flights, which begin in April. The sound is described by Peterson as a "winnowing huhuhuhuhuh," while Audubon calls it an "eerie whistling." Old World European farmers thought snipe sounded like bleating goats, while Eskimos thought the sound was akin to the voice of the walrus. For those of you who don't remember your walrus songs, walrus make an "avik" sound. Thoreau pegged it best, though, calling it a "spirit-sug-gesting-sound."

The snipe produces this sound when air rushes through its tail feathers as it dives. The tail feathers hum at speeds between 25 and 50 miles per hour. The male careens through the sky in a series of dives and climbs trying to impress females. The male has even been seen gliding at high speed upside down to attract a prospective mate (a bachelor friend tells me this works with human females, too, but I suspect that's why he's still a bachelor). Around Manitowish, snipe court actively all day, though the books say they court at dusk and dawn.

Other notable snipe traits include a flexible upper bill that allows the bird to probe around in the mud to capture insects. Snipe also parent in a way I've never heard of. When the young hatch, the male shows up and leads half of the brood away to his own nest nearby, where he raises his batch while the female raises hers. This amounts to divorce without lawyers. I hope humans don't hear about this.

Goshawks and Shrikes

Peter Dring, a naturalist who lives near Land O'Lakes, discovered a northern goshawk hunting his feeder during the winter of 1995-96. The effect of the goshawk's presence was the instantaneous disap-pearance of all nearby songbirds.

Northern shrikes were quite common that winter as well. Peter bands birds, and one day he captured his fourth northern shrike of the year. In the 30 seconds it took Peter to get to his trap, the shrike killed three other birds that had also flown into the trap. Shrikes are known as the "butcher bird" for their habit of impaling songbirds on thorny branches in preparation for dining. Shrikes have a toothlike structure on the cutting edge of their upper bill, much like that of a falcon. They often kill their prey with a series of sharp bites, which severs the neck vertebrae of their victims. Because they are not equipped with talons like a hawk or an owl, shrikes depend on their bill for killing prey.

Wooing Woodcock

This is the time of year to look and listen for the male woodcock wooing a female. Listen at dusk in open areas for a consistent sound best characterized as a nasal "peent." The male will offer this sound for several minutes, then leap into the air and spiral upward some 300 feet in widening circles, hover momentarily while chirping, then drop down in a series of swoops like a falling leaf, still chirping away in liquid song. This courtship flight occurs again and again until it becomes too dark, and is then resumed at dawn. Here's a trick to try: Once the male woodcock ascends, run to the spot he took off from; huddle down, and see if he doesn't land close to you. I've tried this many times, but the woodcock around my place always lands about 15 yards away, then starts up again. I'll keep trying this technique, but I suspect that the woodcock in Manitowish haven't read the book, which insists that the birds will land on the same spot they took off from.

New Eagle Nest

One April morning in 1992, Mary made the discovery of the spring. She spotted a new eagle nest, built in the dead top of a white pine along the river near our house. With our spotting scope, we were able to watch the nest from the comfort of our kitchen. The pair failed to produce any young that spring. We never really knew if they had actually laid eggs.

In the spring of 1993, the nest blew down. A pair of eagles perched in the tree and around the nest site, but failed to rebuild. We guessed that they renested nearby on the river, but we have not been able to find a nest.

As of 1996, there is no sign that the eagles returned to that tree or to our area for rebuilding. Still, we see eagles cruising the river nearly every day in the spring. Where they are nesting remains a mystery to us.

First Sightings of the Year

During April, birds seem to reappear continually, the month proceeding like a magician who sweeps his cape and reveals yet another magical apparition. We keep notes on what we see, though we don't claim to see all we should—or to even to be out every day looking. The business of life too often precludes the more pleasurable pursuit of bird-watching. Still, our records offer a fair picture of the seasonal comings and goings of birds in our one small spot. I enjoy looking at the records, and I try to understand their discrepancies. For example, a killdeer arrived two weeks later one year than another. Why? Answers seldom distill from the questions, but the mysteries add as much to our pleasure in watching birds as the resolutions. Here are examples of a few April records.

52

First April Sightings, 1995

Song sparrow	April 1	Great blue heron	April 16
Killdeer	April 4	Flicker	April 16
Common loon	April 15	American bittern	April 16
Fox sparrow	April 15	Yellow-bellied	
Turkey vulture	April 15	sapsucker	April 17

First April Sightings, 1993

Male red-winged		Great blue heron	April 3
blackbirds	March 30	Ospreys	April 7
Killdeer	March 30	Wood ducks	April 7
Grackles	March 30	Common mergansers	April 8
Dark-eyed juncos	March 31	Sandhill cranes	April 10
Tree & song sparrows	April 2	Scaup	April 10
Common loon	April 2	Tree swallows	April 11
Northern harriers	April 3	Phoebe & winter	
Woodcock	April 3	wren	April 11

First April Sightings, 1992

Great blue herons	April 1	Albino evening	
Killdeer	April 5	grosbeak	April 7
Bluebirds	April 5	Common loon	April 9
Woodcock	April 6	Fox & song sparrows	April 11
		Northern harrier	April 12

FIRST APRIL SIGHTINGS, 1991

(The weather gyrated in its usual spring dance. High of 20°F on March 29; high of 75°F on April 7).

Hooded mergansers	March 30	Cliff swallows	April 5
Mallards and geese	March 30	Wood frogs	April 5
Dark-eyed juncos	March 31	*Mosquitoes!*	*April 5*
Tree sparrows	April 2	Spring peepers	April 6
Killdeer	April 3	Fox sparrows	April 6
Song sparrows	April 4	Wood ducks	April 6
Purple finch	April 4	Flickers	April 6
Northern harrier	April 5	Red-tailed hawk	April 6
Sandhill crane	April 5	Turkey vultures	April 8

53

Nearly every day brings a new find, scratches a memory, makes the field guides dogeared for a while again. If you're not out poking around, someone better check your pulse.

Sightings

Chipmunks are back out, mating and active (and hanging out in our bird feeders, naturally); red squirrels are madly chasing one another in courtship; pussy willows are popping; the male goldfinches at our feeders are molting into their yellow spring plumage; the buds of the silver maples along the river are swollen and ready for leaf-out; the runways of voles and mice that had lived under the snow all winter are readily apparent in dry areas; otters have given birth in their river dens, usually producing two to four cubs whose eyes won't open for another month; snowshoe hares are in molt and mating; grouse are drumming; the ice on the lakes is turning black; trailing arbutus has emerged from the snow and is soon to bloom. While April is often cold, wet, and muddy, the lack of biting insects and the opportunities for quiet exploration with few others around are ample compensation.

Tundra Swans

Look for tundra swans to migrate through northern Wisconsin in the first week of April. One April 7th, 20 stopped over on Oxbow Lake, a widening of the Turtle River located north of Mercer.

April Musings

The world is full of beginnings now, and beginnings are often more interesting, sometimes even more important, than what follows. The vernal change has started.

But the great change comes now before the full flowering. Now is the deep wonder, for the bud itself is the miracle . . . Spring is there in the flower within the bud, but the miracle is in the beginning, the way that bud opens. You see a birch on the hillside, its buds fat against the sky. You watch the . . . tip appear, when the tree stands in all the delicacy of April's green mist . . . Or the way bloodroot comes to flower, opening that fat green bud . . . That, to me, is April, the swelling bud, the beginning.

-Hal Borland

Notes

April 16 to April 30

Transitions

There may be no time period of greater, concentrated change in the northwoods than now. The whole bulk of winter snow and ice is transforming from crystal to liquid and rushing into rivers.

The catharsis sweeps through our minds and hearts as well. If we could bud and leaf out, we would. There is ground to smell. It is "just spring when the world is mud-luscious," as e.e. cummings wrote. I am as full of life now as the marshes are full of water. Every stream waves me over to check its edges for life returning.

Maples, hazelnuts, alder, and willow are flowering; bluebirds are arriving; walleyes and musky are spawning; morel are coming out; bucks are growing their antlers; muskrat young are being born; blue herons are nest building; kestrels are lined up every mile on telephone lines, watching for prey; chorus frogs are tuning up; and the ice should be off the lakes. Get outside and enjoy this resurgence before the mosquitoes get serious. The first wood ticks usually appear around April 21, too, in case you'd forgotten.

Late April Musings

Let the boys at Canaveral hurl their rockets at the moon and at whatever swirling worlds there are. I respect their discipline and their sense of high adventure, but in the cold, pre-dawn of the Buena Vista, as I listen to one of the last authentic, truly wild American voices, I achieve my adventure.

-Paul Olson
of the Dane County
Conservation League
after watching prairie chickens boom. He subsequently launched the Prairie Chicken Foundation, which helped purchase the lands necessary to save the prairie chicken in Wisconsin.

Counting Sandhill Cranes

Wisconsin's annual Sandhill Crane Count Day usually occurs on the third or fourth Saturday of April, provoking early-morning expeditions into the marshes of every county in our state. The weather tends to vacillate from year to year, ranging from sunny 50s to snowy 20s; generally, we encounter more wind than we would in the slipstream of a jet. One morning before first light, Mark Jaunzems and I waded through a foot of fresh snow on the dikes of Vilas County's Powell Marsh. We were rewarded with seven cranes, adding them to the state total.

58

The count began in 1982. Fifty to 70 counties are surveyed, depending on the volunteers available. About 2,600 people do the count every year. The highest total number of cranes counted was 12,308 in 1995. Heavy fog in 1990 and rain/snow/wind conditions in 1991 held the count numbers way down. The snow conditions Mark and I experienced dampened the statewide totals in 1992 as well. The cranes are in the marshes by this time of year, though; if we can overcome the weather, we can adequately count them. The crane population in the central counties of Wisconsin has reached a saturated plateau, while numbers in peripheral counties like ours are showing a 20 percent annual increase.

Cranes are sometimes confused with herons. In flight the long, outstretched necks and trailing legs of cranes clearly differentiate them from herons, which fly with their necks tucked in an "S" shape. Each of their calls is distinctive, too. The herons produce a primordial croak, while cranes generate a unique unison call on the ground and a bugling call in flight.

Cranes arrive early on the marshes, regardless of snow and ice conditions, building simple platform nests on the ground. Pairs mate for life and return to the same nesting area each spring. Usually two eggs are laid in late April, hatching in 30 days. Four years later the juveniles, driven away from the nest area after their first year, form pair bonds and mate in a new territory.

Cranes are extraordinarily long-lived; a bird 30 to 35 years old is not uncommon. One Siberian crane at the International Crane Foundation in Baraboo, WI, lived into his mid-eighties!

Early Birds

Bird migration is in full swing by late April. While we might like to think of them as "our" birds returning home, it's more often the case that southern bird species are visiting the north country for a brief breeding season. Compared to the southern wintering grounds, the northwoods in summer offers longer days for gathering food, less competition for nesting habitat, a moderate climate and, if you hadn't noticed, a rich and diverse insect population. We may view the insects as a plague, but the birds see them as a horn of plenty. About 140 bird species will return from Central America, the West Indies, and South America to breed in our region.

Early migrators may appear to be taking unnecessary risks with "spring" weather. (I write this on an Easter morning, looking out my window at six inches of fresh snow, with more falling.) But breeding, nest building, and incubation often must take place early on, so the young will be born when the amount of available food is at its peak. The young must also have enough time to mature before they migrate in the fall. If some birds didn't breed until the insects were hatching, the number of insects could be greatly diminished by the time the birds were born.

As I watch my feeder, I wonder how many of these early migrants are back again from last year. Most birds return each spring to the same nest site, a behavior known as "site fidelity." But site fidelity isn't automatic. It's dependent on variables like previous breeding success, the physical stability of the nest site, and the sex and age of the bird. Individuals within a species may not return to the former site if they failed to bring off young. The species that build nests in unstable areas like beaches, sandbars, and riverbanks exhibit less site fidelity than species that nest in stable areas like rocks, buildings, or secure forests. For example, barn swallows exhibit good site fidelity, while bank swallows exhibit poor site fidelity. Barns are stable nesting sites, while banks erode.

The larger question for me is, how did the birds at my feeder find their way back to Manitowish, a tiny spot on any map or landscape? How do birds navigate a course directly to their historical nesting site,

59

often traveling thousands of miles? While the question has been partly answered by science, it remains one of the miracles of animal behavior. Different species use different cues in different orders to get "home." Through various experiments, ornithologists have shown that birds employ five means of determining direction: stars; sun; topographic features, including wind direction; magnetic fields; and odors. On overcast nights, birds orient by using wind direction, but they often head the wrong way. When they're "lost," how do they know how to compensate for their mistake?

Once here, most birds sense that it is time to start breeding by the lengthening of days. The increasing photoperiod, or duration of light, brings the birds to the starting line, but the weather and the amount of available food serve as the final gun. One experimenter demonstrated that if red-winged blackbirds were given substantial food, they would lay their eggs three weeks earlier than red-wingeds without supplemented diets. So keep your feeders full, in case a white Easter decides to stay awhile.

Prairie Chickens: Boom with a View

After years of procrastination, in 1995 I finally drove down to watch prairie chickens boom in the Buena Vista Marsh. The Central Wisconsin Environmental Station near Amherst Junction offers a program there called "Boom with a View." For $35 you can listen to a talk on the chickens (they're really grouse) in the evening; sleep (although not for very long) in the dorm; and in the early morning (up at 3 a.m.) stumble out to your designated blind on the marsh. Three hours later, they pick you up.

We saw 16 males and 11 females on our booming ground between 5:20 and 7:40 that morning. When the females finally left, the males immediately fell into silence, as if they had lost all ability to speak.

The males dance and display to protect their territories and to entice a female into mating. For their part, the females wander slowly about with general disinterest, fanning the hormonal flames of the males, which woo all the more intensely when a female approaches. I suppose if you wanted to compare this endeavor with human behavior, you could say this is the ultimate bar scene. Thankfully, though, the air is clean, the music is far more appealing, and the landscape stretches well beyond four dingy walls.

Today Wisconsin supports only about 2,000 prairie chickens. Approximately half live in the Buena Vista Marsh area, a 12,000-acre patchwork of protected grasslands scattered within nearly 38,000 acres of agricultural land. The prairie chicken is on the state's threatened species list, but it seems to be declining in marginal territories that can't quite maintain the needed habitat structure. Comparatively speaking, we're lucky; Michigan has no prairie chickens left whatsoever.

If you enjoy birds, make a commitment to see the booming this spring. I recommend very few things that involve a 3 a.m. wake-up call, but this is absolutely one of them.

61

First Swim and Spotting Kingfishers

My earliest-ever swim of any year happened on April 21. I hope I needn't add that the dip was unintentional. We had bought a solo canoe in Minneapolis, and I got up the next morning raring to go. I put in below our house on the Manitowish, and immediately flipped over on my face in two feet of water. It seems the craft was a bit tippy. I shlucked up onto shore, looked around quickly to make sure no one was in the midst of hysterics after seeing my abortive launch, and then squished my way home. As a phenological note, I might add that the water is very cold on April 21.

Two geese were just downstream when I tipped. I wonder what they thought as they watched this human fall into the river, then come up gasping and saying impolite things.

Upon finding dry clothes and explaining to Mary why I was in the basement doing laundry when just five minutes ago I had left to go canoeing, I was back on the river. Solo canoes, when upright, are wonderful. Ours is 15-1/2 feet long and weighs 36 pounds. It's quick and quiet, particularly when compared to our former aluminum Grumman, which is like riding in a bass drum.

Anyway, I saw my first kingfisher of the year that morning, though

I know they return earlier than April 21. Kingfishers are the punk rockers of the bird set. Their feathers stand up on top of their heads; a white band that looks like a scarf circles around their necks; and the long, daggerlike bill protrudes dramatically, looking as if it should tip them over on their noses. I paddled to within 100 feet of one bird. It behaved characteristically by flying downriver while giving its rattling call, then perching on a branch overhanging the river. This behavior was repeated three times as I came nearer, until the kingfisher swung around and flew back upstream. A kingfisher's feeding territory covers about 500 yards, and this one had apparently escorted me to its boundary when it rattled me a goodbye. Unfortunately for the kingfisher, I later paddled back upstream and invaded its territory once again. This time it flew off into a side slough and watched me struggle upriver.

Listen in April for the rattle of kingfishers, which sounds to one writer like the amplified clicking of a fishing reel.

House Finches Appear

The sudden appearance of house finches at our feeder in the spring of 1993 was predictable. In 1940, caged-bird dealers in southern California, where house finches are native, illegally shipped these birds to New York, where they were to be sold as "Hollywood finches." U.S. Fish and Wildlife agents stopped the trafficking, but the dealers released the finches somewhere in New York City. They spread rapidly. The house finch was first reported in Illinois in 1971; in Michigan in 1976; in Minnesota in 1980; and in Wisconsin in 1983. The first Wisconsin house finch nests were reported in 1986 in Madison and Milwaukee. Price County sightings occurred in 1989, and the finches have doubtless been seen in Vilas, Oneida, and Iron counties over the last few years. However, my 1993 sighting marked the first I had seen of them. They are now regulars at our bird feeders.

House finches nest in cavities, in dense foliage, in old bird nests, on the ground, in tin cans hanging on posts . . . in other words, just about anywhere. Eighty-six percent of their food is weed seeds, supplemented by some berries, according to the *Encyclopedia of North*

American Birds. Their competition with house sparrows in the Northeast appears to be a major factor in the sparrow's decline. They otherwise appear to be unusually benign for an introduced species—although we may not yet understand their detrimental effects.

Spring Ups and Downs

In 1992 the constant cold throughout April postponed many of the "firsts" of spring by about two weeks. Spring arrived relatively early in 1991, though it gyrated like most Aprils—75°F on April 7, and snow on April 9. But the 1992 April was particularly cold. Here are a few comparisons to illustrate the variations that occur in spring returnings and beginnings:

63

	1991	1992
Tree swallows	April 2	April 20
Song sparrows	April 4	April 10
Wood frogs chorusing	April 5	April 20
Spring peepers chorusing	April 6	April 20
Fox sparrows	April 6	April 10
Flickers	April 6	April 21

On the other hand, some species came back at nearly the same time:

	1991	1992
Juncos	March 31	March 30
Killdeer	April 3	April 5
Sandhill cranes	April 5	April 8

Some species return like clockwork, regardless of the weather, while others sniff the wind a bit before deciding to move on. We had fox sparrows at our feeder for 2-1/2 weeks one spring. They showed little inclination to move on to Canada while the weather remained poor. Who could blame them?

As always, our dates for "firsts" are highly localized. They're also dependent on how frequently we've been able to get out, and whether we're in the right place at the right time. I would happily volunteer to spend all day every day noting the rebirth of spring in the northwoods, in order to assure accuracy in my recordkeeping. The real world of work intervenes in my case, but someone should be hired to do just such a task each spring. Over time, the record would become a fascinating and valuable research data base. God knows our government pays money for far less useful tasks.

Most marshes and streams are open by early April, but many lakes remain iced up until the end of the month. The advantage of this prolonged lake ice is that we can see large concentrations of waterfowl in the open areas. Mary and I frequently hike or canoe along Powell Marsh and the Turtle-Flambeau Flowage in April. While parts of both are always still locked up tight with ice, other areas are open and flush with ducks. Large rafts of scaup (bluebills), bufflehead, common and hooded mergansers, ring-neckeds, goldeneye, geese, and mallards, with interspersions of coots, pintails, wigeon, shovelers, wood ducks, and blue-winged teal are often numerous on these water bodies, with smaller numbers of red-breasted mergansers, horned grebes, and cormorants.

The Peverly Bird

White-throated sparrows return in late April, adding their simple, crystal-toned song to the melodies of spring. Their song is most often said to sound like, "Old Sam Peabody, Peabody, Peabody." But one story has it that a farmer named Peverly couldn't decide when to put in his wheat one spring. He heard a bird suggest an answer to his dilemma from a nearby woods: "Sow wheat, Peverly, Peverly, Peverly." Apparently he later reaped an abundant harvest, and farmers have since been prone to call white-throated sparrows "the Peverly bird."

One beautiful passage by Stewart Edward White appears in his book, *The Forest*, and best distills the bird's song: "It is night, very still, very dark . . . Suddenly across the dusk of silence flashes a single thread of silver, vibrating, trembling with some unguessed ecstasy of emotion. Ah! 'poor Canada, Canada, Canada' it mourns passionately, and falls silent. That is all."

64

A Bachelor's Party
of Sharp-tailed Grouse

I traveled to Crex Meadows Wildlife Area in northwestern Wisconsin in mid-April, 1995, to watch the spring courtship dance of the sharp-tailed grouse. The DNR offers blinds on the brush prairie of the wildlife area for anyone interested in seeing one of the most fascinating avian rituals anywhere. I'd read and heard a lot about the dancing "sharpies," but the actual show was even better than its rave reviews. Seven males flew in before sunrise, at about 6 a.m. I was in the blind by 5:30. The males immediately began to exhibit a variety of courtship behaviors and associated calls—all intended to woo a female onto their dancing grounds.

65

The most tame aspect of courting behavior came when an individual would thrust his head forward, cock his tail straight up, inflate the expandable, featherless sacs at the sides of his neck into a small violet balloon, then coo like a deep-voiced dove. Sometimes the bird would also produce a sort of "gobble" or "chilka-chilka" sound. Then two males would often rush at one another and fly in the air for a brief clash, coming right down again and facing off across from each other in a stare-down.

The most remarkable courtship display was their tail-rattling dance. The male spreads his wings in a downward arc, pushes his head forward, inflates his violet sacs, flares a yellow stripe above his eyes, lifts his tail up straight and white (much like a deer lifting its flag), then pistons his feet as fast as they can go. He spins around in a circle, emitting a clattering or rattling caused by the vibration of his feathers. The others often join in. The sight of five or more grouse, all spinning in a circle and rattling away, is not one likely to be forgotten. The males are just as likely to stop on a dime, as if a switch had been turned off, and just stand there—or sit down and face off with some nearby male. After a short time, they'll pop up and again engage in one of the series of ritualized behaviors that are supposed to impress females lurking on the periphery.

These behaviors continued for over two hours without letup, and without sign of any females. Every so often, the males seemed to stop and look around as if perplexed, and my anthropomorphic mind assumed they must be wondering where the hell the ladies were. The females never showed up. The party was a bachelors-only affair, with enough posturing to attract a whole women's auxiliary but nothing to show for the effort.

Biologists estimate that only 1,000 sharp-taileds are left in Wisconsin. They're found mostly on 11 state wildlife areas, where the open brush prairie habitat the birds require is maintained. Sharpies are spotted on open bogs, old burn sites, large clear-cuts, and abandoned farms, but large open prairies seem to be the habitat of choice. Four habitat needs must be met. They need open grassy uplands for dancing; grassy areas with shrubs to provide shade for nesting; trees and shrubs around grass for rearing their young; and deciduous or coniferous forest with ample buds and catkins for wintering.

Historically, sharp-taileds were very numerous, and were a staple food for pioneers in open prairies or burned cutover. But as forests have regenerated and prairies have been planted, the populations have dwindled dramatically. Only 50,000 acres of Wisconsin barrens remain, and a parcel of at least 10,000 acres appears critical to the maintenance of a sharp-tailed covey.

Four areas in the state provide blinds for public viewing of sharp-tail dancing: Crex Meadows in Burnett County; Namekagon Barrens in Burnett County; Pershing Wildlife Area in Taylor County; and the Wood County Wildlife Area. Riley Lake Wildlife Area and Kimberly Clark lands, both in Price County, are known sharp-tailed sites, but blinds are not provided. Powell Marsh in Vilas County used to host sharpies, but I don't know if the birds are still there.

If you wish to join the Sharp-tailed Grouse Society or get more information about sharpies, call (715) 834-2627 or write Box 1115, Cumberland, WI 54829.

Finding Spring
When Winter Won't Give Up

My wife Mary, my eight-year-old daughter Callie, and I spent six days one early April visiting nature sanctuaries and wildlife preserves, mostly in southern Michigan. We hoped that spring might already have sprung there, but snow, ice, wind, and rain followed us wherever we went. Still, southern Michigan typically offers many remarkable sites for the spring-starved northern Wisconsinite. If spring seems reticent here, you might want to follow up on these suggestions:

For wildflowers: Southwestern Michigan contains several exceptional old-growth hardwood stands, surrounded by prolific spring wildflower displays. The two best are Warren Woods Natural Area in Berrien County, a 200-acre climax beech/maple woods that has been designated a Natural National Landmark; and Dowagiac Woods in Cass County, a 220-acre tract that hosts over 50 species of spring wildflowers and is considered the best wildflower site in all of Michigan.

For waterfowl migration: The Erie Marsh Preserve, owned by The Nature Conservancy, is a 2,168-acre wetland on Lake Erie in far southeastern Michigan. When I pulled into the main parking lot along one of the dikes, eight great egrets stood within 50 yards of the lot! Point Mouillee State Game Area, a DNR parcel in Monroe and Wayne counties north of the Erie Marsh, offers miles of dike-walking along Lake Erie. The species of particular interest I spotted during just two hours of wandering included the caspian tern, Bonaparte's gull, horned grebe, and more great egrets. You might also explore Saginaw Bay on Lake Huron, where at least five areas contain exceptional concentrations of waterfowl.

Really Rough Ruffed Grouse

Rolf Ethun, who lives on Hiawatha Lake near Winchester, reported that a "killer" ruffed grouse attacked his truck one April whenever he drove down Hiawatha Lake Road on the way to his home. The grouse flew against the back window of his pickup and beat the window with its wings; or it flew alongside the truck, apparently escorting the vehicle out of its territory. Rolf asked other visitors to his home whether they experienced the same treatment. They had, which dispels the possibility that the grouse simply didn't like the make of Rolf's truck.

Laying Square Eggs

Mary and I canoed onto the Little Turtle Flowage on April 21, 1991. Ducks galore greeted us—ringnecks, buffleheads, hooded mergansers, mallards, pied-billed grebes. We saw our first osprey of the season; we were hoping to see black terns and yellow-headed blackbirds, but they had yet to return.

The pied-billed grebe's call is quite remarkable. The books say it sounds like a series of loud "cow-cow-cow" notes, but that description is too tame. The call is wild and maniacal. Once you hear it, I can't imagine how you could forget it. Pete Dring, a naturalist and bird bander in Three Lakes, says it sounds like a bird trying to lay a square egg, if that helps you imagine it.

Pied-billeds can also do a great submarine imitation. Many years ago, when Mary and I saw our first pied-billed, it simply sank when it saw us. No dive, just a submergence. We were in disbelief at first; then it surfaced and performed the same disappearing act again. We laughed for five minutes. It was as if someone had pulled out the bird's cork. As it turns out, pied-billeds can squeeze air from their feathers, reducing their volume while maintaining their mass, and thus overcome their buoyancy. Having no recall of high school physics, that explanation leaves me a bit confused. I prefer the cork image. Their unique talent has earned these birds the unusual but descriptive nicknames of "hell-diver" and "water-witch."

Eagle Wars

Carl Ashe from Lac du Flambeau called me in mid-April one year to share a sighting he and Gil Willms had experienced on Long Interlochen Lake. An eagle was being chased by a half a dozen crows. It landed on the ice and began crying up at them while the crows made passes at it. Another eagle landed on the ice several minutes later, but the crows continued their harassment. Then a third eagle landed. The crows must have sensed that the odds had changed, because they flew off.

Romatic Cottontail Dating Rituals

In late April, *Lakeland Times* editor Dean Showers called to describe two cottontail rabbits that had engaged in most unusual behaviors in his backyard. At 5:45 a.m. in Dean's backyard, the two squared off. They then ran headlong at each other, as if to butt heads (a la bighorn sheep); at the last instant, one jumped in the air while the other ran beneath. This was repeated about six times.

After I wrote about this scene in my column, a reader, Jane Lueneburg, wrote to describe similar sparring scenes she had watched while growing up in a semirural area near Racine. She said the jumping rabbits resembled popcorn popping, because one male jumped so high. She further noted that, as she watched one evening, "the male jumped and emitted a fine spray (urine?) as the other ran beneath him."

69

I had read about this urine spraying among snowshoe hares, but not among cottontails. While this behavior may be old hat to cottontail experts, it was news to me. It's just another example of the unusual lengths animals go to during the spring breeding season, and it amply illustrates how the definition of romance varies among species.

Banana-Loving Butterflies

Peg Trotalli from Lower Trout Lake called to say that butterflies were returning to her yard on April 17, 1996. Peg puts out mashed bananas with the skins split to attract butterflies, and she has had great success over the years in luring them in to feed on her banana brew.

Deer Hair Loss

Peter Dring from Three Lakes wrote one spring to tell me he had seen a yearling deer with a great deal of hair loss on its flanks. The exposed skin was turning black and crusty, a condition caused by a protozoan parasite called Sarcocystis, which forms nodules under the skin in the muscle tissue of deer and other animals. If the nodules are close to a nerve ending, the irritation can be so severe that the deer lick or scratch themselves down to the skin. The condition seems to occur primarily during late winter at overpopulated feeding stations. The parasite is usually transmitted to the deer through canine fecal material, which is often deposited around the feeding stations, then inadvertently eaten by the deer. The condition, while ugly and painful, is seldom fatal to adult deer, but it can be fatal to young deer.

Brief Sightings

A sharp-shinned hawk visited our bird feeders one late April. It even tasted a sunflower seed or two while the other birds flew far away. We watched snipe mate within easy view in the marsh below our house on April 22. We put a beaver carcass about 30 feet from our bird feeders, trying to entice an interesting visitor. I glanced out our window just as an adult eagle picked up the carcass, which was by then rather picked over by ravens, and carried it away. Female red-winged blackbirds won't usually come to our feeder until late April. They return many weeks after the males have arrived; we usually see males by March 21. Look for yellow-rumped (myrtle) warblers flitting around by April 17—they're usually the first warbler to return to the northwoods.

Redpoll Mania

Linda Thomas called on April 18, 1996, from the Sayner area. Linda said she had upward of a thousand birds in her yard, most of them redpolls! The 18th was the first of several warm days in a row we experienced that spring, and I suspect the birds had been backed up just south of here, waiting for their chance to get north. A thunderstorm late that afternoon may have grounded their flight temporarily, and many of them seem to have known Linda's address.

Woody Hagge in Hazelhurst reported seeing some 400 redpolls appear at his feeder during the same time period, arriving he said like leaves falling in an autumn storm. He fed them eight to 10 gallons of sunflower hearts per day—a king's ransom to keep the red army fed.

Teaming with Wildlife

Many conservation groups and outdoor recreation businesses are championing a user fee called the Fish and Wildlife Diversity Funding Initiative, which could raise $350 million a year nationally. The user fee would take the form of a modest surcharge on outdoor recreational equipment, similar to the user fees that hunters and anglers have long paid on their equipment and accessories under the Sport Fish and Wildlife Restoration acts. All of the funds would be dedicated to state-based wildlife conservation, recreation, and education. The proponents envision it as a way to enhance hiking, canoeing, nature trails, wildlife viewing blinds and towers, and nature centers. It could also increase the availability of on-site naturalists, brochures, viewing guides, and educational materials for schools, parks, museums, and wildlife management areas. Outdoor equipment such as backpacks, canoes, mountain bikes, binoculars, guide books, bird feeders, and the like would be targeted for a user fee that would range from 1/4 percent to five percent.

I like the idea. It's time the nonhunter/angler population carried its share of the economic weight required to conserve and protect our most valued resources. There's a host of details to this initiative. If you'd like to know more, contact the International Association of Fish and Wildlife Agencies, 444 N. Capitol Street NW, Suite 544, Washington, D.C. 20001.

Hopefully, the law will be enacted in the near future. If it's still in limbo, consider offering your support.

Complete, Partial,
or Irruptive Migration

Migration is a way that birds exploit seasonally abundant resources and avoid seasonally difficult times. There are three migration patterns that birds may follow. Complete migrants leave their breeding range entirely during the nonbreeding season. An example is the Eastern wood pewee, which breeds from southern Canada down to the Gulf Coast of the U.S., then winters in Central and South America. Complete migration is mostly a North American phenomenon—South American birds don't migrate north to our hemisphere to get away from their winter. The reason for our migrational monopoly is that there's very little land south of 55° in the southern hemisphere; therefore, most birds below the equator needn't fly far to escape their winter.

Partial migrants, which participate in the second migratory pattern, have overlapping breeding and winter ranges, resulting in a middle, year-round range. Red-tailed hawks and song sparrows are good examples of this group. Some members of these species migrate, while others don't.

Irruptive migrants are the third group, and these are the birds we often see during the northwoods winter. They are not seasonally or geographically predictable. They may migrate one year but not the next; the distances they fly and the number of migrators will vary from year to year. Great gray owls and northern finches are good examples. Their movements are adaptive, just like partial and complete migrants, but their motivation is not always clear. Food shortages often cause movements of irruptive migrants. Northern finches eat the seeds of only a few trees, while northern shrikes are dependent on the lemming population. If either of these food sources fail, the birds have to move.

As is the case with most processes in the natural world, there are many exceptions to the three migrational categories. Some birds, like the white-winged scoter, migrate along a route that is more east and west than north and south. They breed in Alaska and western Ontario, but they migrate to the eastern coast of the U.S., flying nearly due east.

Some birds leapfrog their compatriots. Northernmost breeders may go farther south than the same species of birds that breed in southern areas. Peregrine falcons that breed in the tundra migrate to the neotropics, while temperate-breeding peregrines don't migrate at all, or travel only a short distance.

Then there's the matter of differential migration. Members of a species may exhibit different migratory behaviors, based on their age and sex. For example, female dark-eyed juncos migrate farther south than males. Immature herring gulls migrate farther south than adults—first-year birds may fly to Florida, while a four-year-old winters in the Carolinas. Immature male snowy owls migrate farther south than adult females.

73

There's a hot debate about why differential migration occurs. Social domination apparently plays a role—bigger and older birds dominate the resources nearby, forcing smaller, immature birds to travel farther away. Female birds of prey are often larger than males, possibly explaining why immature male snowy owls are usually found farther south in winter than the females.

Another hypothesis says that males of some species stay north of the females in order to acquire the best breeding sites in spring. Neither explanation works for all species, but each may apply to some species.

Food availability appears to be the driving force behind all migration. A number of songbirds no longer migrate as far as they once did, because so many people feed birds throughout the winter. Thus migration is a flexible behavior—inherited and instinctual, but plastic and moldable.

Osprey Return Dates

Woody Hagge of Hazelhurst annually watches a pair of osprey that traditionally nest on his Foster Lake property. As of April 12, 1996, Foster Lake was still covered with 28 inches of ice. When the ospreys returned on April 14, an argument may have taken place between them:

"I told you there was too much ice for us to come all the way back."

"Oh, don't worry. We've toughed it out before." And so on.

I had thought ospreys returned right at ice-off, but Woody thought they returned a week before. Well, it's always nice to have a few statistics to prove just how poor our recollections can be. Woody looked up his osprey data and found the following:

In 1990, the ospreys returned on April 11. The lake opened on April 11.

In 1991, they returned on April 4; ice-out occurred on April 14.

In 1992, they returned April 9; ice-out April 27.

In 1993, returned April 17; ice-out April 28.

In 1994, returned April 14; ice-out April 18.

In 1995, returned April 16; ice-out April 18.

If one can safely generalize from seven years of data (longer-term data would be better), it appears that the ospreys return any time they damn well please.

Ospreys have a tougher go of it when they return than eagles, because they rarely eat carrion. Ninety-nine percent of their diet consists of fish, so they probably work the rivers until the ice disappears.

Arctic Owl Update

The winter of 1995-96 was exceptional for seeing Arctic owls. The Wisconsin Society for Ornithology summarized the number of confirmed sightings of Arctic owls in Wisconsin that winter: great gray, 40 or more; boreal, 15 or more; hawk, 3.

Loon Migration

Loons appear on northern lakes as soon as the ice is off. "Our" loons winter on the Atlantic coast; by the end of March, they have flown up the coastline to somewhere north of the Carolinas. They turn inland in loose flocks that fly at various altitudes, and at distances of up to one-quarter of a mile apart, quite unlike the tight formations favored by geese and ducks. Anywhere from several to a few hundred loons may travel together. They probably become acquainted in areas where the loons are backed up waiting for ice-off.

Loons follow lakes and rivers during migration, because they can't land on anything other than water if they hope to take off

> ## Late April Musings
>
> *No spring returns but that I wish I might live again through the moment when I went out in the woods . . . to learn not only the name, but the ways and the range and the charm of the windflower [wood anemone].*
>
> -Donald Culross Peattie

again. Their exact pathways are unknown, but by early May the hotspot in the Midwest is the Whitefish Point Bird Observatory near Sault Ste. Marie, MI. Thousands can be seen there on peak migration days. May 2 was the peak date in 1995, when 1,486 common loons passed by the observatory. A record total of 9,284 common loons were counted between April 15 and May 31 in 1994.

75

MAY

The Ojibwe word for May is wabigwungizis—wabigwun meaning "flower," gizis meaning "month." These two words amply sum up the bounty of May. The ice usually goes off northern lakes just prior to the first of May; then many trees and shrubs form blossoms and leaves in a wondrous explosion of scent and greenery. The first flowers that come into bloom in the sandy soils of southern Iron County include round-leaved hepatica, trailing arbutus, wood anemone, large-flowered bellwort, marsh marigolds, and barren strawberry. In richer soils than our depauperate sands, look for Jack-in-the-pulpit, spring beauty, trout lily, Dutchman's breeches, and bloodroot—all of which seem to magically appear in the woods, sometimes in numbers that defy simple calculation.

Forest flowers race into bloom in May because they must. Once the tree canopy leafs out, the sun becomes a rare commodity on the forest floor, seen only in a flecking that moves with the wind's fluttering of the leaf umbrella. After seven months of frost, the smell of rich, damp decay emerging from the soil as life renews itself is something close to holy.

STOCKTON IS.

MINNESOTA

INTERSTATE 35

ST. CROIX RIVER

WISCONSIN

GOVERNOR KNOWLES WILDERNESS AREA 7,348 ACRES

black flies
little black
flies

always
the
black
flies

no matter
where you
go...

skeeter

MAY 1-15

May 1 to May 15

A Blessing in Disguise

During any northwoods spring, the snow's seemingly endless presence tests us psychologically. The longest winter Mary and I have experienced in the northwoods happened in 1996. On May 6, snow was still prevalent throughout the woods; the ice didn't go off most of the lakes until the second week of May (May 17 on Trout Lake). The snow seemed like it would never leave. Still, as difficult as it may be to accept, the snow's long refusal to melt is actually a blessing in disguise.

> ## May Musings
>
> *Few people know how to take a walk. The qualifications . . . are endurance, plain clothes, old shoes, an eye for nature, good humor, vast curiosity, good speech, good silence, and nothing too much.*
>
> -Ralph Waldo Emerson

Back in the 1920s, the Northern Highlands/American Legion State Forest was created. Many reasons were given for its creation, but one of the most important was to protect the forests in the headwaters region in order to prevent flooding. Consider what might have occurred in late April of 1996 if our huge snowload had melted in one large pulse. Our rivers were quite high from the previous autumn, even without the addition of all the melting snow. Massive flooding could well have resulted.

Thankfully, our watersheds are almost entirely shaded forestlands. If our lands were in agricultural production or concrete development, neither would shade the snow and slow the meltwater. The forests also act as a sponge to absorb the water into the soil. The bottom line is, we would face dramatic flooding nearly every spring if our snow didn't melt slowly.

Sightings

On May 1, photographer Jeff Richter from Mercer observed a lapland longspur, usually more of a western grasslands migrant, feeding among the sparrows in the snowy grass by his home.

One memorable day in early May, Bob Kovar from Manitowish Waters watched dozens of birds knocking themselves silly by flying headlong into one of his picture windows. It happened just after our last major snowstorm of 1996, and Bob suggests it may have been a mass "bird-a-cide." Perhaps they couldn't take the winter any longer.

Look for indigo buntings by May 7; veeries by May 8; eastern gray tree frogs calling by May 8; redstarts by May 11; brown thrashers by May 12; chipping sparrows by May 13; catbirds by May 14; scarlet tanagers on May 16; goslings by May 16; and white-crowned sparrows by May 19.

Trailing Arbutus, the Plymouth Mayflower

Mary's grandmother used to gather trailing arbutus in the woods across the river. She shipped the tiny, fragrant blossoms in sphagnum moss to her sister in California, who missed the beautiful Wisconsin springs. Early settlers in Boston used to sell bunches of arbutus on the city streets, calling it the "Plymouth Mayflower" because it was thought to be the first flower seen by the Pilgrims.

To survive northern winters, trailing arbutus evolved leathery, hairy, evergreen leaves that creep along the forest floor. Late spring frosts have little luck damaging such tough leaves. The flowers, too, are tolerant of the cold. We've sometimes seen the blossoms surrounded by snow, still perfuming the spring air.

Gathering Wild Leeks

One early May, Gil Willms from Lac du Flambeau led Mary and I on a trip to gather wild leeks in the Chequamegon National Forest. We filled a five-gallon pail with the beautiful leeks, which were growing amidst a throng of trilliums, Dutchman's breeches, and other wildflowers. Leeks should be picked in May, because once the flower has blossomed in June, the flavor of the bulbs becomes undesirably strong. Try potato-leek soup for a wonderful, wild food meal during the cool nights of May.

Hepatica and the Doctrine of Signatures

In the woods around Manitowish, hepatica is usually the first wild-flower blessing of the spring. The genus name Hepatica originates in the Greek *hepar*, or liver. The leaves of the plant are three-lobed, and were thought to resemble the lobes of the liver. Centuries ago, people believed that God had created plant shapes to indicate the manner in which He desired us to use them—a concept called "the Doctrine of Signatures." God's signature was thought to be upon all things, if only we could see it. Thus, hepatica was considered the cure for liver ailments. Today's medical terms for liver-associated ailments, like hepatitis, are derivations of this original name. As with most applications of the Doctrine of Signatures, the plant's shape has proven to be of no value in determining its medical use.

81

Soils: It All Starts Here

Hepatica, wood anemone, and trailing arbutus are the first flowers Mary and I usually see in bloom in spring. Many springs, they are the only wildflowers, except for leatherleaf in the bogs, that we see blooming in our sandy soils in early May. At the same time, it's not uncommon for friends in the Gurney area—some 45 miles northwest where the soil is heavier—to have carpets of trout lilies and spring beauties in bloom, as well as bloodroot, Dutchman's breeches, marsh marigolds, white violets, dwarf ginseng, and bellwort.

The difference in the presence and populations of species of wild-flowers can be remarkable when areas of light, sandy soils are compared to areas with clay or loam soils. Some species, like Canada mayflower and wild sarsaparilla, are generalists that grow in either soil type. But many wildflowers are specific in their habitat requirements.

Trillium is a classic example. I have seldom seen a large-flowered trillium growing in sandy soil, so we almost never see them in our area. They are prolific, however, in the heavier soils of northern hardwood forests all around us, even though the climate is the same.

We may miss out on the community of plants associated with rich deciduous soils, but on the other hand, our friends in Gurney express envy over our trailing arbutus and barren strawberry, which grow best in pine/sand country.

A rule to remember about the natural world: Never say never, and never say always. Most plants are found in specific habitats because they are able to outcompete other plants in the same conditions. That doesn't mean they can't live in other soil or climate conditions, if the competition is reduced. A good example is tamarack, a true bog species adapted to wet, cold, acidic conditions, but one quite capable of surviving in dry uplands like my backyard, where we have transplanted one that's doing very well.

Counting Frogs

On May 1, I perform the first of my three annual frog counts for the Wisconsin DNR. I stop at 10 different sites in Vilas County, and I listen for five minutes to determine which species are calling and in what general numbers. Most folks laugh when I say I'm going out to count frogs. A man was once parked at Jag Lake, one of the sites I survey. He came over to my car to ask a question. I felt I ought to explain why I was sitting in my car with a chart in my lap, so I told him I was counting frogs. To his credit, and my relief, he didn't fall apart into a series of belly laughs. But he undoubtedly enjoyed a few chuckles with his wife about the "frog guy" when he got home.

The Wisconsin frog count began in 1984, and takes place on permanent survey routes in every county within the state. Why does the Wisconsin DNR count frogs? Like any species, frogs are an important link in the food chain. Because they live in wetlands for much of their lives, their increase or decrease can tell us much about the health of our wetland areas. Frogs and toads are sensitive to environmental changes, so they can be used as an index of environmental quality.

Some frog species, like leopard and cricket frogs, are now significantly declining for reasons as yet unexplained.

I have been running my survey route since 1988, listening for frogs in the early spring, late spring, and midsummer. Spring peepers usually lead the chorus at each of my wetland survey sites. Peepers are a little more than an inch long, sport a dark X on their backs, and have toe pads like all tree frogs. Each female lays 800 to 1,000 eggs, which hatch in two to three days. By early June, the tadpoles have already transformed into adultlike froglets.

In early May, I usually hear a total of five species calling—spring peepers, wood frogs, chorus frogs, American toads, and northern leopard frogs. The males woo the females through their calls. At a few sites, the decibel level gets so intense that local noise ordinances must be broken.

83

The calls are very simple to learn. Once memorized, they help you sort out the din of a spring night. Most people unfamiliar with frog calls give credit to "crickets" for all the racket, though crickets aren't even on the scene yet. The call of the wood frog sounds like a soft quacking. Leopard frogs produce a series of low-pitched, guttural "snores," lasting several seconds and sounding somewhat like rubbing a finger over a wet balloon. To me, it actually sounds more like the growling of a hungry stomach. Toads give a long (often 15 to 30 seconds), high, trilling call, while the call of chorus frogs sounds like someone raking a finger across a comb—sort of a "creeeeek" sound. Peepers just peep over and over again, chorusing often day and night. Soon to join the orchestra are Eastern gray tree frogs, mink frogs, green frogs, and bullfrogs, each of which has a distinctive call that is easily remembered. Those nine species are generally the only ones you need to know in the northwoods.

Toads usually start trilling during the second week of May, and leopard frogs began calling soon afterward. Leopard frogs are one of the frog species that have been in significant decline over the last two decades, not only in Wisconsin but in several areas of the United States, England, and Europe as well.

Make Your Ears into Satellite Dishes

There's an easy trick for amplifying calls, so you can hear quiet singers like wood frogs. Cup your hands behind your ears and push your ears out, a la Dumbo. It seems to nearly double the sound volume, much like facial disks must do for owls.

Dying with the Black Flies

Black flies, little black flies,
Always the black flies no matter where you go,
Dying with the black flies picking on my bones,
In North Ontario, in North Ontario.

84

So goes the chorus of "The Black Fly Song" sung by folksinger Bill Staines. That refrain pops into my head every year at this time, when the female black flies swarm in search of the blood meal they require prior to laying eggs. In contrast, the males—peace-loving souls that they are—enjoy sips of flower nectar, then lounge in the wetlands. I imagine they're engaged in reading the classics.

To their only credit, black flies make no sound during their attacks (I hate the whine of mosquitoes), but they lack etiquette in all other respects. They prefer to fly in your ears, up your nose, down your shirt, and behind your glasses, biting right along your scalp line. Like mosquitoes, they inject an anticoagulant into their prey's blood, but they must use the super octane mix, because their bites hurt a lot more and last a lot longer than mosquito bites.

The female eventually lays her eggs on vegetation or rocks near a fast-moving stream, where the larvae hatch and begin the 11 month larval period of their life. They cling to underwater rocks by means of hooks and suction, and then filter the water for food particles as it flows by.

Prior to the hatch, the larvae spin a cocoon structure. They then float to the surface in air bubbles, which prevent their wings from getting wet. Once hatched, their numbers and hunger can drive people and animals from the woods. Repellents seem to offer no succor, and often the only way to find relief from their attacks is to don a full, mosquito-netted body suit.

Mosquitoes Hatching

Mosquitoes usually hatch soon after ice-out. One early May a heat wave (90°F—a miracle!) lasted three days, escalating the mosquito numbers into an army of Biblical proportions. We weren't happy in the least, but I assume the birds were thrilled. Songbirds make up over half of all birds, and most are predominately insect-eaters. In one researcher's stomach analysis of 80,000 North American birds, insects were found to comprise 88 percent of all animal foods. Nine species of shorebirds feed on mosquitoes; a killdeer or sandpiper might consider 50 to 500 mosquitoes an adequate meal. Mosquitoes play an important role in the food chain; however, when I'm trying to look at a wildflower or listen to a bird and the 'skeets swarm around my face, ecological value is seldom foremost in my mind.

85

Wisconsin Point

Mary and I experienced a rare bird sighting one early May in 1994 along Wisconsin Point, a two-mile-long sandbar that juts into Lake Superior. According to a sign at the site, this point is the world's longest natural sandbar. In the sleet and snow of that normal, northwoods spring day, two flocks of white pelicans (each including about eight members) huddled and flew, then huddled some more against a biting north wind. White pelicans have been sighted in about eight of every 10 years in Wisconsin since 1939; most years, there are one to four reports. No evidence of breeding pelicans existed for Wisconsin prior to 1995, though they had begun nesting in Green Bay as of 1996. These birds must have been on their way north to a breeding area in northcentral Canada or west to western Minnesota, where a few colonies breed.

During our hour or two of birding that day, we were additionally rewarded by large rafts of various species of ducks, along with smaller numbers of cormorants, tundra swans, and horned grebes. Wisconsin

Point is considered one of the best birding spots in Wisconsin. It is particularly good during rainy weather, because migrating birds may be grounded there for days. As many as 24 species of warblers have been seen there on a "socked-in" May morning.

Brockway Mountain Drive
Hawk Migration

During the first week of May in 1995, Mary, Callie, and I traveled to Brockway Mountain Drive, located near the tip of the Keweenaw Peninsula in Michigan's Upper Peninsula. We wanted to watch the spring hawk migration. Because most birds dislike crossing large bodies of water, the Great Lakes act as barriers that constrict the broad flow of migrating birds, often forcing them into very narrow corridors. When birds flowing through our general area reach Lake Superior, they often follow the Superior lakeshore, trying to find a land crossing or at least the narrowest passage across the lake. Many thus end up at the tip of the Keweenaw. Just south of Copper Harbor, the hawks like to ride the warm updrafts sweeping up the face of Brockway Mountain, a steep ridge that runs for nearly 10 miles to Copper Harbor. Brockway Mountain Drive is advertised as the highest American road west of the Alleghenies and east of the Rockies. The panoramas of rich forest, inland lakes, and Lake Superior are genuinely breathtaking.

We were told that the first weekend in May is often one of the best for seeing migrating hawks, so we took our chances and headed up. We got lucky. On Sunday, May 7, 1995, the hawks were coming through hot and heavy. Many of them were at eye level, or below eye level in the valley to our east. The northeast wind was not all that favorable for a crossing over Lake Superior, so the hawks weren't rushing by. They often passed over our heads very slowly, and many even hovered over us for awhile. One sharp-shinned hawk flew so close that we could have touched it. Within an hour we saw broad-winged, rough-legged, sharp-shinned, Cooper's, and red-tailed hawks, northern harriers, kestrels, turkey vultures, and bald eagles, plus a few skeins of geese and some songbirds, among them yellow-rumped warblers. In total we saw a minimum of several hundred raptors during that one hour, though we weren't counting.

One kettle of broad-winged hawks included 36 individuals. Broadwings often migrate in groups, called "kettles." As they fly north, the birds circle on thermals within the kettle, seemingly going in two directions at one time. Spring flights can be significant, but broadwings are best known for their huge fall flights over Hawk Ridge in Duluth. The single-day record there is 47,922!

The northwoods' most common hawk, broadwings are the smallest of the buteo hawks, and are about the size of crows. When soaring, broadwings may be identified by their chunky, short bodies; their long, rounded wings; the three black and two white bands on the tails of adults; their clear wings with black edges; and their whitish bellies with dark, vertical streaks. Their plaintive, high, whistled call, which sounds somewhat like that of a wood pewee, makes identification easier.

87

There was still snow in patches on top of Brockway Mountain when we were there. Road signs indicated that the drive was closed, but the locals said the highway department just hadn't gotten around to removing the signs. The Keweenaw, as you probably know, receives more snow than any other area in the Midwest, and the last snowstorm there usually comes between May 1 and May 15. The hawks don't mind the snow, and peak migrations occur from mid-April through May. If nothing else, Brockway Mountain provides what could be the most beautiful scenery in the upper Midwest.

Martian Owls

While camping in early May with some high school students on the Manitowish River, we heard a saw-whet owl. The call is unmistakable once you learn it. The saw-whet issues a continual series of beeps that sounds to me like a dump truck backing up and to others like the Martians just landed in the swamp. The male is wooing the female; once they have mated, the saw-whet will lapse into silence again until the next spring.

The saw-whet is the smallest owl of the eastern U.S., only seven to eight inches long. It prefers lowland coniferous woods and is seldom seen.

We were also treated to the calls of several barred owls, performing the familiar "who cooks for you" call with a wonderful maniacal twist at the end. They sounded like an evil witch in a late-night spook show.

Wildfowl Welfare

Goslings usually hatch out on about May 9 in this area. Carol Hanneman, who lives on Echo Lake in Mercer, reports that wild pairs come to her yard with their young every spring, feeding on grass and Carol's handouts. Carol works at the local school and brings home scraps from the cafeteria for the geese and ducks every day. They have no qualms about Carol's welfare system, and come running when they see her. In our goose-starved area, Carol's house is the best guarantee for seeing geese in the spring.

Mallards, Wood Turtles, and Loons

On May 5 one spring, Dave Picard, a friend and inveterate explorer, was startled when a mallard hen flushed from an old, charred pine stump. She had deposited 11 eggs inside the stump, the eggs resting a foot down or so in the three-foot-high stump. Mallards usually nest in the grassy areas of a marsh, or on a sandy ridge. The nest is most often just a scrape built of matted grasses, so this was an unusual sighting.

In the Upper Peninsula of Michigan on that same day, Dave watched six wood turtles, a threatened species. Four of the turtles were on a hillside. The other two were copulating in about two feet of water, staying underwater in that position for some five minutes (perhaps they were newlyweds).

A friend who wishes to remain anonymous watched a loon lay an egg on an equally anonymous lake in our area. I suppose the loon would also prefer to be anonymous in this story. The unnamed female was nesting on a platform built by the landowner, and one egg already resided in the nest from the previous day. The loon had been offering a tail end profile for over half an hour to my friend, who was just about to give up attempting to photograph this bird, since rear ends don't sell well. The loon suddenly leaned forward and lifted her tail end up high, almost arching her back, and began to strain. She then settled back down, but in about 15 seconds leaned forward again, lifted her rear and strained. Up and down she went, and in 15 minutes the egg finally emerged. The female stayed in her tail-up position for several minutes after the egg was laid, then stood up, turned around, and flopped down on the eggs so hard that my friend thought she could have broken them.

89

Loons typically lay two eggs, one day apart. Incubation lasts about 30 days, so most young will hatch in mid-June.

Flickers: It's a Jungle Out There

Every morning in early May, male flickers make a heck of a racket outside my window. The male's jungle call, a very loud yuck, yuck, yuck or woika, woika, woika, depending on your level of phonetic acumen, is enough to raise the dead. Courtship is further enhanced by head bobbing and weaving, a la Muhammad Ali in his prime.

Flickers eat more ants than any other North American bird. They are our only ground-feeding woodpecker, and they use their long, sticky tongues to collect the ants. One researcher counted 5,000 ants eaten at one feeding by a flicker.

To identify flickers, look for their conspicuous white rump patch. The males have a black "moustache," while females are clean-shaven.

Flocks of Yellowlegs

I love to paddle on the Manitowish at this time of year, because the ducks are thick in just about every slough along the way. Blue-winged teal and mallards are most common, but I see many green-winged teal, hooded mergansers, and wood ducks as well. The beauty of the male wood ducks is startling, but the male green-winged teal and hooded mergansers are wonderfully "painted," too. They often surprise me by how close they allow me to come before they scatter in flight.

The birding highlight for me, though, is usually a flock of 10 or more greater yellowlegs, feeding in the mud flats along the shoreline. Yellowlegs are a large shorebird with very long, yellow-orange legs. Like many waterbirds, they fly a short distance downstream when disturbed, then settle down again. I invariably come around the next bend and kick them up again. Off they go, as if we're playing an ongoing game of hide-and-seek. Yellowlegs nest in Canada, so they only pass through our area for a short time; then they're gone until their southerly migration occurs in August. We often see them in good numbers in the early fall on Powell Marsh, where they feed in the mud and shallow water created when the DNR draws down various water impoundments.

90

Northern Harrier: The Marsh Hawk

Marsh hawks, or northern harriers, are now at their peak of migration through the north. Many will nest here. They are easily identified by their white rump patches and low-flying maneuvers over wetlands. Harriers fly back and forth, often covering 100 miles a day as they search the wetlands for rodents, small birds, frogs, crayfish, and snakes. While harrier numbers appear strong here, their numbers are down throughout their nesting range, because of the nationwide loss of wetlands and the use of pesticides.

Mary and I regularly watch marsh hawks working the river wetlands behind our house. The genders can easily be distinguished by coloration. The male is a light blue-gray, while the larger female is brown above and streaked with brown below. Harriers nest on the ground in marshes, using grasses for their dominant building material.

Scissor-tailed Flycatcher

Harvey Posvic, who lives just south of Hurley, called one May 6 to say he'd been watching a scissor-tailed flycatcher perched on his fence for most of the day! For extremely rare sightings like this, it generally pays to be skeptical, but a scissor-tailed flycatcher can't be confused with any other Wisconsin bird. Its tail measures nearly nine inches, comprising about two-thirds of its total body length. When it flies, the bird's tail opens and closes like a pair of scissors. I have never seen one, and I didn't realize just how rare the scissor-tail is until I looked up the record of sightings in Wisconsin. It has been reported in Wisconsin only nine times since 1980, and it wasn't until 1956 that it was first seen here. As the state bird of Oklahoma, it has little business chasing insects in Hurley. What a kind gesture on the scissor-tail's part to allow a few northerners a glimpse of it.

Stockton Island Bears 91

In mid-May, Mary and I had the opportunity to camp for several nights on Stockton Island, one of the islands in the Apostle Islands National Lakeshore near Bayfield. The Sigurd Olson Institute runs a series of three-day schools on the island, and we escorted 15 sixth-graders so they could experience the island and Lake Superior. Stockton may be most remarkable for the 25 black bears that live on it, which is an average of about two per square mile. That's the highest density of black bears to be found anywhere in North America. A high density for our area is usually two bears for every three square miles. The carrying capacity of the island appears to be exceeded, as the yearling bears are vastly underweight. The major question facing DNR researchers is this: What is the limiting factor on how high the population can get? They also want to know whether the bears will migrate to other islands (they can swim quite well), starve, or resort to cannibalism. Something has to give, and only time will tell.

Wisconsin Wilderness: How Much Is Enough?

The Turtle-Flambeau Flowage is remarkably rich in birdlife. It harbors the highest densities of eagles, ospreys, and loons of any water body in Wisconsin. In 1995, 12 pairs of eagles, 18 pairs of osprey, and 25 pairs of loons nested here. The easternmost one-fifth contains the highest concentration of these species within the flowage, offering five eagle nests, five osprey nests, and six loon nests. A black tern colony and a merlin nesting pair are also found here.

The master plan for the area, written in the spring of 1995, has designated the easternmost one-fifth as a "voluntary quiet area," a classification bound to create user confrontations between those who wish to roar around in large motorboats and those who come expecting quiet due to voluntary compliance.

Such a compromise appeases most people on different sides of the issue, but it fails to address the long-term needs of this portion of the flowage and the large number of people who seek wilderness experience. The issue of wilderness, like many issues, often comes down to one value-laden question: How much is enough? My answer is simple: Since there isn't any more wilderness being made, we had best save the few remaining vestiges.

Some would argue that we already have enough. Here's the facts, so you can judge for yourself. The State of Wisconsin manages four designated wilderness areas: The Manitowish River Wilderness Area, a 5,460-acre area in the Northern Highlands State Forest; the Flambeau River Wilderness Zone, a 13,560 acre linear protection zone along the shorelines of the North and South Forks of the Flambeau River; the Governor Knowles Wilderness Area, 7,348 acres of shoreline along the Wisconsin side of the St. Croix River; and the Big Block Wilderness Area in the Flambeau River State Forest, encompassing 1,354 acres of what was the best example of old-growth forest in Wisconsin until a windstorm nearly leveled it in 1977. The Big Block is now more of an experiment in natural recovery.

Wisconsin also contains five federally designated wilderness areas within its national forests. The Nicolet National Forest offers three areas, totaling 33,000 of its 658,000 acres. The Chequamegon National Forest includes two protected areas, covering 11,050 acres of its 850,000 acres.

One might fairly ask why we need more. Add the numbers together and you'll find that Wisconsin lags far behind other Midwestern states in providing wilderness recreational areas for silent sports users such as cross-country skiers, canoeists, kayakers, snowshoers, and dog sledders. Minnesota, by comparison, has set aside 804,000 acres of federal wilderness; Michigan offers 248,000 protected fed-

92

eral acres; Wisconsin contains about 72,000 acres in combined state (27,722 acres) and federal lands (44,350 acres). Wilderness designation eliminates motor use, but allows all other activities currently taking place, such as fishing, hunting, trapping, and camping.

The northwoods can't be all things to all people, or it will cease to be anything to anyone. To set aside land requires vision and courage. The number of people using the northwoods continues to rise, and the future of most public waterways is one of overcrowding, particularly during the highly sensitive nesting season, which lasts from the opening of fishing season through Memorial Day. Too many people, even if they're paddling canoes, means "consumption" of the resource, because people create disturbance. These decisions only become harder as more and more people come to know an area. I hope we can soon let go of our "needs" long enough to grant precedence to the needs of the Turtle-Flambeau Flowage's pristine flora and fauna.

May Musings

It was rare and comforting to waken late and hear the undiminished shouting of the water in the night. And at sunup it was still there, powerful and incessant, with the slant sun tangled in its rainbow spray, the grass blue with wetness, and the air heady as ether and scented with campfire smoke. By such a river it is impossible to believe that one will ever be tired or old.

-Wallace Stegner, while camped by a wild river.

3:45AM

5:14AM

8:37PM

LET
THERE
BE LIGHT!

cotton grass • leather leaf • trillium • lilac • pussytoe • spring beauty • labrador tea • star flower • gaywing • clintonia • honeysuckle • phlox • cow vetch • tall buttercup • columbine • forget-me-not • twinflower

22,197

The Preacher

MAY 16-31

AEL

May 16 to May 31

Remember, This is May

One May 16 my wife Mary, myself, and twelve hearty souls canoed from Murray's Landing on the Turtle-Flambeau Flowage into the portion of the flowage that is now designated a "voluntary quiet zone." The wind had whipped up whitecaps at the landing before we even put in, but we pushed through them, hoping to find some protection on the lee side of islands. There was little calm to be found, and equally little time for looking around if you didn't want to be blown back to the landing. We were greeted several hours later by a brief

> ### Late May Musings
> *They tell us that plants are perishable, soulless creatures, that only man is immortal, but this, I think, is something that we know very nearly nothing about.*
> -John Muir

snow flurry after surfing with the wind back to the landing. This was another in a long history of personal experiences demonstrating the vagaries of May weather in the northwoods. Expect the unexpected.

Singing to Woo and Warn

Bird song is at its height in late May. The males sing on their nesting territories to advertise for females, to strengthen bonds with an established mate, and to serve notice to other males that this territory has been claimed. Songbirds do sing songs, defined as consistently repeated patterns of sounds, but they also produce calls—short sounds with no pattern. The calls serve different purposes than the songs. Calls help them maintain contact within the flock, alert others to predators, and serve to ring the dinner bell when food is found to share.

Some females sing, too—notably song sparrows, rose-breasted gros-beaks, and cardinals—but all genders and ages give calls.

Songs can be long and wonderfully intricate. A winter wren's song lasts for eight to 10 seconds, a seemingly impossible task for a bird so small. The larger brown thrasher has 3,000 song-types, and can sing in a manner that seems continuous for several minutes. Many songs, though, are short and not the least bit musical, like the woodcock's "peent" or the least flycatcher's "che-beck."

Most birds sing in the early morning and late afternoon, but some sing all day. Mary and I took an early afternoon walk in a mature hemlock-hardwood forest one May weekend. A black-throated green warbler sang for virtually the entire time. One researcher counted 1,680 songs produced by this little warbler in a seven-hour span. But the red-eyed vireo may hold the world record for one day, a perfor-mance of 22,197 songs. The vireo earns with ease its title of "the preacher bird."

Some birds communicate through nonverbal song substitutes. The ruffed grouse drums on a hollow log with its wings to produce the equivalent of a song, while a male snipe dives through the air to create a winnowing sound through his tail feathers.

Birds vocalize through their syrinx, a resonating chamber that can allow them to sing two different pitches simultaneously. When slowed down on a recording, the song of a veery is really two songs per-formed at once, creating a rather indescribable, ethereal, flutelike song.

Every bird species is born with an "auditory template," which al-lows each species to concentrate solely on learning its song in the midst of all the other melodies available on a spring morning. Experi-ments that involved placing nestling birds in a soundproof chamber have demonstrated that, while calls are innate, most songs are par-tially or entirely learned.

After a long, silent winter, I know of no one who does not love the songs of spring floating in through an open window on an early May morning.

Snoring Can Be a Song, Too

Leopard frogs have an odd song, though "odd" may be a peculiar term to use. What is "normal" for frogs, after all? Leopard frogs seem to snore; sometimes they sort of chuckle; but then again, they produce a quick, knocking sound characterized by some as the sound of rubbing your hand slowly along a balloon. The English language fails me (or I fail it) when I try to describe many sounds that occur in the natural world, and the leopard frog's vocabulary joins that long list.

If you had a leopard frog in hand, you'd discover a medium-sized frog with two or three rows of irregularly spaced brown spots outlined in a cream color. Leopard frogs were once the most common frog in Wisconsin, but their populations have decreased dramatically. They are most often heard or seen breeding in open, quiet bodies of water.

97

Hummingbird Extremes

I often watch ruby-throated hummingbirds approaching our nectar feeder in May, and the male is one very territorial guy. When another male tries to come to the feeder, the first male drives him off, then goes into his "celebratory dance," flying back and forth in an arc as if he were attached to the end of a pendulum. This behavior also occurs prior to copulation with a female, but in my observations, I have not seen any females in the vicinity.

Probably no other family of birds has such unique extremes of physiology and behavior as hummingbirds. Hummers have the most rapid wingbeat of all birds, exceeding 4,000 beats per minute. While hovering, their wings are blurred at 55 beats per second; while they move backward, the wings beat at 61 beats per second; and while the birds move forward, the wings beat at 75 beats or more per second. They have the largest heart size, relative to body weight, of any warm-blooded animal. They also have the most rapid heartbeat of all birds, thumping away at nearly 500 beats per minute while at rest and 1,000 beats per minute when active. Their normal body temperature is approximately 105 to 109°F, among the highest of all birds. Hummers are the only birds capable of prolonged hovering and rapid backward flight. They are able to do so because they can reverse their primaries through rotary movements at the shoulder, wrist, and in the bones supporting their outer primaries. Last but not least, they frequently eat more than half their body weight in food per day, and they may drink eight times their weight in water each day.

Their nests are usually constructed largely from spider webbing, lined internally with willow cotton, and decorated on the outside with lichens and bark, thereby blending into the branches on which they are placed. The female usually lays only two eggs, and she does all the incubating and child rearing. The male is liberated from such duties in order to pursue his promiscuity. Nests are often used for several seasons, and they are refurbished annually.

Hummingbirds were collected for "ornamental purposes" in the late 1800s by upper-class Europeans. During one month in 1888, more than 12,000 hummingbird skins were sold in London alone. Today such a practice seems like an impossible conceit, but one wonders what people a century from now will think of some of our current environmental values.

Woodcock Drama

The woodcock's courting ritual is quite a performance, and it's enacted virtually every night and early morning in open patches throughout the northwoods. The male begins his nasal peent at dusk, when the light level reaches 0.05 foot-candles. He calls sporadically for a minute or two, then lifts off the ground, flying in wide circles and creating a twittering sound with his three outer primary feathers. He levels off at 200 to 300 feet, then descends to earth, zigzagging back and forth and chirping for all he's worth until he alights on the spot where he began. Here he struts around, bobbing up and down and fanning out his tail for the adoration of a lady he hopes is watching. Then he begins his less than melodious peenting once again. Aldo Leopold wrote about the woodcock's aerial display in his Sand County Almanac: "The drama of the sky dance is enacted nightly on hundreds of farms, the owners of which sigh for entertainment, but harbor the illusion that it is to be sought in theaters. They live on the land, but not by the land."

Cliff Swallow Nesting

Every May, upward of 80 cliff swallows busily make their flask-shaped mud homes under the Highway 47 bridge near my house. From a puddle near my driveway, they gather mud in their beaks, their wings drawn back and fluttering like angels. With a little dab of mud in their mouths, the swallows swoop back under the bridge and engineer a home, traveling back and forth more than a thousand times before the nest is ready.

99

Watching them gather mud is enjoyable. Equally enjoyable is walking onto the bridge and watching them all pour out from their nests and wing around you. Swallows look like they have a great time flying, slicing down inches above the river with their tiny mouths wide open to catch insects. Being in the midst of their swarming is exciting—they'll often brush close by your head. This might be a territorial display; on the other hand, they may simply be taking advantage of all the mosquitoes humans usually attract.

Catbirds and Thrashers: Bird Mimics

I canoed a section of the Manitowish through an early morning mist one late May. At one of the many beaver lodges along the route, I could hear the kits inside squealing. I approached the lodge, but a series of low grunts and growls seemed to clearly indicate that I wasn't welcome. Shortly after that, I heard a deer snort loudly as it bounded behind the ubiquitous willow shrubs of the Manitowish. Also apparently unhappy about my intrusion, the deer snorted continuously at me for a minute or more as I drifted past its hideout.

One animal that didn't mind my presence was the catbird singing from the top of some shrubby willows and alder. If creativity can be measured by lack of repetition, the catbird might well be the most creative bird. Catbirds distinguish themselves through their disjointed medley of notes and phrases that, put together, can loosely be called a song. Their singing contains an interspersed call that sounds like a cat "mewing," which gave rise to their name. Catbirds can also imitate the calls of other birds in the area like jays, hawks, kingfishers, various songbirds, and even tree frogs. Catbirds offset the richness of their call (though some consider it merely loud) with their distinctly uncolorful appearance—a slate-gray body with a black cap.

Along with catbirds, brown thrashers are members of the mockingbird family. Although their call is similar in many ways to the catbird's rollicking, free-form interpretation and mimicry, thrashers are easily distinguished because they repeat nearly all their phrases twice. One writer characterized their song as a telephone conversation: "Hello, hello, yes, yes, who is this? who is this? I should say, I should say, How's that? How's that?" and so on. Thrashers are remarkable mimics of birds as diverse as flickers and wood thrushes. Their long, cinnamon-brown tails, heavily striped breasts, and downcurved bills make them strikingly pretty.

100

Downy Woodpeckers

A downy woodpecker pair uses a nest cavity in a teetering, dead black ash just below our house. When the adult comes in to feed the chicks, they squeak and holler like it's their first and last meal.

Downies are small, averaging only six inches from the tip of their beaks to the tip of their tails. Due to their size, they can excavate very small holes in tree limbs that are only four to five inches in diameter. This is an important ability, because it helps them avoid predation of their young by starlings. The starlings are expert nest robbers, but they're too big to enter the downy's front door. The nest also serves as the male's roost hole. He forces the female to roost elsewhere at night while he tends the eggs and the young.

Downies are the most common woodpecker in Wisconsin, because they are quite tolerant of humans. They find nesting sites in small, dead limbs that fastidious city dwellers might not notice. They feed in forests and open spaces on tall, weedy plants, a versatility that allows them to fit into just about any urban or rural habitat. The male feeds extensively on tiny branches and tall weeds, unlike the female, which prefers to comb over tree trunks and larger limbs. If you see a downy feeding on a tall goldenrod stem, you can bet it's a male.

The adjective "downy" derives from the white stripe that goes down its back. The feathers there are soft, like down feathers; they lack the barbs typical of wing feathers. The downy's look-alike cousin, the hairy woodpecker, also has a white stripe down its back, but its feathers are a bit hairier.

I always forget which bird is the little one (the downy) and which is the bigger one (the hairy), so I use a memory device—diminutive downy, huge hairy.

101

Tundra Swans in the Light of the Full Moon

Bob Kovar, a Manitowish Waters native, saw goslings in mid-May on Little Trout Lake. Interestingly, the geese nested right under an active eagle's nest on Bob's property, thus probably shortening their life span. Most surprising was Bob's sighting of a pair of tundra swans on Little Trout Lake on May 22. He watched a pair of tundras a week earlier, swimming on Powell Marsh as a huge, orange full moon rose and bathed them in its light, an absolutely beautiful sight. It's quite odd to see tundras in our area this late in the year. They ordinarily pass through in early April.

Northern Bobwhite Quail

A bobwhite quail appeared under one of our feeders on May 8, 1995, and sang near our house until late that summer. Bobwhites don't breed here, being a more southern species, but apparently they are being released in the area by a hunting guide, in order to train his dogs. A few have escaped their fate, and somehow one male found his way to my feeder. He sang his "bobwhite" song all day long throughout the summer, even in hot weather. He didn't return the next May, though. Bobwhites just aren't adapted to the extreme winter conditions of the northwoods.

Flowers Blooming

The list of flowers that bloom in our area in late May is a long one. Here are a number of the most common flowers to look for:

102

Starflower	Blueberry
Goldthread	Gaywing
Bog laurel	Cotton grass
Leatherleaf	Bog rosemary
Trillium	Wild strawberry
Lilac	Pussytoe
Cherry trees	Spring beauty
Currants	Labrador tea
Bluebead lily	Canada mayflower
Honeysuckle	Nannyberry
Highbush cranberry	Red-osier dogwood
Gray dogwood	Bunchberry
Phlox	Alternate-leaved dogwood
Blackberry	Cow vetch
Wintercress	False Solomon's seal
Mountain ash	Tall buttercup
Yellow bullhead lily	Hawkweed
Tall meadow rue	Columbine
Wild calla	Baneberry
Blue flag	Yarrow
Sarsaparilla	Three-leaved false Solomon's seal
Twinflower	Forget-me-not

Cotton Grass

I recommend taking a late May drive along Highway 47 north of Lac du Flambeau, where Powell Marsh opens up along both sides of the road into hundreds of acres of bog. Here, cotton grass is in flower in a waving snowstorm of white blossoms. Below the tall stalks of "cotton," bog laurel is in its full pink regalia. If you're willing to risk wet feet, the hanging, globelike flowers of leatherleaf and bog rosemary can be seen close-up, too.

Trilliums

Trilliums paint a wondrous, white-silk tapestry in the May woods. Found almost exclusively in mixed hardwood forests with deep, moist, neutral soils, trilliums need a shady, undisturbed woodland in which to flourish.

Ants distribute trillium seeds by dragging them back to their nests, where they eat an attachment to the seeds. The ants then discard the seeds, which are not damaged. Although the seeds germinate the next spring, the trillium won't produce its first blossom for six years or more.

Historically, picking trilliums was illegal in Wisconsin. Since the passage of the Endangered Species Act, only those species listed as threatened or endangered are protected. Do the trilliums, the woods, and yourself a favor, however, and leave the trilliums where they belong. A trillium bouquet wilts quickly. As with most things, the most beautiful flowers are those seen in their natural habitat.

103

The Wave

Columbine comes into flower in late May, often blooming in inhospitable habitats like rock ledges. Like most wild plants, columbine has been used historically in many ways, though none of its users were more interesting than the Omaha and Ponca Indian men who considered it an aphrodisiac. The pulverized seeds were rubbed into the mens' palms, and each suitor would try to contrive a way to shake hands with the woman he desired. For the Omaha and Ponca women, I suspect this may have been the necessary incentive for inventing the wave hello and goodbye.

Marsh Marigolds

Marsh marigolds carpet wet areas in May with their brilliant yellow flowers, set off by large, dark green leaves. The tall, waxy flowers are arranged in a shallow cup, creating the overall effect of a large buttercup. The leaves are glossy, roundish to kidney-shaped, and are held up by thick, succulent stems.

I expect to see Dorothy, the Cowardly Lion, the Tin Man, and the Scarecrow skipping along one of our northern creeks someday. The profusion of flowers in wet areas makes them look very much like a "yellow brick road."

Dandelions

Engaging in the rite of lawn mowing is fruitless in late May, given the usual ample rain and heat. The dandelions in my yard are back in bloom within two days of any cutting I've done. The truth is, I kind of like dandelions, but if that's too much to stomach for the lawn manicurists among you, you might at least respect your nemesis. Dandelions are escape artists extraordinaire. Their leaves lay flattened along the ground, immune to mower blades. The period when the flower and seed head open is the only time in a dandelion's life when it becomes vulnerable to the guillotine. If you don't get the flower head immediately with the mower, the flower stalk soon becomes flaccid and collapses to the ground where it's safe once again. Then when the seed head is ready, the dandelion springs back to life in a growth spurt of five to six inches that occurs within a day or two. Even if you manage to get the first bloom, the plant will simply produce another bud, and flower again.

Dandelions were originally well-adapted to barnyards and pastures, where their thistlelike leaves and bitter white sap made them distasteful to cattle. Lawns have provided an even better habitat.

What's the best way to rid yourself of dandelion madness? Let your grass grow long. Grass hugging plants like dandelions can't tolerate shade, so they will soon become a rare flower in your yard. Skeptical? Compare their numbers in unmown meadows to manicured lawns.

Avoiding Mosquitoes

If dandelion madness is upon you, then you must certainly suffer from mosquito madness as well. Because we know that mosquitoes are drawn to movement, dark color, odor, and carbon dioxide, some mosquito-avoiding strategies are available. If you have dark hair, wear a white hat—this reduces attacks by 75 percent. Be a good listener, because the big talkers are releasing CO_2, and mosquitoes are attracted to CO_2. Stay cool—the skeeters are drawn to heat sources, too. If you own a bug zapper, give it to your neighbor—preferably a neighbor you don't much like. Studies have shown that the zappers' ability to attract mosquitoes exceeds their ability to kill them. Yards with zappers have more mosquitoes than those that provide peace and quiet.

Let There Be Light

By the end of May, the sun will rise around 5:14 a.m. and set at 8:37 p.m., bathing us in nearly 15-1/2 hours of daylight. Birds are now singing outside my window at 3:45 a.m.

105

Canoeing in the Rain

My family and a large group of friends canoed a short stretch of the Manitowish River one Memorial Day weekend. The weather was threatening, and we probably wouldn't have gone had not one of the children challenged us by calling us "a bunch of wimps." We couldn't let that shoe fit, so we embarked, and within 15 minutes, the rains were upon us.

There are two good things about being out in the rain. One is that virtually no one else is out there to disturb your experience; secondly, the wildlife seem less prone to conceal their activities. Thus we had many excellent sightings of eagles and various ducks. We saw both widgeon and common mergansers on the river—the first time I had ever seen these species on the Manitowish. I assume that both were late migrants, because few widgeons nest in our area and common mergansers are usually found on large inland lakes or the Great Lakes.

We were cold and drenched by the end of the trip, and none were worse off than the child who had accused us of wimpishness. Suffice it to say, she has not thrown out that charge since then.

Tennis, Anyone?

Killdeers nest in open gravel areas. We've seen nests right along highways, but the most unusual site we ever saw was a nest built along a fence separating the tennis and basketball courts in Mercer. It was flush with four eggs to hatch if the balls mercifully kept bouncing away. Remarkably, the eggs weren't crushed, and I assume the little kill-deers hatched and skittered around the courts for the rest of the summer.

Habitat for Humanity, Avian Style

If you're in the habit of feeding birds, you may also want to help them raise new homes by putting out nesting material. Stuff like drier lint, yarn scraps, dog and cat hair, and sheep's wool is quickly collected by birds and incorporated into their nests. One spring we watched numerous birds glean dog hair from an outdoor mat, a favorite lounging spot for our shedding husky. I also found two nests one spring that included layers of pink fiberglass insulation. More than likely, the birds filched the batting from an open shed where we store some old insulation. I hope birds don't get itchy touching the stuff, like we do.

I certainly wouldn't recommend putting out fiberglass insulation, but use your imagination in providing a variety of natural materials. For instance, northern orioles are particularly fond of white yarn, and may make their nests almost entirely of the yarn. If you put the yarn in the same wide screen baskets that you probably used all winter for suet, you can watch birds collecting housing materials while you feed them.

Migration Triggers

Spring migration is a bit of a misnomer. It's hardly spring when gyrfalcons return to their arctic breeding grounds in February; likewise, it's hardly spring when some sedge wrens finally return to their breeding grounds in July.

Fall migration is an inaccurate term, too. Some shorebirds begin their southerly migration in early July, while some waterfowl wait to head south until November, just before ice-up. We'd be better off using post-breeding and pre-breeding as the terms for fall and spring migration, but the terminology is hardly important in May, when the world has suddenly come alive with morning bird song and flashing avian colors.

Wintery weather slows bird migration, but many still return early in the season, seemingly oblivious to the vacillating temperatures. The behavior has prompted questions from both scientists and curious observers for many years. What controls their timing? How do the birds navigate and orient themselves to the same nesting sites every year?

Consider your response if I said you would have to make a trip from South America for thousands of miles to a specific hole in a tree in North America. Not only that, but you would have to do the majority of your traveling at night, as most migrating birds do, using the stars or magnetic fields for guidance. And you would have to forage along the way for whatever foods you could find—no money or credit cards allowed—while sometimes traveling enormous distances, such as 500 miles across the Gulf of Mexico without any food at all. You would have no maps and nothing to guide you except your experience last fall in flying to your winter home in South America. There would be big predators, 20 to a hundred times bigger than you, all along the way—voracious killers of cute little things like you.

107

It's more than remarkable that any of the birds return at all. I surely couldn't do it. I try hard to be appreciative of those birds who arrive every spring, because they are true adventurers, worthy of our esteem.

What triggers the onset of migration for these world travelers? A combination of things, including the length of daylight (called the photoperiod), weather, food availability, and social factors. How does a warbler wintering in South America know what the weather is like on its breeding grounds in northern Wisconsin? It can't, so neotropical birds like red-eyed vireos, redstarts, Canada warblers, and Swainson thrushes seem to have a built-in caution dial. A study in Massachusetts demonstrated that long-distance, neotropical migrants often arrive three weeks later than short-distance migrants like white-throated sparrows, yellow-rumped warblers, and hermit thrushes, which winter in the U.S. They have evolved to know it is better to arrive late than not at all, probably through a natural selection process costing the lives of countless early risers and Type A personalities.

Social dominance factors enter in, too. Male warblers of over 20 species arrive several days before the females, presumably to get a jump-start on competing for nest sites.

Departure dates are also clearly influenced by weather factors. Birds are masters of flight. They make numerous decisions concerning when to fly, how far, how high, and in what direction. They must be acutely aware of prevailing wind conditions, because a wrong response to weather can easily prove fatal.

108

In a nutshell, then, it appears that spring departure dates are influenced by the photoperiod (a genetic trigger that varies among species); the expected weather on the breeding grounds as it relates to the food supply (warblers won't arrive until the insects should be plentiful); and local wind conditions.

Warbler Migration

Thousands of wood warblers return to nest in the Lakeland area every May. Birders live for such times, when a major pulse of birds comes through all at once. In mid-May of 1996, I hit the migration just right. One day I counted 10 species in the shrubbery of the Powell Marsh; a friend saw 14 species on the Turtle-Flambeau Flowage that same day. Without putting in substantial time or effort, I saw 14 warbler species the following two days, including black-throated green, black-and-white, magnolia, yellow-rumped, chestnut-sided, American redstart, bay-breasted, pine, palm, yellow, Wilson's, Nashville, common yellowthroat, and ovenbird. I'm certain that top birders who worked at observing different habitats saw well over 20 warbler species during the same time period.

The species numbers were high, but the number of individuals was even more remarkable. The warblers seemed to be everywhere. I'm amazed when I think about how many birds that actually represents, since I only visited one small area. One radar study of nocturnal migrating birds along the Gulf Coast counted up to a million songbirds passing through a one-mile-wide corridor in five hours—about 200,000 per hour. So when birders speak of a "pulse" of migrating birds, the numbers multiplied onto a larger landscape can be astonishing.

In mid-May, only quaking aspen trees have really leafed out. The bare tree limbs provide an open canvas for the best birdwatching of the year. Warblers are easily seen, because they flit around constantly in search of food. The average long-flying songbird puts on 40 to 70 percent of its body weight in fat every day while migrating, so the morning after a long flight is one of great activity.

I recommend slow and quiet walks in the early mornings of May, equipped with good binoculars and well-tuned ears. You may not know all the birds' songs, nor all their physical identifications, but just being among them is joy enough.

109

Nocturnal Migration

Warblers migrate at night, as do most songbirds. The setting of the sun appears to be the alarm clock that nudges nocturnal migrants into motion. In laboratory studies where the lights in the lab could be manipulated to simulate sunset at any time, caged migratorial birds became very restless, hopping incessantly after each "sunset" in an apparent attempt to initiate migration.

Migration usually begins 30 to 60 minutes after sunset, reaching its peak between 9 p.m. and 1 a.m. It was thought that most birds migrate at night to avoid predation, but geese, ducks, and herons also migrate at night, and they have limited fear of predation. Two more plausible hypotheses exist. One explains nocturnal migration by noting that birds need to eat prior to migrating, and most birds can obviously do this best during the day. The exception (there are always exceptions) are some nocturnal migrating owls, waterfowl, and shorebirds, which ordinarily forage at night.

The second theory says night is the best time for flying. The night atmosphere is cooler and smoother. Chilly air helps cool down birds that generate a great deal of heat in making long-distance migration. It also reduces water loss through the skin and through respiration. In fact, the loss of body water may be the greatest limiting factor in migration during long, non-stop flights.

Night also offers the smoothest air. During the day, the sun heats the earth, and warmed air rises in columns called thermals. Vertical gusts within the thermals can reach 10 miles per hour, providing superb flying conditions for soaring migrants like hawks. But migrating songbirds must rely on powered flight, constantly flapping their wings to maintain altitude and thrust. For them, an atmosphere that allows them to maintain a straight and level course is the most energy-efficient (a tailwind helps greatly, too). Tiny birds like 1/2-ounce warblers get buffeted around by thermals, forcing them to lose energy in fighting the wind and making navigation difficult.

110

Thus the vast majority of birds that use powered flight—warblers, tanagers, vireos, orioles, kinglets, thrushes, gnatcatchers, most sparrows, cuckoos, catbirds, thrashers, shorebirds, owls, herons, and waterfowl—navigate nocturnally. The exceptions are red-winged blackbirds, cowbirds, grackles, finches, crows, and blue jays, all of which migrate during the day or are crepuscular, meaning they migrate just before and after sunrise.

Shorebirds at Powell Marsh

The mud flats in Powell Marsh can provide exceptional shorebird activity. One late May a birder friend and I wandered out on the dikes to a number of shallow wetlands, where we saw numerous dunlins, short-billed dowitchers, greater yellowlegs, and semi-palmated plovers, and an individual black-bellied plover and ruddy turnstone. We also watched numerous, distant flocks of small sandpipers, which frustrated our best attempts at identification.

The shorebirds were just stopping off on their way to their breeding grounds in the farthest reaches of northern Canada, a migratory journey that takes them thousands of miles from their wintering grounds in South America. One of the longest journeys is made by red knots, which winter near Tierra del Fuego and breed in the Arctic. Their annual round trip covers over 18,000 miles. High-quality rest stops, usually much more extensive and richer than Powell Marsh, provide essential refueling along the way.

Memorial Day Abundance

On Memorial Day, just about every animal in the northwoods awaits the birth of their young. It's a time of great fertility for everything. Quaking aspen, birch, maple, willow, and hazelnut are fully leafed out. Fern fiddleheads are up through the leaf litter, and many are already unrolled. Warblers are all back—they usually peak a week on either side of mid-May. Young woodchucks and cottontails are leaving their dens. Robin, blue heron, mallard, and killdeer eggs are hatching. Wood ducks are fledging. Loons are incubating their eggs, and beavers are born. Green frogs begin their banjo twang. Fawns are born. Swallowtail butterflies arrive in our yard during the last week of May. Aspens and willows distribute their gossamer seeds in snowstorms throughout the northwoods. Silver maples set their helicopter fruits. Fireflies are flashing. Whip-poor-wills are calling. The list just goes on and on.

111

This is an important time to keep your dogs tied up and your cats corralled. Our husky jumped a newborn fawn one Memorial Day weekend, nearly killing it. We've never let her loose in the woods over Memorial Day since that time. Do the emerging wildlife a favor by doing the same.

Late May Musings

For forty years the loons have been coming to our lake. I like to think it's the same pair, or at least their descendants. When the loons are calling, things seem right with the world.

-William Mennell

from Warrenville, Illinois, in a letter describing his love of the northwoods.

JUNE

The Ojibwe word for June is *odeimin*, meaning "strawberry." Wild strawberries come ripe in mid-June; though they're usually tiny, they pack more flavor into one bite than seems possible. Isaak Walton had the final say on wild strawberries when he said: "Doubtless God could have made a better berry, but doubtless God never did." As the summer progresses, blueberries, Juneberries, raspberries, thimbleberries, and finally blackberries will come ripe.

113

JUNE 1 - 15

June 1 to June 15

Sex in the Pines

Pine pollen can be everywhere in June. Clouds of pollen settle on the shores of lakes, on sidewalks, on everything. It was particularly abundant in the summer of 1995, undoubtedly because of the exceptionally hot, dry weather. It's likely that no more pollen was produced in 1995 than is normal, but in an ordinary year rains wash much of the pollen from the male cones before it becomes airborne. That summer there was little rain, and the amount of pollen produced seemed enormous. I watched gusts of hot winds shake many pines, creating a billowing yellow fog all around the trees.

All conifers are wind-pollinated—unlike most wildflowers, which rely on insects to carry their pollen. Most people don't realize that conifers have both male and female cones. In spring, before the pollen cones have shed their pollen, the season's new, immature, female

> ## June Musings
>
> *When I close my eyes and make a picture in my head of the river, it is always June, the water sparkles with sunshine, and dragonflies are soaring in the golden air. They are shimmer and sheen, bulging heads that are all eyes, glistening wings, long, slim bodies in bright metallic colors, a body-shop paint-salesman's inspiration; candy apple, seaflake, peacock fire.*
>
> -Sue Hubbell,
> Broadsides from the Other Orders

seed cones are small and soft, and their scales are slightly separated. When the pollen is released, it sifts down between the scales, coming to rest on one of the two ovules attached to the bottom of each cone scale. The cone scales then grow together. Pitch seals the outside of the cone, and it gradually grows to full size. In the meantime, the male pollen cones shrivel and dry up; many fall off and come to rest on forest trails. The next time you walk a trail, notice all the tiny (about 1/4-inch-long) pollen cones on the ground. Male and female cones are found on the same tree in all conifers except yews and junipers, which grow separate male and female plants. The individual pollen grains are extremely small—on the order of 1/250 of an inch—and a scanning electron microscope is required to make out their details. When the grains alight on the surface of a lake, they form a temporary film, but they soon sink to the bottom. The grains are nearly indestructible, becoming microfossils that remain unchanged for thousands of years in the bottom layers of accumulating sediments. By studying these grains, paleobotanists can accurately describe the history of the vegetation in an area, and thus can theorize the historical regional climate. I assume that some future scientist will have no trouble reading the historical pollen record for 1995.

Yellowing Pines

Along many of our highways in 1996, the needles of numerous pines were yellow or brown—some trees to such a degree that they appeared dead. The trees were probably suffering from winter scald. Scalding occurs when evergreens, in particular pines and white cedars, suffer severe water loss. Their root systems often freeze in the late winter. The freezing, combined with drying winds, means the foliage can't replace lost moisture. The lengthening daylight in spring also increases the rate of photosynthesis, which further reduces available water.

Trees growing in exposed areas, such as those along roadsides, are most susceptible to winter drying. South-facing trees tend to be more susceptible yet, because they receive the most sunlight. Trees growing back in the woods show little scalding, because neither wind nor sun can easily dry them out.

A number of the trees Mary and I have planted became scalded, too, but they eventually grew. To prevent winter drying, you should thickly mulch around the base of your exposed trees, in order to minimize moisture stress. You might also wrap the trunks of newly planted trees with burlap. Once the frost has gone out of the ground in spring, you can replenish the moisture levels around the tree by watering for about 12 hours with a slow-running hose.

Ephemeral Wildflowers

Many of our forest wildflowers—like violets, spring beauty, marsh marigold, hepatica, trailing arbutus, and wood anemone—have already gone to seed by early June. About 70 percent of northern woodland flowers bloom prior to June 15. When they die back, most leave little trace of their existence. Most woodland flowers are called "spring ephemerals," in reference to their short life spans. They have to leaf out, flower, and get their fruit on before the canopy of leaves fills in above them. It's a race, and photosynthesis is the sought-after prize.

Mary and I took a walk on the Fallison Lake Nature Trail in the Northern Highlands State Forest one early June. The following flowers were still in bloom along the trail:

117

White baneberry
True Solomon's seal
Starflower
Canada mayflower
Sarsaparilla
Yellow violet
Labrador tea
Wood betony
Twinflower
Clintonia (bluebead lily)
Yellow and orange hawkweed
Gaywing
Pink lady's slipper
Oxeye daisy
Yarrow
Red-berried elder
Cotton grass

False Solomon's seal
Three-leaved false
    Solomon's seal
Barren strawberry
Common cinquefoil
Blackberry
Bunchberry
Columbine
Calla lily
Common buttercup
Yellow bullhead lily
Bog laurel
Twinflower
Forget-me-not
Purple clematis
Wild oats
Bladder campion

My list is sure to be incomplete or inaccurate for many of you, depending on where you live. Variations in soil, temperatures, moisture, light, and other conditions produce different blooming times and different species altogether.

Lilacs in Bloom

By early June, lilacs have usually been in blossom for several weeks, and cuttings grace our table nearly every night. A European import, lilacs arrived in the U.S. in the 1700s. Thomas Jefferson and George Washington transplanted lilacs into their gardens, and colonial women dyed fabrics lavender by boiling the leaves.

Lilacs were also thought to enhance a woman's beauty. If a woman washed her face on May Day with the dew from lilac blossoms, it was believed that she would be beautiful for the rest of her life.

In Germany, lilac blossoms were placed on the roofs of homes to protect the household against lightning. If rodents plagued a house, an incense from lilac blossoms was employed to get rid of them.

I'm predisposed toward native plants, but I'm planting lilac shoots all around our house. I'll set aside my bias in exchange for the lilac's unbeatable fragrance.

Cotton in the North Country

In the bogs in early June, cottongrass blossoms are often so dense that the bogs appear to be covered by a thin layer of snow. If you're from the Deep South, I suspect the bogs look like a ripe cotton field. Put your bog boots on and get out and take a look. The going is usually a bit tough, because most cottongrass grows on mounded hummocks, or tussocks, in the bog. These mounds are like a pot-bound flower without the pot. The hummocks may live for over a century, enlarging slowly over the decades.

The cottony material is thought to be used in nests of songbirds like yellow warblers, which line their nests with downy materials. The "cotton" was also used by pioneers as pillow stuffing, but feathers were more desirable and required less work to gather.

Naming Flowers

Flower names range from logical to just plain strange, and the lore surrounding how flowers received their names is fascinating. Hawkweed was apparently given its name from a folktale in which hawks ate the flower to improve their vision. It's often referred to as "devil's paintbrush" as well, because it invades farmer's fields and spreads quickly by rhizomes. Note the profusion of yellow and orange hawkweed along our roads, usually interspersed with oxeye daisy. Hawkweed exudes a chemical that kills other plants around it, giving it an exceptional competitive edge.

119

Lupines grow in poor soil. They were believed to destroy the soil, when in fact they are simply adapted to growing in marginal habitats. Because they were seen as "wolfing" nutrients from the soil, they were named after the wolf—which is *lupus* in Latin.

Marigolds were said to be a favorite of the Virgin Mary, so their name literally means "Mary's gold." I wonder, though, what they were called before the Virgin Mary.

Daisies are named logically—they are "the day's eye." But the name does not refer to their resemblance to the sun. The English daisy closes at night and opens at sunrise—hence the name.

If you wish to know more about how plant names were derived, the best resource I know of is a book by Mary Durant, entitled *Who Named the Daisy? Who Named the Rose?*

Highbush Cranberry

Highbush cranberry is flowering now along riverbanks and in lowlands. This "cranberry" really belongs to the honeysuckle family and is unrelated to the familiar bog cranberry. The brilliant red clusters of berries in the fall are eaten by bears, foxes, squirrels, grouse, cardinals, cedar waxwings, pine grosbeaks, thrashers, and many other creatures. Some folks still make an exceptional jelly from the fruit, which is rich in vitamin C. The raw berries are bitter, however, demonstrating how sugar can make just about anything taste good.

Northwoods Tomatoes
and Black Ash Leaves

Black ash trees finally begin to leaf out in the lowlands by mid-June. They are the last tree to accept the idea that summer is really here. When the black ash leaves below our house turn green, we know that we may now safely plant our hot weather garden plants. For low-lying areas, June 15 is usually the magic date. Over the years, we've discovered that frosts can occur on any day before then.

120

Migratory Stopovers

From 1989 to 1993, Tom Nicholls from the U.S. Forest Service conducted a migratory bird study near Fifield in Price County. He and his crew captured and banded birds in 14 different habitats during the spring and fall migrations. The purpose of the research was to determine which habitat types serve as important stopover sites for migratory birds. Many of "our" migrants are in decline, not only due to loss of habitat in wintering areas and nesting areas, but also because island stopover areas that provide food and shelter along the migration routes have been lost.

The research concluded that the most important habitats were shrubby lowland areas comprised of species like alder, willow, and sedges. Up to 60 different species utilized these habitats during migration. The poorest habitat was red pine forest that supported no understory of protective shrubs. Only six species utilized this habitat on their way farther north. Red pine plantations are often referred to as "ecological deserts," and Nicholls' research clearly supports the derogatory label.

Breeding Ducks

Larry Gregg, who works out of the Park Falls DNR office, has been coordinating a study of duck ecology in northern Wisconsin since 1989. The objective of the study is to determine breeding densities and habitat use in the northern forests. Northern lakes are traditionally less productive than southern lakes, but they are becoming more important as wetland areas in southern Wisconsin continue to diminish. According to 1989 statistics for the 689 northern lakes, 51 rivers, and 11 wetlands surveyed, mallards comprised 76 percent of the breeding pairs. Wood ducks were second, accounting for six percent of all the ducks seen.

Not-So-Common Terns

One early June, Mary and I watched a flock of 35 common terns vigorously feeding just a few feet offshore along Lake Superior. At the time, we were looking for shorebirds along Wisconsin Point in Superior. What began as a few terns diving for fish soon grew into a major flock that was hovering, diving, splashing, and rising again to hover en masse. The sight was remarkable, particularly because common terns are rare in Wisconsin. The species has been listed as endangered in Wisconsin since 1979, when only one nesting location was found in the entire state.

121

Whip-poor-wills

Whip-poor-wills usually call loudly and repeatedly on early June evenings. I stress loudly! Their Latin name is *Caprimulgus vociferus*, the latter part referring to the remarkable clamor they produce. Whip-poor-wills begin sounding off around dusk, then sometimes work themselves up to calling once per second from about 2 a.m. until dawn. Fifty to one hundred repetitions are common, but their record is 1,088 consecutive calls—about 18 minutes without letup. All animals have evolved strategies for survival over thousands of years, but it's hard to know what strategy is served by this incessant calling. Possibly they're just delighted to be in the northwoods in June, like the rest of us.

Sandhill Cranes

Just below our house on the Manitowish River, we saw and heard a sandhill crane for the first time in 1992. We've also watched a pair feeding several miles away, in one of the few farm fields of southern Iron County. For most counties in Wisconsin, the sight of sandhill cranes isn't a rarity. Central counties like Wood and Waushara contain hundreds of pairs, but the northwoods tends to be rather poor habitat for cranes, presumably because we lack the farmland they prefer. As of the 1993 count, Iron County had only three pairs; Vilas County had six pairs.

A 1991 article from *Passenger Pigeon*, the much-recommended journal of the Wisconsin Society for Ornithology, states that the sandhill population has shown a six percent annual increase in breeding pairs since 1983. Only 25 pairs were counted statewide in 1936, but today Wisconsin boasts over 10,000 individuals.

If you've never seen sandhill cranes, they are truly spectacular birds with a wingspan of six to seven feet. Great blue herons are often confused with cranes, but they are easily distinguished by coloration and in flight. Herons pull their necks back in an "S" shape during flight, while cranes extend their necks straight out. Cranes are gray in spring, but they rub mud over their feathers to camouflage themselves on the nest, and so are brown at this time of year. Herons are blue-gray.

Killdeer

By early June, killdeer young are racing around many northwoods residents' lawns and fields. Generally born in broods of four, they eat insects, which make up 98 percent of their diet. The parents commonly pretend to have a crippled wing, in order to lead intruders away from the young. It's a great act, but once you know its purpose, you can find the chicks by often looking in the opposite direction.

The Man in Red
and the Value of Baths

One June morning, Gil Willms of Lac du Flambeau was sitting in a chair wearing his favorite red pants. As he was watering his flower bed, a male ruby-throated hummingbird flew up and sat on his thigh. It then flew into the spray from his hose, hovering as if it enjoyed the experience, and returned to his thigh. The hummer repeated its flight into the spray and back to Gil's leg about 12 times before it headed for Gil's nectar feeder.

Two other local residents wrote me, both describing hummingbird scenes similar to the one experienced by Gil. While they watered their lawns and flowers, hummingbirds flew into the fine mist, hovered, exited, and then returned, in the obvious pursuit of a bath. In one case, the hummer followed the man around while he was using a sprinkling can.

Why would a bath be of value to a bird? No one really knows for sure. Cleaning the feathers doesn't appear to be the bath's main function, but helping spread oil during feather preening is a possibility, because preening oil spreads more readily over damp feathers. Feathers become more flexible when they're wet, so bathing might also help restore feathers to their original and proper shape.

123

Most birds bathe, so the act must be of some importance. Even hawks have been known to come to birdbaths. As an alternative to water bathing, many birds take dust baths. I suppose this is analogous to going to the dry cleaner. Dust baths are thought to help reduce parasites in the feathers. In the case of quail, the dust absorbs excess preening oil. Feathers of quail that are prevented from dusting quickly become oily and matted.

Birds like swifts and swallows take their baths on the wing, dipping into the water during flight, while woodpeckers and nuthatches simply stand in the rain, extending their wings and spreading their tails. Waterbirds like ducks, swans, and geese may bathe on the surface of the water or while diving, spreading their feathers and wings.

Most birds need to dry off after a bath. Songbirds simply shake themselves like the family dog, while cormorants stand around with their wings spread like laundry on a line. We've watched eagles in a similar pose, wings spread to dry, apparently after having struggled with a bigger fish than they could handle and taking an undesired swim.

If you wish to attract more birds to your yard, set up a bathing area. The birdbath can be as simple as on overturned garbage can lid filled with water, or as complicated as a rock-lined, hand-dug pool. As the movie line goes, build it and they will come.

A Hummingbird's Appetite

Hummingbirds may just be the most unusual member of the bird family. Their energy output per unit of body weight exceeds that of any animal in the world. An average, 170-pound human burns about 3,500 calories a day; if the daily output of a hummer was adjusted to reflect the weight of the average human, that person would need to burn about 155,000 calories. Translated into food, keeping up with a hummer would require eating 285 pounds of hamburger a day—or 370 pounds of potatoes if you're a vegetarian.

124

In order to keep their internal engines stoked, hummingbirds must feed every 10 to 15 minutes. At night, the hummer must go into a state of torpor, reducing its energy consumption to one-twentieth of day-time levels. Nevertheless, a hummer in its version of torpor uses an amount of energy equivalent to that of a vigorously exercising human.

The hummingbird's tongue, which can be extended beyond the bill, is split at the end into two parallel tubes that suck nectar from flow-ers—just like straws. The outer edges are also frayed like a brush, in order to gather insects. Nearly 25 percent of a hummer's diet is in-sects, in case you have wondered how these birds can survive on sugar water.

Hummers are the avian version of the pollen-carrying bumblebee. When a hummingbird dips its head deep into a flower blossom, pollen is often transferred onto the bird's head. As the hummer feeds, the pollen is spread to other flowers. Thus the hummingbird is one of the most important pollinators of tubular flowers.

Loon Hatchings

Loon chicks usually hatch out in mid-June. By late June, they are two to three weeks old. The chicks are often seen riding on a parent's back, which protects them and conserves energy. Please observe them from a distance. The chicks are easily exhausted if harassed.

Surveying Frogs

In late May to early June, I conduct my second frog survey of the year in Vilas County. I usually find that American toads, leopard frogs, chorus frogs, and wood frogs have stopped calling, while spring peepers continue to call. Eastern gray tree frogs, mink frogs, and green frogs are usually still in full voice; the green frogs are the most recent additions to the choir. The bullfrogs are the last to join in, but their bellicose song makes up for their late arrival at the party.

One of the highlights of the surveys is that I usually hear whip-poor-wills at three of my stops. Their incessant call often makes it difficult to hear the frogs, but one should not quibble with gifts when they are given.

125

Gray Tree Frogs

The Eastern gray tree frog sings at night, and many people confuse its song with a bird call. The song is a short, musical trill lasting only a second. The males often sing from a perch on logs, or from branches that arch over water. Richard Vogt, the author of *Natural History of Amphibians and Reptiles of Wisconsin,* a book I rely on for much of my understanding of amphibians and reptiles, writes that gray tree frogs have the "most beautiful call of any species of Wisconsin frog . . . a musical trill." In this case, I beg to differ. The song of the gray tree frog is a harsh staccato that can be extremely loud. It's often confused with a bird call because it bursts forth from above the water, but it just doesn't rate as melodic.

When Eastern gray tree frogs breed, the male climbs onto the female's back and squeezes her middle. As she releases her eggs, he fertilizes them. A female may lay up to 2,000 eggs, often in loose clusters attached to vegetation just under the surface of the water. By August in the northwoods, young gray tree frog tadpoles may be seen swimming about.

Once breeding is completed, gray tree frogs head for the woods, where they forage for insects in trees and shrubs. You might want to thank the next frogs you see for their insect consumption. Just one tiny cricket frog, for instance, consumes nearly 5,000 insects a season.

It's somewhat difficult to identify the Eastern gray tree frog, because it can change its color from gray to brown to light green to dark green. Its "choice" of coloration apparently depends on the ground color and how the frog wishes to camouflage itself. One source encourages you to verify this ability by catching several Eastern grays, putting one in a dark bottle (with airholes, of course) and the other in a lighter bottle. After an hour, compare the differences in color.

Some people refer to the Eastern gray as a tree toad, but we have only one true toad in the northwoods, and that is the American toad. Toads are distinguished from frogs by their dry, bumpy skin and their short, weak rear legs. "Regular" frogs like the northern leopard frog, wood frog, or green frog have smooth, slimy skin, long and strong rear legs, and big webbed feet for swimming. Tree frogs like the Eastern gray, spring peeper, and chorus frog have suction cups on their toes, which help them climb trees.

126

Dragonfly Metamorphosis

Mary and I watched dragonflies emerge from their larval bodies one June 11. The aquatic larvae swim out of the water and attach themselves to blades of grass, pier posts, or rocks. Eventually the exoskeleton splits down the back, and an adult dragonfly crawls out. When the adult emerges, it pumps air into its body, expanding its size. It also unfolds its wings, which are like soft cellophane. Within about 10 minutes, the wings are hard enough to support flight. Away it goes, leaving the crispy larval shell clinging to its supporting structure. We collected several dozen that day along a 20-foot stretch of Manitowish River shoreline. Take a look along the shoreline rocks, pilings, and driftwood of your favorite lake or river, and you are likely to find dragonfly husks.

This metamorphosis takes place just above the surface of the water. Mary and I both observed that the "no wake" law, designed primarily to prevent shoreline erosion, is also a lifesaver for hatching dragonflies. One strong wave would surely have drowned the newly emerging, helpless adults. Because dragonflies eat mosquitoes and serve as prey for a host of frogs, birds, and fish, we profit when they survive.

Dragonflies are a good indicator of water quality. A field study of the North and South Forks of the Flambeau River revealed a startling difference in the species abundance of dragonflies. Eighteen species of dragonflies were collected on the South Fork, which is seldom disturbed by humans; only three species were found on a section of the North Fork located below a dam and paper mill.

Damselflies, which are classified in the same family as dragonflies (Odonata), also emerge in enormous numbers in June. While paddling along the Manitowish one day, I was escorted the entire way by a variety of species of damselflies, which were lifting off from the bank vegetation in search of prey. Damselflies look like a fragile version of a dragonfly, and are easily identified by how they hold their wings when at rest. The damselfly's wings are held back behind its head, while the dragonfly's wings are held out like the wings of a plane.

127

The Mosquito Army

In early June, the lowly mosquito earns the title of the most talked about wildlife species in the north. To enter your home near dusk requires an Olympian sprint for the door, in the hope that the little demons can't quite keep up with you. The skeeter population boom often backfires, though. Most warm-blooded creatures that can stay inside, or at least out of the deeper woods, do so, fearing for their lives.

Scientists are not sure exactly when mosquitoes evolved mouth parts for sipping protein-rich blood, but one female with a blood meal still in her belly was found in amber dating back 25 to 40 million years. She probably fed on small mammals and birds, since humans had yet to appear on the scene. Today, about 3,450 species of mosquitoes populate the earth, three-fourths of them living in the tropics and subtropics where they originated. The United States "only" provides a home for 170 species; Canada supports a mere 70 species; and the Arctic hosts a relative dearth of less than a dozen species.

Before you pack your bags for the Arctic, you should know that no place on Earth has a greater concentration of individual mosquitoes.

The Arctic permafrost prevents water from seeping deeply into the soil, resulting in a landscape dotted with thousands of square miles of tundra pools. Above these pools, mosquitoes often blacken the sky. I use the word "blacken" conservatively, too. In the name of science, some crazed Canadian researchers exposed their bodies to the mosquito hordes, reporting up to 9,000 bites per minute, or 150 bites per second. If they had continued their research, they would have donated half their blood in two more hours—and they would have died. I'm not aware of records concerning human deaths due to mosquitoes, but young, domesticated animals have been killed by mosquitoes in prime skeeter habitat.

128

The adult female mosquito must tap a protein-rich blood meal in order to make eggs. As large, slow, easily prickable sacks of protein, humans must present an extremely pleasing vision to a mosquito. Once the female has collected her tiny measure of blood (one-millionth of a gallon per sitting), she waits two days while her eggs mature, then lays them in and around water. When her eggs are dispatched, she enters the fray again, seeking another donor for another round of eggs. A female may feed and lay eggs a dozen times during her month-long life span.

Stretch sensors tell the female when to stop her bloodletting. The female's abdomen distends greatly, holding up to four times her own weight in blood. As one researcher says, she looks like a tiny Christmas tree light. If the nerves that connect the sensors to the brain are cut, she will feed until she pops.

Normally, various receptors sensitive to heat, carbon dioxide, and other factors excite the female into a rapid and often risky search for a host. But once she's had a full meal, a hormone is released that renders her unaware of nearby protein sources, thereby reducing risky behavior until she can lay her eggs.

We're not the only ones that suffer from mosquitoes. Young, unfeathered birds in the nest are very vulnerable to mosquito bites, as are adult birds at night, which are bitten around their bills and eyes. A roosting bird tries to tolerate the mosquitoes, because fluttering can give its location away to predators. Herons and other wading birds are also bitten extensively on their exposed legs and heads while they silently stalk fish.

We can take solace in the fact that our blood is an inferior brand, low in the amino acids that mosquitoes require. Other animals provide a higher octane fill, though our dominance on the planet must surely please the opportunistic mosquito. Perhaps we're the equivalent of a junk food diet.

What possible good can mosquitoes be? Well . . . they are part of the food chain, providing food for many birds, bats, frogs, and other animals. Some trout fishermen apparently know how to tie six different mosquito flies in order to lure a rainbow or brookie, so skeeters also feed fish. Researcher Lewis Nielsen reports that mosquitoes are the main pollinators of bog orchids in the Arctic. He discovered pollen grains from over 30 species of flowering plants on individual mosquitoes, so skeeters may be far more important as pollinators of wildflowers than anyone ever suspected.

129

If water levels are low during the summer, mosquito populations are usually kept down. Mosquitoes breed in permanent and temporary pools, so the less water standing around the better.

As all good insect chauvinists know, the female is the only gender that seeks our blood donations. She is also the only one to produce the high-pitched wing music we so appreciate prior to our loss of blood. The male's wings emit a lower hum that we don't hear. The sexes actually identify one another through the different wing pitches. The male is sexually attracted to the high whine of the female in flight. It's a convenient adaptation, but couldn't they have used color instead?

Zap Your Bug Zapper

A Notre Dame study found that only three percent of the insects killed by a bug zapper on an average night were female mosquitoes. The rest were mostly harmless insects like moths and beetles. The finding makes sense, because most biting mosquitoes are not attracted to light. How many mosquitoes have you seen flying around a light bulb in the evening? Mosquitoes are attracted to heat, carbon dioxide, and ammonia scent, all of which indicate warm-blooded prey. Bug zappers don't give off these signals. So, while it may be "entertaining" to hear the little zips and zaps produced when insects get fried, the actual value of the zapping appears to be minimal.

Life's Tough for a Turtle

Turtles lay eggs in upland areas during June. Various predators like coyotes, mink, otters, skunks, foxes, and raccoons become instantaneously busy digging up the eggs and eating them. Look for holes with what appear to be shriveled pingpong balls lying around them—the remains of the eggs. If the eggs survive predation, gulls, crows, herons, and even red-winged blackbirds may eat the hatchlings during their trek to the water. If the hatchlings make it to the water, they are preyed upon by many fish until they grow too large for fish jaws. Then it takes eight to ten years before most turtles begin to reproduce. The moral of the story? Appreciate the adult turtles you see—they've had a job making it this far.

Black Terns
and Yellow-headed Blackbirds

One early June I canoed on the Little Turtle Flowage in Iron County, a 1,200-acre flowage/wetland created in 1971. Over 60 small pothole lakes, each about one-fourth acre, were dug out to provide territorial sites for waterfowl. The uplands around the flowage were clearcut; since 1981, controlled burns have been used to prevent reforestation and to maintain the herbaceous growth of the perimeter.

The long and short of all this intensive management is an area brimming with birdlife. Possibly the two most pleasant sightings I had that day involved colonies of black terns and yellow-headed blackbirds. The terns provided several hours of entertainment as they hawked for insects and small fish all around my canoe. They did raise their voices a few times when I apparently came too close to their nests; at these junctures, several would swoop near my head and scream at me. I got the message. I've heard stories about researchers who needed helmets to get to the nests, so I backed my canoe off and poked into other cattails and sedges.

The yellow-headed blackbird's call is just plain fun to hear, I suppose in part because we have so few around here. They proclaim their presence loudly and harshly, leaving little doubt as to who occupies their bit of wetland turf.

Other sightings/soundings I experienced that day included pied-billed grebes, American bitterns, kingfishers, ospreys, great blue herons, tree swallows (dozens of these), many pairs of wood ducks and blue-winged teal, geese, snipe, common yellowthroats, mink frogs, and enough mosquitoes at the landing to send the average person screaming for shelter.

131

A loon even came in for a landing about 15 feet over my head while I was looking elsewhere; the rush of its wings was louder than any bird I have ever heard.

The osprey pair I saw was occupying a natural nest in a dead tree, across from an empty platform that a pair of ospreys had nested on for many years. In fact, I had seen an osprey pair on the platform just two weeks earlier. One of the ospreys carried a stick to the new nest while I was watching, so I assumed it was the same pair renesting, though I have no idea why they chose a different nest site.

A June marsh like the Little Turtle Flowage exudes action and noise in the early morning. If you're seeking meditative quiet, head elsewhere.

Caprice

Our oldest daughter Eowyn and I canoed the Little Turtle Flowage another time in early June. By July, the flowage becomes a shallow wetland that is nearly impassable, due to dense stands of cattails, bullrushes, and sedges. In June, though, it is a maze of young cattail "islands," which harbor birds and muskrat.

Black terns, yellow-headed blackbirds, and red-winged blackbirds sang, swayed, and flew from nearly every clump. We heard a number of loud calls we couldn't identify; these caused us to poke around excitedly, trying to discover the singer. An osprey soared and fished above us for over an hour, while black terns darted all around the canoe, either in defense, curiosity, or simple indifference to our intrusion. A mink hunted from one bank, while muskrats plopped into the water whenever we approached their feeding areas.

Mary, Callie, and I repeated the trip the next weekend, putting in just as threatening skies began to produce drizzle. We ended our trip not long afterward, sodden with rain. As so often happens, I talked up how great our trip had been the previous week, in particular about the terns and yellow-headed blackbirds. Of course, not one of them was in evidence during the rain. Fortunately, Mary is used to the capricious side of nature, but I wonder about all the other folks I've taken out over the years, who didn't experience the wildlife show I had described. It's one of the reasons I like plants so much—they're almost always where I say they are, doing what they had been doing the day before. It's also one of the reasons I enjoy animals so much—their unpredictability makes their appearances more precious.

132

Fish Spawning Draws Eagles

Mary, Callie, and I saw four bald eagles in trees along a very short stretch of the Manitowish River one early June. They had apparently gathered to partake in the annual spawning of redhorse in the rocky rapids. From our canoe, we could see the redhorse swimming together, and I'm sure the eagles' view was much better from their white pine perch.

Just a week earlier, an acquaintance had stopped at our house to say he had seen 10 eagles in the same spot. We speculated then that they were feeding on the sucker run. In future early Junes, you may wish to watch for eagles near the rapids area to the west of where the Highway 51 bridge crosses the Manitowish, just a few miles north of Manitowish Waters.

Of Fawns and Adult Deer

Most fawns are born between Memorial Day and mid-June in the northwoods. One to three fawns may be born per doe, each one usually weighing four to eight pounds. The fawns will spend the first few weeks of their lives close to home, relying on natural camouflage and their lack of scent to protect them.

The deer herd in Wisconsin numbered over 1.5 million in 1995. Overall density in the northwoods is up. In many management units north of Highway 64, deer are at least 20 percent above population goals. The farm areas south of here are experiencing an even greater degree of crop and browse problems.

Still, there are few things as beautiful to watch as the leap of a deer. A New York biologist measured a deer's running broad-jump. The deer leaped 29 feet, while clearing a seven-foot-high windfall. A buck was once seen sailing over an eight-foot fence without even taking a preliminary step. Eat your heart out, Michael Jordan!

133

A Big Appetite

Jack Bull of Winchester called in June to describe a bear he observed on his property. The bear was limping badly from an injury to its right foreleg, and it was eating from meat scraps that Jack puts out to feed a red fox. When Jack realized that the bear was in such poor condition, he unloaded his freezer; before the night was out, the bear had eaten 30 pounds of meat, a loaf of bread, and a pail of corn from Jack's deer feeder. It came back three more nights, each night improving physically, but failed to return on June 6. Hopefully, the bear healed sufficiently to survive on its own.

Jack once watched an osprey swoop down, grab some of the meat scraps, and land on a nearby tree to dine. That's unusual behavior for ospreys, which dine on fish 99 percent of the time. Eagles commonly scavenge meat, but I have seldom heard of an osprey with a taste for red meat.

The Long Lake Monster

One June several alarmed people reported seeing a 20-foot-long serpent on Long Lake in Iron County. It turned out to be a family of young otters swimming tail to tail, dipping and undulating in the water, appearing for all the world like the Loch Ness Monster.

Northern Lights

Northern lights can occur during any month, but one early June we had several nights in a row of exceptional displays. They pulsed and shimmered all the way down onto the southern horizon. I spent half an hour lying on my back in the middle of State Highway 47 at 2:30 in the morning, watching them. Fortunately, no police car happened along. It wasn't until the fog started rising off the river and the coyotes began yelping nearby that I got up, the otherworldliness of the moment imprinted upon my mind.

134

Ancient people ascribed supernatural origins to the northern lights. Eskimos believed departed ancestors were playing wild ball games in the heavens. The Norse regarded the lights as Valkyrie riding across the sky. The Valkyrie were the beautiful maidens who brought souls to Valhalla, the hall of Odin, where heroes slain in battle and others who died bravely were received. The Old Testament described the lights as spectral horsemen riding their fiery steeds. In Roman times, the northern lights fooled the Emperor Tiberius' troops into believing that flames were beyond the horizon, signaling the burning of the colony of Ostia. During the Middle Ages, the lights were dreaded as harbingers of coming misery.

The Roman naturalist Pliny was the first to suspect that the lights were of natural origin. Today, scientists tell us that the aurora borealis is generated when electrically charged particles from the solar wind enter the Earth's magnetic field. There are also southern lights in the southern hemisphere, the aurora australis, which are strikingly similar and occur simultaneous to the northern lights—almost like two halves of an apple.

The display can come in many colors, which are determined by the nature of the incoming molecules and atoms and by the energies of the collisions. Molecules of oxygen glow red or green, while hydrogen molecules produce red. Nitrogen atoms generate purple.

Ultimately, scientific explanations are much too earthbound for such a phenomenon. To me, northern lights are the natural world's far better answer to Fourth of July fireworks. Perhaps the 19th-century polar explorer Charles Hall deserves the final say on northern lights: "Who but God can conceive such infinite scenes of glory?"

Aroundthebenditis

I was paddling on the Manitowish one June when it became clear to me that I suffer from "aroundthebenditis," an affliction seen in canoeists who just can't control their curiosity. The Manitowish is contorted in ribbons and oxbows that can transform a one-mile-by-crow trip into a four-mile-by-canoe journey. For me that's addictive, because there's always a bend in sight; if I just go around it, I'm sure I'll see that moose, or whatever I've been looking for over the years. The affliction makes for long trips and late arrivals.

135

On this particular paddle, I said to myself, "Just one more bend, then I'll turn around," and it paid off. A big doe was standing knee-deep in the water right on the bend. While hardly an endangered species (some folks call deer "forest rats" because of their high numbers), the doe reinforced my aroundthebenditis for many trips to come. It's an affliction, but better that than traveling in straight lines.

An Answer to How We Can Tolerate Long Winters

Lu Karl, who lives near Boulder Junction, was awakened one June around 3 a.m. by screams coming from his yard. When Lu trained a spotlight on the sound, he saw a bobcat and a red fox squared off. The bobcat kept up a continuous screaming while it circled around the red fox. By contrast, the fox never let out a sound. Lu's wife had been feeding the fox some meat and bones over the last few weeks, so he assumed they were fighting over territorial rights to his back-door soup kitchen. Nearly 15 minutes later, the duo had moved into the woods adjoining Lu's property. By then the bobcat had reduced its intimidating screams to infrequent growls. Neither animal struck the other; apparently both were trying to win the confrontation without risk of injury. Lu went to bed when he could no longer see or hear them, but a loon pair promptly started wailing on the lake, so he couldn't get back to sleep.

Folks sometimes ask how we can tolerate the long winters up here. For me, the reasons are many, but all are rather simple and easily illustrated by Lu's story. Most urban dwellers are awakened by the unwelcome sounds of sirens, traffic, and unruly neighbors; we northwoods types are awakened by mysteries, and we open our windows all the wider to hear. That's why we live here.

Sightings

136

Mark Pfleiger from Harshaw fed sunflower seeds to the "black-winged redbird," otherwise known as the scarlet tanager, at his feeder for over three weeks in May and June of 1996.

That same June I received two calls from people who discovered Cape May warblers drinking from their hummingbird feeders. For several days, Henry Olson on Lake of the Falls watched a pair of Cape Mays eating orange slices as well as sipping his sugar water.

Del Link from Rhinelander wrote to express his great pleasure in seeing, after 20 years of birdwatching, a pair of cardinals appear in his yard during May and June of 1996.

June Musings

I came to learn that worthwhile observations of birds and animals and insects were great in proportion to the smallness of territory covered. . . To be a good naturalist one must be a stroller or a creeper, or better still a squatter in every sense of the word.

-Charles William Beebe

Final Notes on Ice-out

In 1996, the ice finally went off Trout Lake on May 17. I believe that's the record for the latest ice-off in this area. Woody Hagge has kept ice records on Foster Lake near Hazelhurst for 19 years. The average length of ice cover on Foster has been 145 days over those years, but the lake kept its ice for 178 days in the winter of 1995-96. That's 33 days longer than the average!

Woody has also kept records since the late 1980s on the number of days between ice-out and the first nesting of Foster Lake's resident loon pair. The average time has been 26 days. So if you have nesting loons on your lake, you can expect to see them 3-1/2 weeks or so after ice-out. Incubation takes 26 to 31 days. After an average winter, the first loons usually hatch around June 10.

137

June 16 to June 30

Summer Solstice

Summer solstice occurs between June 20 and June 22, offering us the gift of 15 hours and 42 minutes of sunlight. The sun is now 35° north of the equator, meaning it is much higher in the sky than during the winter solstice, when it is 35° south of the equator. The sun will set for a week or so after June 21 at around 8:53 p.m.; then the inexorable solar swing south begins.

> ### Late June
> *Every landscape has its own acoustical ecology. The music of a place is as invitingly distinctive as the aromas of a household kitchen.*
> -Peter Steinhart

Important Mosquitoes in History

Mosquito numbers were down in 1994 in the Lakeland area, and what a pity that was. When the snow thaws and the spring rains cause temporary pools to form, spring mosquitoes lay their eggs on the ground. But our snow melted early that spring. The rains never came, and late May brought hard frosts—all of which in concert appeared to keep the little buggers in check. Different species of mosquitoes do overlap in their breeding cycle, so even if June supports few mosquitoes, we are seldom without a persistent whine around our ears until the first frosts in late August.

On an acre of good breeding habitat, mosquitoes may number between one and nine million individuals. Remember that an acre is only 208 feet on a side. According to one estimate, there are 41,000 mosquitoes for every man, woman, and child in America—all 250 million of us. I've purposely not done the multiplication to see how many mosquitoes this really means. The number would be frightening! On the brighter side, we have the exceptional good fortune of not having to worry about getting malaria or yellow fever from mosquito bites. Around the world, two people die every minute from mosquito-borne disease.

While being driven from the woods by an army of mosquitoes, one might not take the time to appreciate the historically invaluable role mosquitoes have played in American politics. Without their influence, we might today inhabit a differently shaped U.S.A. In 1800, France wrestled control from Spain of all the lands situated roughly between the Mississippi River and the Rocky Mountains—much to the dismay of the American colonies, which feared that France would shut down trade through New Orleans. By 1802, Napoleon was equally fearful that the colonies would prevent him from taking total possession of Louisiana. Napoleon dispatched 33,000 troops to New Orleans under the leadership of his brother-in-law, Charles Leclerc. The troops were ordered to reinforce his claim to Louisiana; along the way, they were also expected to put down a slave insurrection in Haiti. But the plan went awry. Mosquito-borne yellow fever annihilated the French expedition, killing 29,000 of the troops. This debacle helped convince Napoleon to sell 828,000 square miles of land to the United States for a mere $15 million, or four cents an acre (native Indian tribes were obviously not consulted regarding the deal). Thus, the United States doubled its existing territory, due in large part to the intervention of the lowly mosquito.

Mosquitoes have played a significant role in world trade, too. The French gave up on an attempt to build the Panama Canal in the 1800s, after losing 23,000 men to yellow fever. But with the discovery of quinine tonic to cure yellow fever, the U.S. was able to complete the canal in 1914. Incidentally, the tonic cure was so bitter that the men learned to cut the taste with gin—creating the gin and tonic. This may be the only mixed drink ever contributed to civilization by an insect, though the honeybees came first with mead, made of fermented honey and water.

140

About the only way to deal with mosquitoes is to laugh about them. Roger Welsch, a folklorist who writes for Natural History magazine, collected some mosquito stories that are worth passing on:

"The oldest mosquito story is the one about the hunters who are camping and see shadows against the canvas of the tent, and one guy gets up and sees two giant skeeters outside the tent talking. The one mosquito says, 'Shall we eat them here or take them with us?' And the other says, 'Let's eat them here, because if we take them back, the BIG ones will take them away from us.'"

Welsch writes about mosquitoes being the state bird in Minnesota: "I was fishing on the Boundary Waters a couple of years ago and a mosquito got so much of my blood, I got a Father's Day card from him."

141

If all else fails, remember that if you like solitude, you need mosquitoes. You seldom have one without the other. By their presence, mosquitoes have probably kept more wilderness pristine than any legislation humans will ever write.

Sexing Mosquitoes

You'll be happy to know that we have 52 species of mosquitoes in Wisconsin, and that their life cycles are arranged in an overlapping order. Thus we have some species breeding and biting virtually throughout the spring and summer.

If you have ever wondered how to sex a mosquito (as I'm sure you all have), the male's antennae are quite bushy, while the female's are not. Of course, this is a moot point given that only the females will land on you, searching for a blood meal while the males are out drinking nectar. But if you're a truly masochistic naturalist, you may want to look through your hand lens the next time you're getting bit (sucked is actually the more appropriate verb), in order to confirm the gender of your attacker.

Deerfly Strategy

Deerflies are out in late June and biting with relish, too (in fact, we may taste like relish to them). Their mode of attack involves circling your head enough times to thoroughly confuse you, then bite. And they hurt! The female is the culprit, needing to gorge on blood in order to lay clusters of eggs on wetland plants. The eggs hatch out in one to three weeks. The larvae then drop into the water or mud, living a predatorial existence throughout their aquatic stage, which lasts through the fall and winter. In spring they crawl onto dry soil, where they pupate for one to three weeks, emerging in June as adults to bedevil anything with warm blood.

Here are some tricks for avoiding deerflies. Deerflies always go for the highest point, and they tend to cluster around the trail leader. Try to walk with tall people, and always bring up the rear. Hunch over, claiming a bad back. Don't read this section of the book to your trail companions.

Remember, deerflies are prey for numerous insects, birds, fish, and frogs, so they do serve a purpose beyond inflicting pain. However, you are close to sainthood or psychosis if you can appreciate their ecological role while they're mobbing your head.

Clean Water Isn't Always a Good Thing

The good news about black flies is that by late June they are pretty much a fond memory. We could probably eliminate the little fiends, though, if we just polluted our water systems more thoroughly (I'm not advocating this, of course). It's ironic that the Clean Water Act has improved our water quality so much that black fly populations are doing better than ever. Most species of black flies can't survive in polluted waters.

We're fortunate that only 10 to 15 percent of all black fly species include humans as their prey, because their bite raises a welt that itches for days. I don't know if black flies use a better brand of anticoagulant when they bite than mosquitoes, or if they just run more of the juice into us, but their bites have quite a punch. They disappear at this time of year because the females have found their needed blood meals and produced their eggs. The eggs are laid on rocks, sticks, or vegetation, in or near a flowing stream. They hatch into aquatic larvae that grow through some seven stages until the following spring, when they pupate and rise as adults in an air bubble to the surface of a stream, to begin feasting all over again. One species of black fly is so specialized that it takes blood only from loons, but deer, bear, and moose are more typical victims.

Spittlebugs

The glob of "spit" you may see on many species of trees and flowers houses the nymphal stage of the spittlebug. We have two species in the area: the pine spittlebug, which is found in spittle masses above ground; and the Saratoga spittlebug, found in spittle masses below ground, on the roots of plants like sweet fern and blueberry.

The spittlebug manufactures its spit by sucking juices from the host plant and mixing them with an ingredient from its abdomen. A clear mixture is then excreted, and air is blown through the liquid by a pump-like structure beneath the abdomen, producing bubbles one at a time until the liquid becomes a froth. If you gently probe through the spit with your fingers, you will find the spittlebugs enjoying another day in a controlled, almost predator-free environment. It's an unusual but apparently effective adaptation. It doesn't offer the spittlebugs much of a view, though.

Pine spittlebugs are not a significant problem, but the Saratoga adults feed on new and old shoots of pines, damaging the tissue with a toxic injection of saliva. Characteristically these pines look "flagged" with dead foliage, and may ultimately be killed.

Northwoods Tigers

The Canadian tiger swallowtail butterfly graces our woods edges, gardens, and fields in June. Its striking pattern of yellow and black and its 3-1/2-inch wingspan make this tiger swallowtail as recognizable as the monarch butterfly. Adults feed on the nectar of many flowers, and often engage in "puddling," a social behavior in which dozens may hang out at the local mud puddle. They are also attracted to manure or decaying animal flesh. Swallowtails recognize that dung

143

and carrion are excellent sources of nitrogen, sodium, and amino acids. One might feel that the beauty of swallowtails is diminished by such impolite behavior, but the female needs nutrients for her eggs, and the source is immaterial. The eggs are most commonly laid on the green leaves of a cherry or ash tree.

Duped by a Duck

While walking on the Powell Marsh dikes in June, our husky Keena kicked up a hen mallard; the dog went galumphing off into the vast marshes of the Powell, in vain pursuit of the much more intelligent mallard. The hen did an "unable to fly far" routine, akin to the broken wing act of a killdeer. The bird fluttered ahead about 30 yards, landed, waited for Keena to come within about 10 yards, then sputtered ahead another 30 yards. Ignoring our calls, Keena followed the duck for nearly 15 minutes; soon she could only be seen with binoculars. Keena eventually tired, and we could see her walking slowly toward the duck. The mallard must not have had enough of the sport. She swam back toward Keena, encouraging her to take up the chase again, and off they went. The hen must have thought she had a real rube on her hands. She played Keena for all she was worth until I finally caught up with the duo by taking another dike to intercept them. At that point, the hen swam to several other mallards loafing nearby, took off, and flew back to her original site, undoubtedly laughing as only a duck can.

I was impressed. I've seen female hooded mergansers pull a similar act when we've come too close to their broods in our canoe. These theatrical ruses are called "distraction displays." The practitioners make themselves as conspicuous as possible when approached by a predator, rather than relying on cryptic coloring to camouflage themselves. The displays take the form of feigned injuries, exhaustion, or even illness to divert the predator from the nest or the young.

Ground nesters, like many shorebirds and waterfowl, may employ broken-wing displays. These typically involve the spreading and dragging of a wing or tail, while slowly fluttering away from the nest or young—usually accompanied by equally exaggerated calling.

The timing of displays varies from species to species, depending on when the need is greatest. For altricial birds (those whose young are incapable of moving around on their own and must be taken care of) like robins and sparrows, distraction displays are most theatrical just before fledging of the young. For precocial birds (those whose young are capable of moving around soon after hatching) like mallards and killdeer, adult displays are most conspicuous at hatching. As the risk to the young declines, the displays also decline, until they are no longer needed.

In general, most ground nesters are precocial, while most tree nesters are altricial. Altricial comes from a Latin root meaning "to nourish," while precocial comes from the same Latin root as the word precocious, meaning "to ripen early." Truly altricial birds are hatched with their eyes closed, and have little or no feathering. All our songbirds are born this way. On the other hand, truly precocial birds hatch out covered with down, eyes open, and leave the nest within two days. All of our ducks are precocial.

145

There is a gradient between these extremes, and some species seem to fall right in the middle. For example, some young may be able to walk or swim away from the nest, but they nonetheless remain at the nest to be fed by their parents. Some young are covered with down and have their eyes open, but are unable to leave the nest and must be fed by their parents (great blue herons, for example). From this perspective, humans are an interesting hybrid. We are born precocial—our eyes are open, we are "furred," and we have large brains. Yet we are altricial in our need to be nourished for a very long time prior to assuming full independence—too long for some teenagers, as well as some parents.

Big or Little Families?

Another "decision" for animals is whether to have lots of young or just a few. If they produce a whole lot of young, the parents must leave the offspring to survive on their own, because caring for all of them would be too much. Having only a few young means the parent can stay around and take good care of them. Fish, frogs, and turtles use the first strategy. They lay a pile of eggs, and hope that a few survive predation. A snapping turtle that lays eggs in a dug-out sand hole, then leaves them to their good fortune, exemplifies such an evolutionary strategy.

Birds and mammals usually employ the other philosophy. They have a few kids and try to take care of them to ensure that they survive. Black bears are probably the most extreme northwoods example of this strategy. The sow breeds every other year, usually raising just one or two cubs, and she takes very good care of her young.

Pleased to Meet You

The song of the chestnut-sided warbler is one of the most commonly heard birdsongs in June. Its loud "pleased, pleased, pleased, pleased to meet-cha" song emanates from second-growth woodlands and brushy, cut-over areas—habitats found in abundance in the northwoods. According to breeding bird surveys of northern Wisconsin, the chestnuts are outnumbered among warblers only by ovenbirds and common yellowthroats. If you're unfamiliar with their call, listen to a bird tape, then visit a young forest and listen. You'll almost assuredly hear them. They are quite handsome, adorned with a yellow cap and chestnut-streaked sides.

Common Warblers

Learning to identify warblers is one of the more difficult tasks for amateur birders. We have five quite common nesting warblers in the northwoods, and they are easily identified once you adopt the right search mode. In more mature forests, the black-throated green warbler, the black-and-white warbler, and the ovenbird sing persistently throughout the day. The black-throated green sings from the upper canopy. It's often tough to get a good look at one, but its song, "zee-zee-zee-zoo-zee" or "trees-trees-trees-murmuring-trees," clearly indicates its presence. The black-and-white is most often found in the understory, about 10 to 15 feet above ground. Birders can call it in close by "pishing" or "squeaking." Its song, a thin "weesee, weesee, weesee, weesee," sounds a bit like a squeaky wheel.

The ovenbird feeds along the forest floor, and is more often heard than seen. Its emphatic "teacher, teacher, teacher, TEACHER" or "pizza, pizza, pizza, PIZZA" call announces its location and leaves no doubt as to its identity.

The common yellowthroat warbler and the yellow warbler reside in shrubby willows, dogwoods, and alders along streams and lakes. The yellowthroat's song, a clear, unmistakable "witchity, witchity, witchity, witch," is heard in just about any wetland area. The common yellowthroat can be called in closer by pishing, but it often darts rapidly from shrub to shrub, so you have to be quick with your binocs.

The yellow warbler is found in a variety of habitats, but it appears to nest almost exclusively near water. Its song is a swift, musical "sweet, sweet, sweet, sweeter-than-sweet."

147

I urge you to listen to a bird song tape if you don't know these songs. Once you learn them, you will be surprised by how common these five warblers are in the northwoods.

Yellow-Bellied Sapsuckers

Look for the cavity holes and listen for the chicks of yellow-bellied sapsuckers from mid-to late June. The nesting cavity is usually located about 20 feet up in older aspens. Some 35 species feed from the holes drilled in trees by the sapsucker, a process called "commensalism." In effect, sapsuckers set the table that allows many other species to eat.

Do the holes injure the tree? It's debatable, but I believe the detrimental effect is minimal. Even if they do cause injury to trees, what is an acceptable price for the benefits the sapsuckers provide?

Robins Nesting

Robins really seem to like human structures for their nest-building sites. They have set up housekeeping in mailboxes, grape trellises, door ledges, and tractor seats. Robins often lay two clutches of eggs. Because of their short incubation period (only 12 to 13 days) and their short fledging time of just 14 to 16 days, there's plenty of summer left to raise a second family. Ninety percent of the first clutches of young are fledged by July 20.

About 57 percent of a robin's diet consists of plant matter—much of it fruits. The other 43 percent is comprised of animal matter like worms, ants, grasshoppers, tent caterpillars, cutworms, and even small snakes.

Summer Bird Feeding

Don't quit feeding birds in your backyard just because the weather has warmed. Bluebirds, thrashers, catbirds, grosbeaks, orioles, towhees, woodpeckers, sparrows, and others will come during the summer if the table is adequately set. Try some of the following foods to attract different birds:

- Push apple and orange halves onto nails that are driven into a tree, stump, or perch. Robins, catbirds, and blue jays are attracted to apples, while orioles, red-bellied woodpeckers, and red-headed woodpeckers will eat oranges.
- Grape jelly placed in a shallow tray will attract orioles, bluebirds, catbirds, and robins. Generic brands work as well as Welch's.
- Ripe bananas, split but left in their skins and placed in a mesh bag or on a feeder tray, will entice warblers, tanagers, and orioles. These birds will eat the fruit, while hummingbirds will visit to eat the fruit flies.
- Peanuts scattered on the ground near brush may draw a brown thrasher as well as chickadees, nuthatches, woodpeckers, and jays.
- Suet cakes may need to be changed frequently, but they will tempt pileated woodpeckers and other woodpeckers, nuthatches, and chickadees.
- Besides hummers, sugar water will attract orioles, nuthatches, and even woodpeckers.
- Niger seed, though too expensive for my wallet, draws goldfinches, pine siskins, and house finches.
- Sunflower seeds scattered on the ground and in cylindrical feeders will attract rose-breasted grosbeaks, purple finches, jays, and mourning doves.

The most successful feeding stations offer 12 to 15 feeders arranged in 3 to 4 clusters; all are placed at least 10 feet from shrubbery, where cats can hide. Water is important, too. It's best if you can provide dripping or flowing water no more than one inch deep.

Mary and I take the simple approach, feeding with sugar water and sunflower seeds. You may notice a pause in the action at your feeders while young are being raised in the nest, but keep the feeders stocked. Once fledged, the chicks often visit feeders with Mom and Dad.

The Turtle River

Several friends and I canoed a section of the Turtle River from South Turtle Lake to Cedar Lake in late June, a trip lasting about three hours. We found "beaver heaven," heaving our canoes over five beaver dams while counting at least 11 lodges along the way. But the birding was excellent. The highlight for me was seeing a scarlet tanager (the black-winged redbird), a bird I seldom spot in the northwoods. In his book *Wisconsin Birdlife*, Sam Robbins lists the scarlet tanager as fairly common, noting that most nests are found in oaks about 8 to 15 feet above the ground. I wish I would see them more commonly, because they are as brilliantly colored as any songbird in the northwoods.

149

Black Bear Mating

The peak of the black bear mating season lasts from mid-June to mid-July. Females only go into estrus every other year. The male runs off any yearlings that are still with the female, but not the cubs, which will enter the den this fall with their mother.

Both sexes are polygamous, but the female is able to fertilize only one cub during a mating session. Thus, if a female has three cubs, each one is probably fathered by a different male.

Females utilize delayed implantation to postpone their actual pregnancy. After copulation has occurred, the eggs are fertilized, but they are not implanted. The fetuses don't develop until six to eight weeks before their February birth in the den. They are born hairless and sightless, and they weigh less than half a pound.

By June, the cubs have filled out to 15 to 20 pounds, and they are quickly getting weaned from Mom onto solid foods like insects, roots, sedges, and fruits. When the sow searches for food, she usually leaves her cubs by a "nurse tree"—often a large pine or hemlock. If danger presents itself, they can climb up the tree.

Swimming Red Squirrels

One June Mary, Eowyn, and I watched a red squirrel swimming at great speed across the Manitowish River. We had seen another one swim right past our canoe many years ago on Clark Lake in the Sylvania Recreation Area. We feared that we were about to be attacked, a la Jimmy Carter and his swimming rabbit. These sightings weren't as unusual as we first thought. Red squirrels can swim quite well, and do so often. One account talks about a red squirrel that swam out to a fellow's canoe, jumped in, ran along the gunwale to the other end, jumped back in the water, and continued onward to its destination.

Bracken Ferns

In the summer of 1992, late June frosts killed a great number of bracken ferns. The brown, upright fronds were an odd sight along highways so early in the summer. Bracken forms a subcanopy of shade in many woodlands and openings. I wondered then if their premature dieback would let other plant species get a foothold where ordinarily they would be shaded out, but the bracken didn't seem to relinquish any territory.

Bracken is so successful due to three factors that allow it to spread rapidly through woodlands:

- Horizontal rootstalks the diameter of a pencil are buried 10 inches into the soil. They proliferate from the parent plant, often extending great distances in one year and sending up new fronds. The root depth protects the plant from virtually every excess of weather.
- The mature leaves are poisonous to livestock, and are left completely alone by deer and other browsers.
- The shade produced by the nearly continuous canopy of fronds eliminates almost all competitors.

Because bracken are rarely found in rich, moist soils, their presence is usually a good indicator of poor soil quality. Bracken ferns are regarded by some as the "weed" of the fern family. Since virtually nothing eats this plant, some researchers have attempted to isolate the substance that makes bracken so unpalatable. It could prove useful as an insecticide.

Grasslands

The parching heat we experienced in June of 1995 had one positive effect—it reduced the need to cut withered grass. I spent a week of that hot spell in western Minnesota, looking at native prairies. The grasses were doing quite well, despite the heat. Native prairie grasses have been selected over thousands of years, adapting themselves to survival in just such a scorching heat. In many cases, half or more of the biomass of every plant in a prairie is underground. Two-thirds of all prairie species produce roots that extend beyond a depth of five feet. Big bluestem reaches down seven feet; switchgrass roots extend nine to 11 feet; and wildflowers like false boneset and blazing star send roots to 16 feet below the surface. It's little wonder that the original prairie settlers had so much trouble breaking the prairie sod, and that the soil, once broken, was so rich.

151

Swamps, Bogs, Marshes, and Shrub-Carr

When I guide walks through various wetlands, I have frequently been asked what the difference is between a marsh, a bog, and a swamp. The answer depends on who you choose to consult. The Army Corps of Engineers, the U.S. Fish and Wildlife Service, and the Wisconsin Wetland Inventory all have different definitions and many levels of classifications. But for the average northwoods nonbotanist, I believe it's easiest to divide wetlands into four categories.

Bogs are acidic, spongy wetlands dominated by sphagnum moss and sedges. There is no outflow of water, and rain and snow serve as the only inflow. Bogs are typically small, pothole lakes that have been gradually taken over by the bog plant community. These plants grow over the water as a shelf of plant material, creating a springy "waterbed" effect if you venture to walk across the mat. The dominant trees in bogs are tamaracks and black spruce.

Marshes are mineral-rich wetlands dominated by tall, emergent (above water) plants like cattails, rushes, and grasses, and very few trees. Water flows in and out, flushing and replenishing the nutrients in this type of wetland. While bogs are nutrient-poor, thus supporting very slow plant growth, marshes contain vast stores of nutrients that support luxurious growth.

Swamps are wooded wetlands that usually flood on a seasonal basis. Typical deciduous swamp trees in our area include silver maple and black ash, while white cedar is a common swamp conifer.

Shrub-carr is a wetland thicket, usually dominated by willows and alder. It often acts as a transitional zone between a water body and an upland. Extensive wetlands along the Manitowish River fit this definition.

There are gradations between the categories and, of course, combinations of supposedly separate communities, but these definitions work as generalities. Marshes in particular are at their flowering peak in later summer. Use that as an excuse to get out, if you need one. See if you can apply these categories and begin to distinguish between wetland plant communities.

Breathing Underwater

Water lilies, both white and yellow, flower in June in marsh habitats. Take note of the marvels of engineering represented by their long stems. Air-filled passages run throughout the stems, providing buoyancy and conveying oxygen to the roots. Yellow water lily stems conduct gases both to and from the roots. The air pores (stomata) are on the top side of the leaves, unlike most plants, which hide their stomata on the leaf undersides. Oxygen is literally pumped down by the younger leaves, and "exhaust" gases like methane and carbon dioxide are pumped up through the older leaves. One study found that 22 liters of air passed through a single leaf stalk in one day.

The stems of white water lilies are often open tubes that allow air to pass through freely; the stems of yellow water lilies are more chambered. Pick one of the white water lily leaf stems and blow through it. It's really little more than a long straw, and you can make bubbles in the water by blowing through one end with the other end submerged in water.

This could be handy someday. Imagine that you've just escaped from the federal penitentiary. The dogs are on your heels, and the only way to get them off your trail is to leap into the water and stay underwater until the guards have passed by. You might breathe through the white water lily stem while you await your chance to double-back on your track, throw the dogs into confusion, and eventually achieve your freedom.

Lupines

Lupines (*Lupis polyphyllus*) may be the most dramatic flowers currently in bloom. Huge, colorful colonies of this domestic garden escapee can be seen along Highway 2 west of Hurley and on Highway 13 going toward Bayfield. You may also encounter a few scattered sites along Highway 51 near Mercer.

153

Because wild lupine (*Lupus perennis*) grows in poor soils, it was mistakenly accused of depleting the soil of its nutrients. Its supposed "wolfing" of the soil's vitality earned it the name Lupus, which is Latin for wolf. The name does not reflect the true value of the plant. Lupus belongs to the legume family, and all legumes actually improve the soil by fixing nitrogen. Wild lupine grows on poor, sandy soils in prairies and dry, open woods, improving soil fertility for future plant communities.

Phenology

Phenology is the study and recording of natural events from year to year and from place to place. Its value lies in its ability to answer questions like "When do the blackberries ripen?" or "When are bear cubs born?" or "When will ospreys begin their migration to South America?"

Written phenology helps one analyze cause and effect in nature. By taking notes on temperatures, rainfall/drought, snow accumulations, wind directions, and other phenomena, one can begin to demonstrate the relationship between physical factors and changes in populations or behaviors.

I enjoy keeping these records, because they allow me to make educated guesses, to anticipate accurately what's soon to come, and to know when I should get out there and look around. When I find pyrola coming into bloom in late June, it makes me feel good. It shows me that I'm paying attention.

Clear Water: Why Here and Not There?

What are the variables that determine water quality in any given northwoods lake? There are many, but one factor most of us don't consider is the height of a lake in the overall topography of a region. Take Crystal Lake, for example—the swimming mecca of the Northern Highlands State Forest. Water clarity may reach 30 feet in Crystal. The primary reason for its exceptionally clear water is that Crystal is "perched" above all the other lakes in the immediate area. Because of its height, little nutrient-loaded groundwater seeps into the lake, and no nutrient-bearing streams flow in. Few nutrients mean little plant life; thus the water has a much greater chance of remaining clear.

Other variables also influence water quality, and some of the variables are both complicated and surprising. For instance, the number of predator fish in a lake may affect water clarity. Follow this reasoning if you will: If a lake has a high number of predator fish, it probably will contain a low number of forage fish that serve as prey. Thus the lake will have a high number of zooplankton (tiny animals that serve as food for the forage fish), because the foragers are scarce. If the zooplankton are high, the phytoplankton (algae and the like) will be low, because they feed the zooplankton. Few plants means clear water. Thus a high number of predators may help maintain water clarity.

However, because nature seems to favor complexity, many other factors enter into a lake's ecology, including weather, fishing pressure, the watershed vegetation, and basin shape. After only a little study, one soon gains great appreciation for the interactions and fluctuations that take place in a water system. One also appreciates the difficulty involved in making accurate ecological predictions over time for any given water body.

154

Regarding the current effect of acid rain in the northwoods, our local rainwater has an average pH of 4.6, making it 10 times more acidic than normal rainwater, which has a pH of 5.6 (a pH of 7 is neutral). At present, there is little evidence that acid rain is harming northern Wisconsin lakes, though it may be the catalyst in releasing mercury from sediments. We are profoundly fortunate in that we are upwind from the vast majority of industrial areas in the United States. If we were not, the negative effects would be much more dramatic.

The Cold Summer of 1992

It was the summer that wasn't. I remember drinking tea to keep my fingers warm as I typed one night in late July, the temperature dropping to 42°F at 11 p.m. I refused to start a fire in the woodstove, on the principle that we ought to be able to do without its heat during at least one month of the year.

The upside to the cold was the exceptional sleeping weather. We never took our winter quilt off our bed during that entire summer. I'll take that sort of weather any day, rather than sweltering in sweat-covered sheets. I think the forests were also given a reprieve from the droughts of the late-1980s. Maybe some trees that were still stressed and suffering gained strength in the absence of heat and dryness.

Mercury

Improvements in the early 1990s in data collection methods have made virtually all data obsolete on mercury contamination prior to 1985, so in many ways, mercury research remains in its infancy. Our lakes average one part of mercury per trillion—an amount so miniscule that our ability to measure it seems remarkable. Unfortunately, through the process of bioaccumulation, that small amount increases as it moves up the food chain, becoming significant in the predator fish (walleye, muskie, salmon, others), and in animals that eat those predators (eagles, humans, others). Half of all the mercury now in the environment is believed to have emanated from the burning of coal. The mercury has been carried around the globe in airborne emissions.

Hope Versus Assurance

Mary and our daughters mountain-biked around Powell Marsh one midafternoon in late June, spotting five adult sandhill cranes, six bitterns, a merlin, several marsh hawks, a loon, and a coyote pup that wasn't the least bit fazed by their presence. Their sightings illustrate how unpredictable wildlife can be. I've been skunked many times on the Powell while biking or hiking in midday; I've even been skunked early in the morning during birding programs, prompting birders to question my truth in advertising after I've described the Powell as a birder's mecca. Aldo Leopold put things in perspective when he wrote: "Things hoped for have a higher value than things assured." Because we never know what we'll find, every hike or canoe trip assumes an aura of adventure, a sense of anticipation that only chance can trigger. Humans have a disturbing habit of becoming bored if chance is removed from the experiential equation. We seek drama, and wildlife complies through its uncommon and unpredictable offerings.

156

Moon Deception

Note how large the full moon appears as it comes over the horizon, and how, within an hour, it appears "normal" size again. The moon seems larger as it rises because we see it next to familiar objects, like trees and houses. These terrestrial objects provide a scale for comparison; the brain perceives the moon to be larger because it has something to compare it with. The moon illusion can be demonstrated by rolling a sheet of paper into a half-inch-diameter tube about a foot long. Look at the enlarged moon through the tube, using one eye. The larger moon will instantly appear to reduce itself to normal size. Now open the other eye while closing the eye you used to look through the tube. The moon will appear enlarged again, because your brain will unconsciously compare it with objects on the horizon. As an alternative, try taking a picture with a camera (don't use a telephoto lens or mix lenses). Then take one later, after the moon has risen. Measure the diameter of the moon in each picture. The lens won't lie.

Hiking with Children

During many of my guided hikes, parents express concern because they don't feel they know enough to teach their children about the natural world. Rachel Carson responded to this feeling of inadequacy in a way that I would like to share: "For the child, and for the parent seeking to guide him, it is not half so important to know as to feel. If facts are the seeds that later produce knowledge and wisdom, then the emotions and the impressions of the senses are the fertile soil in which the seeds must grow . . . . It is more important to pave the way for the child to want to know than to put him on a diet of facts he is not ready to assimilate."

I believe it is enough to take your child into the woods, sharing the pleasure and wonder of it all. Children don't need experts. They need experiences.

Sightings

As June draws to a close, cedar waxwings are finally nesting, great blue heron young are fledging, and monarch caterpillars are hatched and eating milkweed leaves.

157

Late June Musings

Take the first step in ornithology . . . and you are ticketed for the whole voyage . . . Secrets lurk on all sides. There is news in every bush. What no man ever saw before may the next moment be revealed to you.

-John Burroughs

JULY

The Ojibwa word for July is *minigizis*, which means "the month of blueberries" or, more liberally, any berry, fruit, or seed.

Juneberries, blueberries, and raspberries come ripe in July. A friend shared with me this poem (though he didn't know where he learned it), which extols the virtues of wild raspberries:

> If you should ever find me laying on the ground in
>   a heap,
> and you think I is dead,
> just butter up some bisquits,
> or some new made bread.
> Then spread them all over with wild raspberry
>   jam,
> and wander on over to where I am,
> and wave them vittles over my head.
> If my mouth don't open,
> you know I is dead.

July offers the most warmth and sunlight of any month. Even Houghton, Michigan, has an average high of 81°F in July—a remarkable statistic given the cooling effect of Lake Superior.

July 1 to July 15

July 4th

The July 4th weekend usually draws more boats to the lakes and rivers of the Lakeland area than any

other time. Whether you're fishing, canoeing, sea kayaking, or pleasure boating, there's a lot of wildlife to be seen—particularly if you can get out early in the morning, before the boat traffic on popular lakes heats up. What might you see? In terms of

> ## July Musings
>
> *The earth laughs in flowers.*
> -Ralph Waldo Emerson

birds, the "charismatic megafauna," as a friend recently called them, include loons, eagles, and ospreys. Loon chicks have hatched over the last few weeks. During the first two weeks of their lives, the young spend about half of their time being ferried around on the backs of their parents. The parents must feed the chicks for the first month or more. The chicks are so fluffy and light that when they attempt to dive, they pop up like corks. Once they learn to dive, they're still largely unsuccessful hunters until they master the speed and agility necessary to catch fish and other aquatic creatures, which are much more at home underwater than the loons.

Eagle chicks were born around May 1, so they are now about two months old. They are nearly full grown, and they should appear quite large in the nest. Look for them to begin perching on the edge of the nest and soon foraging onto branches in preparation for their first flight, which should happen around August 1. The parents are kept busy feeding these bottomless pits, so they make frequent flights to and from the nest. A brood commonly consists of two chicks, and one is often larger than the other. The larger chick may be the female (adult females weigh 10 to 13 pounds, while males weigh eight to 10 pounds); or the larger may be the firstborn. In either case, the larger chick is the most dominant when meals arrive.

Osprey chicks hatched around June 1, and these parents are also kept busy feeding the hungry young. This is a good time of year to observe eagles and ospreys competing for food. A group of birders and I recently watched an eagle try to steal a fish from an osprey, while another osprey dove at the eagle, apparently trying to drive it away.

162

Great blue herons are commonly seen feeding along the shorelines of lakes and rivers. As the largest wading bird in North America, standing four feet tall with a wingspan of seven feet, the great blue is in a league of its own.

Look for kingbirds and cedar waxwings sallying forth over the water to catch insects on the wing, then flying back to their perches over the water. Kingbirds have earned their common name by their fearless harassment of any bird or other creature that ventures into their territory. Their Latin name, Tyrannus tyrannus, further reflects their behavior.

As for insect sightings, you're fortunate if a patrol of dragonflies and damselflies escorts you through narrow sections of a river or lake. Both prey upon mosquitoes, and both are masters of flight—able to hover, fly backwards, cruise at 35 miles per hour, and stop or start on a dime. Their metamorphosis from an aquatic larvae into a terrestrial flying machine is extraordinary. A group of canoeists and I paddled a section of the Trout River one July. We saw eagles, ospreys, and herons, but I think the highlight of our trip was watching a dragonfly emerge from its exoskeleton and hang limply from a blade of tall grass while its wings slowly hardened and its body unfolded. It was a miracle to behold, and the same event happens along every shoreline of every river and lake in this area. Dragonflies can see objects up to 50 feet away, and their range of vision is a full 180°. Their bulging eyes are the most highly developed in the insect world.

If you're looking for mammals, watch for the furbearers. Look for beavers, muskrats, and otters in the water; check for mink and raccoons along the shorelines. Dawn and dusk are your best bets for sightings, but dawn is the absolute best time of day. Sure, you're on vacation, but if you can drag yourself out of bed to see the early morning fog over the lake, and hear the bird choir that will soon fade, you'll experience the world much as it has always been.

We're Cool

The weather forecast often calls for temperatures in the 90s in July. Humans cool themselves down with fans and air conditioners, but how do the birds stay cool? Maintaining normal body temperature is a critical problem for birds. If the air temperature rises above the bird's temperature (ranging from 98.6°F for a whip-poor-will to 104°F or more for most songbirds), the bird's body may overheat. It will then quickly die, because it takes in too much heat and loses cooling water too quickly. This is one reason why songbirds are conspicuously absent from feeders at midday during a heat wave. They must stay in the shade and remain inactive or risk overheating. The lethal limit for most birds appears to be 113°F, although one house wren's temperature was experimentally raised to 116.3°F before it died.

163

On one 95°F July day, I watched a great egret fly overhead with its mouth clearly open, as if it was panting. It probably was. Birds have no sweat glands, so they do not face underwing deodorant problems like we obsessive humans, who attempt to plug up our natural cooling mechanisms. Instead, avians lose heat through their respiratory tracts by panting or, in nonsongbirds, through rapid vibrations of the upper throat and floor of their mouths, a process romantically called the "gular flutter." Pelicans have the most pronounced gular pouch, but cormorants, owls, pigeons, pheasants, and quail have one, too. Soaring birds employ yet another cooling strategy—they simply soar in the thermals to avoid midday heat.

Fluctuating body temperatures don't affect birds the way they affect humans. We have a "fever" if our temperature goes up 1-2°F, but the body temperature of a robin or a song sparrow may change by 10°F in a day without apparent harm or concern. Thus, while all those feathers seem to present a major disadvantage on a hot day, birds have developed additional strategies to beat the heat.

Discrimination: The Good Kind

On July 1, 1993, 10 bird-watchers took a walk with bird expert Joan Elias, as part of the Northern Highlands naturalist program. We walked to Cathedral Point from the Trout Lake Forestry Station. The avian exuberance of spring had waned, and the full leaf canopy prevented us from seeing many birds, but Joan was able to point out a host of birdlife around us by identifying their songs. She patiently directed our hearing throughout the hike, until we began to discriminate the songs from the "background noise." The comment I heard frequently from those on the hike was, "I would never have heard that!" We were learning to direct our attention, to focus on what had previously seemed a blur of sound; soon we were fine-tuning the sensory filters of our minds.

164

We thus began learning the process of discrimination, which in this context is another word for appreciation. We were learning to distinguish sounds that had always been around us but which, up to this point, had not been heard. I frequently have the experience of seeing or hearing something for the first time, then realizing it had been there all along, but I had been blind or deaf to it. I'm elated with my discovery, but I also kick myself for being so inattentive as to have missed it all these years. This continual discovery process is the gift the northwoods provides all of us if we simply learn to focus our attention and begin discriminating.

Osprey Development

Osprey chicks hatch around the first week of June, and should be about four weeks old by early July. The general timetable for ospreys hereabouts goes something like this: eggs laid on May 1; eggs hatched on June 1; chicks fledged on August 1. Body feathers generally emerge during the first week of July; by mid-July, the young should look very much like the adults.

The Northern Highland/American Legion Forest contains 30 nesting territories, with 13 pairs occupying the Rainbow Flowage alone. If you're looking for ospreys, the Rainbow has the highest density, while the finest water body in Wisconsin for osprey numbers is the Turtle-

Flambeau Flowage, located outside of the forest, which hosts 22 pairs. About 70 percent of the ospreys in our region nest on artificial platforms put up by the DNR. The project was an effort to reestablish the species, and it's a real success story.

Grouse Gizzards

On four occasions in early July of 1991, I saw grouse standing in the gravel along roadsides; on two of those occasions, I saw adults with young. I assumed that they were eating grit in the form of gravel to aid their digestion. Birds that eat plant parts like seeds, grains, roots, and buds have muscular gizzards within their stomachs. The gizzard has ridges on it, much like a millstone. It regularly contracts, literally grinding hard food materials into smaller particles. Grit assists in the grinding action, while supplying needed minerals.

165

Grinding seeds is just "chicken feed" compared to what gizzards are capable of doing. Some diving ducks can swallow clams whole, and the gizzard will grind up the meal. Mallards and wood ducks can swallow whole hickory nuts and acorns; by the next day, the nuts have been ground into mush.

Back in the 1700s, some rather sadistic researchers introduced glass balls, hollow cubes of lead, tubes of tin plate, steel needles, and pyramids of wood into turkey stomachs. All were ground up or crushed flat by the next day.

If grit is unavailable, some birds use pits of wild fruit as substitutes. Some acquire expensive tastes, like the wild ducks that were found in 1911 with gold nuggets in their gizzards, touching off a gold rush in Nebraska.

The type of grit found in a bird's gizzard can even reveal the general area the bird came from—a clue that can be used to discover nesting areas or migration patterns.

Grouse chicks, which usually number 10 to 12 in a brood, hatch around the first week of June. Within a week or so, they can fly short distances and perch in trees. By the first week of July, they have almost finished their diet of insects, and they are turning to leaves and fruit for their summer needs.

Canada Geese

Carol Hanneman has her own resident flock of Canadian geese on Echo Lake, near my home area of Mercer, Wisconsin. Wild populations elsewhere are far harder to come by. Fifteen years ago, we didn't have any resident geese in the Lakeland area. Thanks to a release program back in the late 1960s, Powell Marsh is now possibly the best habitat in this area for nesting success. Fifteen to 18 pairs of geese presently nest on the marsh. Their chicks hatch in early to mid-May. Sometime in late June to early July they'll probably take their maiden flight (fledging is about 45 days from hatching).

Geese are also nesting on the Bear River, the Rhinelander Flowage, the Little Turtle Flowage, the Flambeau Flowage, Lake Nokomis, and the Eagle River Chain. They have been released on the Willow Flowage, Thunder Marsh, and near Johnson Creek as part of a three-year release cycle.

Geese are secretive about their nesting sites, but with luck you may see more wild geese in the northwoods in the near future. If you live in areas that are inundated with "problem geese," don't be alarmed by this prospect. Geese require grassy feeding areas (golf courses are good) in order to proliferate, and the northwoods remains heavily forested.

July Flowers: Bog Orchids

Among the flowers I have seen blooming in our area during early July are:

Rattlesnake plantain	Sumac
One-flowered wintergreen	Pickerelweed
One-sided pyrola	Partridgeberry
Grass pink orchid	Heal-all
Bladderwort	Beech drops
Meadowsweet	Various pondweeds
Swamp candle	Marsh skullcap
(yellow loosestrife)	Harebells
Water shield	Giant bur-reed
Milkweed	Pitcher plant

True Solomon's seal	Speedwell
Greenish-flowered pyrola	Gill-over-the-ground
Tufted loosestrife	Spotted coralroot
Tall meadow rue	Field bindweed
Mullein	Sweet cicely
Lesser stitchwort	Rock cress
Wild rose	Bedstraw
Tick trefoil	Maple-leaved vibernum

The most beautiful of the wildflowers are arguably the orchids. Forty-two species are found in Wisconsin. The word "orchid" derives from the Greek *orkhis*, meaning "testicle." The always imaginative Greeks gave the plant this name because of the shape of its tuberous roots. According to the Doctrine of Signatures, which held that the shape of the plant indicated its use, eating the roots would result in a powerful aphrodisiac effect—and the offspring from subsequent sexual relations would be male. "Satyrion" is another word that was used for orchids, derived from "satyr," the lustful, half-man half-goat woodland deity of Greek mythology.

The grass pink orchid grows in open sphagnum bogs. We see many of them on bog walks in early July. Grass pink was given the scientific genus name of *Calopogon*, taken from the Greek *kalos*, meaning "beautiful," and *pogon*, meaning "beard." Grass pink is distinctive because the "lip" is on the top petal, not on the bottom petal, as in other orchids. Look also in bogs for rose pogonia, which has a beautiful, yellow-bearded lip beneath its magenta petals and sepals.

Pitcher Plants: Bog Carnivores

Pitcher plants flower in the bogs into July. Bogs are notoriously low in oxygen, extremely cold, and highly acidic. They may be the most difficult plant growth environment in the northwoods. Decay occurs slowly at best, preventing the release of nutrients—nitrogen in particular. Pitcher plants have solved the problem of nutrient scarcity by using fragrance to lure insects into their red and green "pitchers," from which they can't escape. Glands then exude enzymes to help digest the insects, and the nitrogen deficit is relieved.

Pitchers are one of our few carnivorous plants, though one source says that the decaying insects are thought to provide food not for the plant, but for the larvae of the flies that cross-pollinate the flowers.

Some insects spend their entire lives in the rainwater of the pitcher plant, apparently immune to the digestive juices. They survive by sharing the insects that drop in. This process, in which one species benefits while the other is unaffected, is called "commensalism."

Columbines

Columbines are still flowering in July. Their uniquely shaped, tube-like nectaries resemble a circle of doves—hence the Latin *columba*, or dove. The scientific genus name, *Aquilegia*, means "eagle," a reference to the spurs atop the nectaries, which are bent like the talons of an eagle.

Old-Growth Pines

Seventeen people launched canoes one July on Vilas County's Dunn Lake, in order to reach the Dunn Lake Pines Natural Area, a stand of old-growth, undisturbed white pines and hemlocks. Kay and Earl Allen were kind enough to allow us access to the site, which is landlocked within the private boundaries of the Natural Lakes development. We came to see big trees, and we were rewarded with a scattered stand of 75 to 100 pines, their diameters ranging from 30 to 42 inches. The pines are about 300 years old. Under the sparse supercanopy of the pines grew large sugar maples, yellow birches, and hemlocks. Very few younger white pines grew in the understory, because white pine can't survive beneath the canopy of a heavily shaded, climax forest. When the old-growth pines fall, the stand will likely convert to sugar maple, yellow birch, and hemlock, perhaps with some basswood mixed in. The seedlings of these species can tolerate living in full shade, awaiting their turn to grow when a gap opens in the canopy.

The Dunn Lake stand represents what many of the "old-growth" forests probably looked like before settlement in Wisconsin. Because white pines can't tolerate shade, the old-growth forests produced only 12 to 15 giant pines per acre. There were some nearly pure stands of pine, but these were an exception to the rule. The belief that the northwoods once consisted entirely of an ancient stand of old-growth trees, and that a squirrel could cross from New York to the upper Midwest simply by leaping from bough to bough, is pure myth. Wisconsin's presettlement forests contained many second- and third-growth trees, as well as the giant pines of Paul Bunyan legend. John Curtis, author of the "bible" on plants in Wisconsin, *The Vegetation of Wisconsin*, estimated that nearly 50 percent of Wisconsin's land surface was directly influenced by fire, some of the blazes accidentally ignited by lightning, others deliberately started by Indian tribes.

169

Another well-known researcher, Forest Stearns, estimated that at any one time, 15 percent of the northwoods was comprised of blow-downs, trees toppled by the wind. Additional agents of mortality like disease, insects, drought, and ice storms also helped keep the northwoods in a constant state of change.

We know this is true because records were left behind by early explorers, and by the first surveyors. In 1847, geologist J.G. Norwood traveled from La Pointe on the Apostle Islands to Lac Vieux Desert, where the headwaters of the Wisconsin River are located, keeping a thorough diary. He described the portage from the Manitowish River to Trout Lake in Vilas County as passing "for some distance over a sandy plain supporting a few scattering pines." He reported that the land around Trout Lake consisted of "drift hills, from twenty-five to forty feet high, supporting a sparse growth of small pines and birch." Norwood observed that the Flambeau Trail, a 42-mile-long portage trail from Lake Superior to Long Lake in Iron County, was "covered with a growth of small timber, mostly pine, with some sugar maple, oak, and a few aspens, while the valleys support a good growth of sugar maple, with undergrowth of the same."

My historical digression is meant to enhance appreciation for the stand of pines along Dunn Lake. Few such stands now remain. Un-fortunately, the demise of these stands is likely to come soon. Pines reaching above the dense forest canopy stick up like feathers. A big wind can easily bring them down, particularly because our pines have shallow roots in the sandy soil. The Big Block in the Flambeau State

Forest, once Wisconsin's finest remaining stand of virgin timber, was partially blown down in 1949, 1951, and 1952. In 1977, a downburst destroyed the entire stand.

If the wind doesn't drop our giant pines, time will simply wear them out. Though white pines may live for 500 years, they eventually succumb to the forces of species succession—the process leading inexorably from sunny openings to closed-canopy, fully-shaded forests, or to disturbance like fire or windstorm. White pines are usually the middlemen in the successional equation, living the balanced life of growing in some sun and some shade, but ultimately yielding to the final stage of succession, the shaded climax forest.

170

In my mind's eye, the beauty of white pine exceeds that of all other species, providing the aesthetic measuring stick by which all other trees may be judged. The Dunn Lake stand provides a reminder of the great size and dignity that trees can attain, if only the forces of human and natural disturbance are kept at bay.

Bryozoans

To reach the Dunn Lake Pines, we had to paddle a tiny stretch of the East Branch of the Presque Isle River. Along the way, we found an underwater gelatinous mass attached to a log. The mass was dotted but otherwise clear, and felt like a hard Jell-O. It was a moss animal called "bryozoa." Bryozoans typically grow in colonies on objects submersed in the shallow, shoreline waters of lakes and streams. Many members of our canoe party had seen such colonies in northwoods waters, but had not known what they were.

Each dot in the mass represented an individual zooid, or group of zooids. With a hand lens or microscope, our group would have been able to see the zooids rotating their headlike cluster of tentacles. Thousands of individual zooids may live in a one-square-foot mass. The average observer would be hard-pressed to discern whether bryozoans are plant or an animal form. Frankly, if I didn't have research books, I wouldn't be sure, either. They fall into the stratum of living things like freshwater sponges and bladderworts, which defy easy categorization. Perhaps more importantly, the presence of bryozoans is an indicator of good water quality. If you see a colony, rest assured that you are traversing unpolluted waters.

Blue Flag Iris

During a wet summer, blue flags may bloom well into July. The blue flag iris is also known as fleur-de-lis, a name commonly thought to mean "flower of the lily." In fact, the name originated when Louis VII king of France adopted a blue flag as the emblem of his house. Over time the "fleur-de-Louis" was corrupted through spelling errors.

The plant's leaves resemble pointed swords, but they are slightly curved, with parallel veins. A thick, fleshy, horizontal rhizome extends underground. Clonal stems grow upward from the rhizome to form new plants, explaining why blue flags are usually found in clonal patches.

171

Night Fires

Fireflies flash in the wetland below our house in July. Their light production has a sexual meaning, and is not intended merely for our visual pleasure. The male emits flashes of light at intervals of five to eight seconds while he flies a few feet above the ground. Females wait on top of low vegetation; if a flashing male comes within six feet, the female flashes back. The exact number of seconds between flashes serves to distinguish the species. The male will only approach a light if it flashes at the proper intervals.

Glowworms

One July I led for the DNR what was intended to be a full-moon night hike; instead, we settled for a full-overcast night hike. Still, I was impressed by how well the moon backlit the clouds, softly illuminating our hike. We had little trouble seeing, except when we were under a full forest canopy.

We found glowworms in the ferns along the road. I initially thought they might be foxfire, until one of the hikers picked some up and said the lights were moving in her hand. We reconsidered, deciding that they were some type of firefly, because the adult females of some species are wingless glowworms. The larvae of many species of fire-flies glow as well. Because adult fireflies were flashing regularly around us, our glowworms were almost certainly members of one of the 50-plus species of fireflies that live in the U.S.

A firefly's light is a cold light, generating no heat. Remarkably, it is 92 to 100 percent efficient and pollution-free. Compare this to a typi-cal light bulb, which is 10 percent efficient and indirectly produces the emissions associated with burning oil or coal to generate electricity.

Mayfly Madness

I was in Ashland, walking along Lake Superior one early July. Mayflies hung by the thousands on virtually every building. A mayfly hatch is a prodigious event, likened to a "summer snowstorm." Tens of thousands may swarm in the air, mating in flight.

Mayflies belong to the order Ephemeroptera, from the root "ephem-eral." They're appropriately named, because the adults usually live for just one day. However, in some species, the aquatic nymph may live underwater for several years. In preparation for adulthood, its mouthparts and digestive system shrink; its sex organs and eyes en-large; and its stomach changes into an inflatable air chamber. The nymph then floats to the water surface, where its back splits open and the "dun" emerges, coated with a water-resistant film. Meanwhile, predators like trout and water striders feed on the mayfly duns. Un-like most insects, the duns have evolved no defenses like stings or bad taste to give them a sporting chance. Those that survive the surface feeding frenzy lift off in a slow flutter that attracts insect-eating birds like swallows, phoebes, and flycatchers, along with other predators such as bats and dragonflies. The survivors of the aerial predators flit into the treetops, attach themselves to the underside of leaves, then wait for nearly a day while they rapidly experience what amounts to their childhood and adolescence. Their ruddering tail filaments grow to nearly twice the length of their bodies; their multifaceted eyes be-come ultrasensitive to movement and light reflection; the female fills with eggs from end to end, even up to the back of her head.

The dun sheds its last water-repellent covering, the final vestige of its aquatic ancestry, and the female "dresses up" in vivid coloration. Her glistening body is easily spotted by the male's light-sensitive eyes. The final adult stage begins in a form referred to as an "imago" or "spinner." Each mayfly joins a nuptial swarm that usually gathers at sundown and "parties" through the night. The females emit a specific pheromone, which sexually attracts males of her own species. The pheromone also acts as the glue that keeps the swarm together even when it passes through a swarm of another species. As the mass rises up and down above the water, the spinners copulate in midair. Females descend onto the males, which usually fly closer to the water. Males reach up with their long forelegs, clasping the female near her head. They also clasp females near the end of their abdomens with a similarly positioned, tonglike clasper. Males then proceed to fertilize her eggs.

173

Shortly thereafter, the spent males drop into the water to die; the females, ripe with fertile eggs and endowed with only slightly longer life spans, plant their eggs in, on, or above the water, depending on the species. They, too, then fall into the water, where they are devoured by surface-feeding insects and fish. The eggs hatch two weeks later, and the tiny mayflies begin their year-long (or longer) aquatic sojourn, undergoing 15 to 30 molts before they emerge as fleeting but elegant flying adults.

Even if a wayward adult attempted to prolong its survival, it would be unsuccessful. Its mouthparts don't even function, so it couldn't take in any food. All told, it's not much of an adulthood.

The adults are highly light sensitive. They can distinguish between a dark, smooth surface, which might hide fish, and a safer, light-colored surface that reflects light. Thus they are drawn to electric lights near water at resorts and restaurants and along streets, where large accumulations of mayfly bodies are often found.

Huge mayfly hatches are not confined to the Great Lakes. While driving home one evening on Highway 51, I suddenly saw silvery-white insects two inches long in my headlights, splattering on my windshield in enormous numbers. I stopped my car and got out. There, clinging to the highway and fluttering in the ghost glare of my lights, were thousands of large mayflies. Their gondola-shaped bodies hovered peacefully in the still air or crawled on the glistening, dark pavement that must have provided the illusion of moonlight on water. I drove through the horde for another mile or more, flinching at every senseless impact, caught in an open-air cave of mayflies that seemed impossibly large. Yet I knew that such hatches were undoubtedly occurring along other waterways throughout the northwoods. I knew also that other hatches of mayflies had preceded this one, and still others would follow, each seeming to appear out of nowhere and disappearing soon afterward.

Dragonfly Eyes and X-Rated Behavior

The dragonfly is known as the "mosquito hawk." It preys upon deer-flies and other nasties, so I feel well-protected and privileged if one is perched on my collar or cap when I'm hiking.

Dragonflies have the most highly developed compound eyes in the entire insect world. About 28,000 six-sided facets in each eye produce a visual range of nearly 180°; dragonflies can accurately perceive moving objects up to 50 feet away. Take a look at one of their eyes under a microscope sometime—it's very impressive.

I've often watched dragonflies and damselflies mating—a task not for the fainthearted, because they contort themselves into something called "the wheel position." The male catches a female in flight with his legs. He curves his abdomen around, hooking it to the back of her head. The male transfers his sperm to a pouch at that spot on the female's body. The female then swings her abdomen around to the sperm pouch, and the two bodies form a rough wheel shape. That's tough enough, but they can fly in this position as well.

Moose

In an attempt to reestablish the once-native moose population, moose were released in 1987 along Michigan's Upper Peninsula. In succeeding years, moose have been spotted in northcentral Wisconsin. Sightings have been reported northeast of Monaco, near St. Germain, and on North and South Twin Lakes. Moose move around a good deal—ranging 15 to 20 miles a day is not uncommon—so the spottings have often reflected the movements of the same moose.

One cow with an ear tag was observed in this area in the early 1990s. It was determined that she was one of the original Michigan moose, released east of Marquette. She had traveled 150 miles. The bulls are particularly active during their rut, which occurs in late September or early October. Birth occurs in May, and a yearling will weigh 400 pounds by fall.

Locally, the big question is, "Are moose residing in the Lakeland area, or just passing through?" A cow and a calf were seen near Little St. Germain Lake in 1992, and winter tracks have been reported in several areas. But the long-term prognosis is poor. A brainworm carried by deer, to which the deer themselves are immune, infects moose and kills them. Because of the brainworm, the territories of deer and moose seldom overlap to any significant extent. We are presently overpopulated with deer in virtually every Wisconsin management district, but reducing the herd size to accommodate moose would make more than a few deer hunters see red.

175

Still, I hope one day to canoe down the Manitowish, come around a bend, and find myself suddenly faced with a bull and a cow browsing the abundant wetland plants. I wouldn't quibble a bit, whether they were transients or residents.

Endangered Species in Wisconsin

As of 1996, 100 wolves in 18 packs reside in Wisconsin. Pups are born in mid-April, and they leave the den site in mid-June, moving to the rendezvous site—an area where the pack often congregates. Road density is a limiting factor in wolf pack survival. About one mile of road per one square mile of land appears to be the maximum density that wolves can tolerate.

There are no known breeding pairs of Canada lynx in Wisconsin, but the lynx may migrate into northern Wisconsin when the snowshoe hare population crashes in Canada and northern Minnesota.

Pine martens were stocked in the Nicolet National Forest from 1975 to 1982, and in the Chequamegon National Forest near Clam Lake from 1987 to 1990. They are reasonably well-established, but nowhere near as successful as fishers, which are now so common in the northwoods that some consider them a problem.

Cougars were last recorded in Wisconsin in 1909, but many sightings have been reported over the last few years. We may have 10 to 20 cougars in the state, but no one is certain where they came from. Is this a reestablishing population migrating in, a relic population no one knew about, or are these released animals from an unknown source? At this point, no one knows.

Common terns are known to nest at only two sites in the state, one in Duluth Harbor and the other near Ashland.

The piping plover is our most endangered species. No breeding pairs have been seen since 1985 in Wisconsin, and only a dozen pairs are known to be breeding in the entire Great Lakes region.

Floods and Trees

Why didn't the northwoods experience flooding like many central and southern portions of Wisconsin, Minnesota, and Michigan did in 1993? Part of the reason is that our rivers are mostly small headwaters and tributaries, joining other rivers along the way to form major river systems. The Manitowish River joins the Bear River to form the North Fork of the Flambeau River; the Flambeau flows into the Chippewa River, and the Chippewa flows into the Mississippi. But even small creeks can flood, so size is not the essential factor. Forests are. Iron County is 85 percent forested. When rains come, the drops are intercepted by the leaf canopy and broken into finer droplets. Those droplets are intercepted again by other layers of vegetation, including understory trees like ironwood and balsam fir and ground layer plants like bracken fern and big leaf aster. The rain that reaches the soil hits with far less speed, weight, and impact than rain that strikes urban streets or rural farmlands. In these open areas, soil and other ground layer materials wash away at a prodigious rate. Gardeners know this principle, and apply it by spraying a fine mist of water onto vegetables, rather than applying a hard stream of water. This helps the soil and water stay put.

Rain that penetrates a forest eventually strikes the forest floor, which is protected by a layer of organic matter and humus, mostly in the form of dead leaves and needles. The humus acts like a sponge, absorbing much of the water, again contrasting sharply with clean rows of corn and city concrete. These act as gutters, funneling water directly to a lower point. Rainwater percolates slowly into loamy forest soil, 50 percent of which is often comprised of pore spaces that allow oxygen to travel. In our sandy Lakeland area soils, the sand has so many large pore spaces that rainwater drains rapidly into the groundwater—a fact noted by any hiker who isn't forced to slip and slide around on mud for days after a hard rain. In other areas, the soil may be clay that packs together when it gets wet. Rainwater won't readily penetrate the clay surface layer, so it pools up or flows downhill.

177

The long and short of it (or the wet and dry of it) is that natural forests store water and release it slowly, while "clean" farmlands and cities serve as giant spillways, speeding rainwater headlong into rivers.

> # July Musings
>
> *The last word in ignorance is the person who says of an animal or plant: "What good is it?" If the land mechanism as a whole is good, then every part is good.*
>
> -Aldo Leopold

Erosion statistics reflect our loss of forests, and they are startling. Every year, one of every five acres in Wisconsin loses twice as much soil as can be replaced; nationally, we lose 3.1 billion tons of farm topsoil annually, enough to fill the Astrodome 34,000 times. The average loss of soil on American farms is one inch per acre every 33 years. In essence, America has already lost one-third of its topsoil. On a worldwide basis, one-fifth to one-third of the earth's cropland suffers from accelerated erosion.

We tend not to notice this loss until brown floodwaters overrun our cities; then we lament the weather. Floods have certainly occurred in natural environments, and they will continue to do so. Other factors, such as topography and soil type, contribute to the flood equation. But we have vastly increased the extent of flooding in our state and our country through the simple loss of forests. The next time it doesn't flood in Vilas, Oneida, and Iron counties, while floods occur downstate, thank the trees.

BERRY
blueberry

bitterns, harriers, & bobolink

FRUIT
bunchberry

Flora & Fauna

OLYMPICS

GOLD

WHITE TAILED DEER

SILVER

ELK

BRONZE

BLACK BEAR

TRACK SPRINTS

PASSPORT -IN- TIME

TANDY

SEED
columbine

JULY 16-31

SUNLIGHT

July 16 to July 31

Northwoods Flora & Fauna Olympics

Mary, Callie, and I should have had our eyes checked after all the coverage we watched of the 1996 Summer Olympics. The media blitz led me to wonder which of our native plants and animals would medal in certain events if we were to host the Northern Flora and Fauna Olympics. Here are my favorites to take the gold in events specially tailored to these athletes:

Fastest Plant. The common bladderwort, which can open and close its trapdoor in 1/460th of a second in order to catch tiny insects and zooplankton. The human eye can observe movement up to 1/30th of a second, so the judging gets a bit intuitive in this event.

Diving. The common loon wins the depth portion of this event, with dives reported in excess of 200 feet. The double-crested cormorant would take the silver by diving down to 120 feet. The "how long can you hold your breath" portion of the competition would probably go to the beaver, which is apparently able to stay underwater for 10 to 12 minutes.

> ### Late July
>
> *The song of the hermit thrush . . . suggests a serene religious beatitude as no other sound in nature . . . it is perhaps more of an evening than a morning hymn . . . he seems to say, "O holy, holy! O clear away! O clear up, clear up!" interspersed with the finest trills and the most delicate preludes. It is not a proud, gorgeous strain like the tanager's or the grosbeak's; suggests no passion or emotion— nothing personal—but seems to be the voice of that calm, sweet solemnity one attains in his best moments.*
>
> -John Burroughs

Fastest Bird. The peregrine falcon takes first by achieving 200 miles per hour while diving on an unsuspecting pigeon or duck. Ordinarily, its top airspeed ranges from 40 to 60 miles per hour.

Marathon Flying. The blackpoll warbler takes the gold in the ultra-lightweight division, flying 2,000 miles nonstop during its autumn migration from Nova Scotia to South America. It's a 40-hour flight if the winds are perfect (a 30-mile-per-hour tailwind). Blackpolls lose half their body weight on the trip, starting at about two-thirds of an ounce and finishing at one-third of an ounce.

High Jump. The white-tailed deer wins easily, clearing eight-foot fences from a standing position.

Long Jump. The cougar, which is known to gallop in long, graceful leaps of 25 feet or more, takes this event.

Highest Flight. The highest-flying, positively identified North American bird was a mallard that was struck by an airplane at 21,000 feet. Worldwide, the highest altitude ever recorded for a bird in flight was a species of vulture that collided with a plane at 37,000 feet over West Africa and damaged one of the plane's engines.

Track Sprint. The recently reintroduced elk could contend for the gold, given its ability to reach 45 miles per hour. However, the white-tailed deer should win by a nose, because it has been clocked at 50 miles per hour. Remarkably, the black bear might take the bronze in this event, though it would be a bit slow out of the blocks. Bears have been clocked at 35 miles per hour. If black bears are this fast, I would put my money on them to win the decathalon.

Wrestling. Pound for pound, no animal has a greater reputation for fierceness than the weasel, or ermine. Weasels have been known to successfully take on animals 30 times their weight. So, for many weight divisions, the weasel would bring home the gold.

Flying Gymnastics. The ruby-throated hummingbird wins the bird division, thanks to its ability to swoop, roll, tumble, stop on a dime, hover, fly backwards, and dive at 60 miles per hour. The dragonfly, which can hover, do somersaults, make about-face turns, fly backward at high speeds, and fly at a sprint of up to 35 miles per hour, wins the insect division.

180

Swimming Sprints. I like the loon again, because it can outswim most fish. The otter wins the mammal division for its ability to outswim quick, elusive fish like trout.

Gliding. The northern flying squirrel wins the mammal division by gliding in excess of 150 feet.

Synchronized Swimming. Families of otters win hands down. Their ability to swim in a line in perfect harmony has led some observers to conclude that we have serpents in our lakes.

Night Vision

181

Wisconsin drivers hit nearly 30,000 deer annually, mostly at night. They would certainly hit many more if it weren't for the reflective nature of a deer's eyes. Why do the eyes of deer and other nocturnal animals reflect light at night? A night animal has a kind of mirror behind its retina, called the tapetum, which aids in night vision. All incoming light is reflected outward again by the tapetum, in effect allowing the light to be sensed a second time. If the eyes of nocturnal animals did not reflect light, cats, coyotes, raccoons, mice, and others would be nearly invisible to us at night.

Nocturnal animals also perceive more light because they are unable to see color. While human eyes contain cone cells to help us perceive colors, nearly all cells in the eyes of night animals are rods, responsive to light but not color. The colors most mammals see are black, gray, and white.

According to research, the nose of a coyote or a bobcat is also nearly 58 times as sensitive as a human nose. Smell serves as a language for these animals, not unlike our oral language. Tone, mood, and implication are written between the lines.

This isn't surprising. On a recent night hike, while we stumbled and inched our way down the darker parts of the trail, predators had to find a meal without alerting prey to their presence. In darkness, they had to hunt with efficiency, power, and acuity. When you think about it, it's an extraordinary ability.

Powell Marsh: Bitterns, Harriers, Bobolinks

I lead a hike on the Powell Marsh every year, and one mid-July morning our group saw three rather unusual things. First we were treated to eight different sightings of American bitterns, which were flying back and forth across the marsh. Bitterns are members of the heron family, and they are ordinarily very secretive and solitary. Even if they are common in an area, one seldom sees them as often as we did that morning.

182

The presence of American bitterns in an area is usually given away by their call, which is best described as the sound made by an old hand pump with bad leathers—kind of a pump-er-lunk. Some say it sounds like the driving of a stake into the ground. It's an utterly unique call, and rather hard to convey to those who have never heard it.

The call is a mating and territorial effort, and nesting had concluded by mid-July, so we didn't have the pleasure of hearing it that day. Nor did we get to see a bittern doing its camouflage trick, during which it stands motionless with its neck pointed straight up in an effort to merge with the surrounding bullrush and cattail. We were very fortunate to see them in flight, and to see them flying so many times.

The second thing we observed with great excitement were numerous marsh hawks, correctly referred to as northern harriers. Not only did we see them in flight many times, but twice we watched one fly across the marsh with something in its talons. When the harrier came almost directly overhead, it dropped its kill through the air to another harrier, which was coming from the opposite end of the marsh. The second harrier caught the food and proceeded to fly well back into the marsh.

The third sighting of note was a pair of bobolinks—a bird species few of us ever see in the northwoods. Bobolinks are relatively common in grasslands, but we hadn't expected to see them in a major northern bog like Powell Marsh. For lovers of birds like us, it was a real find.

Loon Rangers

Every five years in July, Loonwatch conducts random surveys of loons in Wisconsin. Begun in 1985, the project produced the first accurate estimate of the loon population in Wisconsin. The first survey estimated 2,829 loons, plus or minus 248. The 1990 survey estimated 2,790 loons, plus or minus 235.

Minnesota conducted a loon count in 1994, estimating their summer population at 12,048, which easily makes Minnesota the state most heavily populated by loons among the lower 48. As of 1991, Michigan loons are estimated at 1,800 individuals.

Loonwatch always needs volunteers to help conduct the survey, and volunteering is simply a matter of counting all the loons on an assigned lake and day in your area. Call the Sigurd Olson Environmental Institute in Ashland (715/682-1223) if you would like to take part in this survey.

183

July Migrations

Unbelievably—and sadly for lovers of long summers—some shorebirds have begun their migration south by late July. Arctic nesters like the greater yellowlegs have been seen on Lake Superior's Chequamegon Bay at Ashland as early as July 10! Upland sandpipers begin migration in late July also.

Fledging Eagles

Eagles should be fledging soon in the northwoods. Most young eagles leave the nest around August 1, 70 to 98 days after hatching. By comparison, an osprey fledges after 48 to 59 days.

I strongly recommend a paddle on the Rainbow Flowage if you desire to see eagles and ospreys. During one July paddle, after we saw numerous eagles and ospreys, we pulled out at the landing as an eagle and osprey soared together above us. They climbed higher and higher until they reached the rim of a large cumulus cloud, whereupon the osprey stooped on the eagle in an attempt to hit it, then disappeared.

Quick! Three Beers!

I heard an olive-sided flycatcher at the Allequash Lake boat landing one July day, an event of interest only because of this flycatcher's song. It sings three very clear, loud notes that are usually written phonetically as "Quick! Three beers!" Wisconsinites may appreciate and remember this song more readily than out-of-staters.

Avian Surgeons

Woodpeckers have evolved a constellation of special adaptations that support their lifestyle. Banging one's head repeatedly against a wall can earn a human a trip to the hospital—and to an even unfriendlier institution after healing—but woodpeckers may slam their beaks against a tree as often as a hundred times per minute without physical injury or concern for their emotional well-being. Woodpeckers perform a type of surgery upon trees, usually removing destructive, invading insects. One pileated woodpecker's stomach was dissected, revealing over 2,000 carpenter ants.

Woodpeckers apparently depend upon their hearing to detect insect life within a tree. They often tap deliberately around a tree, probably searching for the difference in sound between hollowed-out insect tunnels and solid wood. If woodpeckers selected trees to explore on a random basis, they would have been doomed a long time ago.

How do they carry out their surgery? Unlike other birds, they have spongy tissue between the bones of the beak and skull, and this tissue acts as a shock absorber. Strong neck muscles deliver hammer blows with their chisel-pointed beak, in order to chip away bark and wood layers. Around the nostrils, bristly feathers filter out wood dust, functioning much like a dust mask does for humans.

In order to pound away at a tree, woodpeckers must be able to cling solidly to a vertical surface. Nearly all woodpeckers have sharp, pointed claws; two of the four toes are pointed forward, one points laterally at a right angle to the trunk, and the remaining toe points down the trunk. Three-toed woodpeckers lack the hind toe, but they still manage to hang on to tree trunks.

Stiff tail feathers brace the woodpecker against the trunk. The central pair of tail feathers are apparently molted only after a new pair has grown in to replace them, and after the other 10 tail feathers have also been replaced. This assures the woodpecker of a steady brace throughout the season. The tips of the tail feathers bend and spread into crevices on the trunk, just as our fingers search out cracks for handholds while we're rock climbing.

Woodpeckers' tongues may be their most specialized adaptation. Their long, wormlike tongues extend beyond the tip of their bill—a feature shared in the avian world only by hummingbirds. The tip of the tongue usually comes equipped with sticky barbs or bristles that snatch insects from deep holes. At its other end, the tongue divides into two branches. When it retracts, it slides up over the skull beneath the skin, extending down into the right nostril. The common flicker's tongue is particularly long, and comes coated with a sticky mucous. When the flicker extends its tongue into an anthill, the ants attack what they probably perceive as an invading worm; they then stick to the tongue and are quickly eaten.

185

Six species of woodpeckers are common to our portion of the northwoods: the hairy, downy, pileated, and red-headed woodpeckers, the yellow-bellied sapsucker, and the common flicker. The northern three-toed and the black-backed three-toed woodpeckers are rare in our area. Both reach the southernmost edge of their range here, and the red-bellied woodpecker reaches the northernmost edge of its range here.

July Frogs

Only green frogs, bullfrogs, and mink frogs are still calling and breeding into July, and they, too, will soon wrap up their amour.

I wonder if any call made by an animal is louder per pound than the bullfrog's—or deeper, for that matter. The call has been characterized as an out-of-tune bass fiddle, or as a voice booming "jug-o-rum". Males defend their territory and woo females with this call. If you haven't heard a chorus of bullfrogs on a summer evening, you're certainly missing one of the more remarkable sounds in nature. I recall distinctly the first time I heard bullfrogs calling. I didn't know what they were. I imagined everything from moose in heat to the scenes from the northwoods version of The Night of the Living Dead. I was both relieved and disappointed to discover it was just the sound of bullfrogs in love.

The mink frog is common only to the northern half of the state. Its call is likened to the sound of horse hooves on a cobblestone road. Male green frogs seek companionship by calling throughout the night. Their call sounds like a loose banjo twang. Neither the mink nor green frog's call seems overly romantic to me, but music is in the ears of the beholder. Who knows what the frogs think when some teenager sets his boombox on top of his car at the local swimming hole, serenading them with the love songs of Madonna?

Cool July evenings often put calling male frogs on ice. Romantic intent requires warm evenings, and temperatures in the 40s don't qualify as warm.

Tadpoles

During a children's lake study program one mid-July, we took nets to Big Muskellunge Lake, in order to search for aquatic organisms. We netted dozens of large, almost fully metamorphosed frogs along the shore. All had four legs, but still retained their tails. They appeared to be young bullfrogs. Bullfrog tadpoles metamorphose in July and August of their second year, then take two to three years to mature. When scared, young bullfrogs will take a series of short, fast hops across the water—as these did—before burying themselves in the bottom.

While the tadpoles develop their front legs, they undergo a digestive tract transformation that changes them from (primarily) vegetarians into carnivores. Until their tails are absorbed, however, they won't feed at all. The mouth has to change, the gut must shorten, and the lungs have to develop. The transformation is quite a miracle when you consider it.

Snakes

There are only six common species of native snakes in the northwoods. Three of them, the smooth green snake, the northern ringneck, and the western fox snake, lay eggs in late June. The eggs vary in number from four to 27 per clutch, and they are generally laid in moist areas like the interior of rotten logs or under bark on the ground. Hatching takes place one to two months later.

Our other three species, the eastern garter, the northern water snake, and the northern red-bellied snake, all give birth to live young in August or early September. Before you holler that only mammals can give birth to live young, let me concede that the embryos are not directly nurtured from the mother's bloodstream; instead, they are nurtured from the yolk of the embryo. Think of this system as if the eggs had no shells, and were retained inside the female's body cavity rather than being laid. A garter snake may give birth to between six and 73 young in a clutch.

187

Dragons and Damsels

Damselflies and dragonflies both belong to the same order, Odonata, which means "tooth bearer." In the case of these toothless insects, the name refers to their tooth-shaped jaws and their carnivorous diet. Damselflies are smaller than dragonflies. They have smaller eyes and flutter at a daintier pace. Their front and rear wings are similar in shape, whereas the dragonflies' wings are dissimilar. When at rest, damselflies fold their wings behind them and alongside their back, unlike dragonflies, whose wings extend straight out from their bodies.

About 154 species of Odanates have been identified in Wisconsin, of which 44 are damselflies. One damselfly species that occurs in enormous abundance along our quiet rivers is called the black-winged damselfly (Agrion maculatum). Its wings may be velvety black, or sometimes half black and half clear.

Damselflies flutter rather feebly in flight compared to the jet aircraft style of dragonflies. Literally tens of thousands may currently be seen in and around the overhanging vegetation along the edges of rivers like the Manitowish, the Bear, the Turtle, and the Trout.

Like dragonflies, they catch their prey with their long, hairy legs, which act as a basket to collect an insect. The males and females mate in the familiar "wheel position." The male attaches the tip of his abdomen to the back of the female's head, the female attaching the tip of her abdomen to the second segment of his abdomen.

The female usually lays her eggs on plant stems just below the water surface. The eggs hatch in a week, but the aquatic nymphs remain under water. The mature nymphs emerge from the water in late spring, crawling onto upright objects like plant stems, sticks, or pier supports. The adults emerge from a split in the back of the nymph's thorax, leaving behind the husk of their former bodies.

188

Damselflies eat small, flying insects like gnats and mosquitoes; they in turn are eaten by birds like flycatchers and swallows, thus providing a dual ecological benefit.

July Flowers

Flowers that you can expect to see in bloom in late July include roadside, field, or marsh flowers and a few woodland flowers. Look for the following:

Hoary alyssum
Common tansy
Fireweed
Black-eyed Susan
Cow vetch
Spotted knapweed
Spreading bogbane
Partridgeberry
Bedstraw
Goldenrods (various)
Pineapple weed
Pinesap
Jewelweed
Butter and eggs
Meadowsweet

Pickerelweed
Deptford pink
Checkered rattlesnake plantain
Swamp candles
  (yellow loosestrife)
Heal-all
Yellow avens
Common sunflower
Steeplebush
Common St. Johnswort
White and yellow
  sweet bush clover
Broad-leaved arrowhead
Wintergreen
Blue vervain

Swamp smartweed

Indian pipe

Sumac

Big leaf aster

Wood sorrel

Wild pink

Water parsnip

Grass pink

Evening primrose

Shinleaf

One-sided pyrola

Common and swamp
 milkweed

Pipsissewa

Buckwheat

Boneset

Common comfrey

Common bladderwort

Joe-pye weed

189

The roadsides are often covered with aromatic yellow birdsfoot trefoil and red clover. The bees must be in heaven. Many of the listed flowers come under the rubric of "roadside weeds." Susan Knight, Trout Lake researcher for the University of Wisconsin, friend, and bog expert, says, "A weed is a plant without a press agent." Others have said a weed is a plant we haven't learned to appreciate. Most weeds are pioneers, colonizing disturbed soils and beginning a process of healing the soil. While they may not appear at the time and place we would choose, most are specialists that bring shade and stability to soils in need. While some nonnative species like purple loosestrife are profoundly invasive, most native weeds have clear ecological value, functioning as the first stage in a long successional transition from bare ground to mature habitat.

Tansies, or golden buttons, qualify as a "weed," and are extremely common along Highway 51 south of Minocqua. They were cultivated in Europe during the Middle Ages for their reputed medicinal value. Unfortunately, tansies are poisonous, and deaths have been caused by drinking too much of a tea made from the leaves. The tea is described by one naturalist as "perfectly vile tasting and worse than the ailments it was intended to cure." Tansies were thought to cure rheumatism and the measles. Because of their bitter taste, animals seldom eat them.

Finding woodland flowers at this time of year is usually a fruitless (flowerless?) endeavor, except in the sandy pine habitats of Oneida, Vilas, and southern Iron counties. In our pine forest habitats, nearly

50 percent of all flowers bloom after July 1; in hardwood forests, 70 percent of the flowers bloom and die by June 15. In the pine forests, look for the blooms of wintergreen, various pyrolas, pipsissewa, rattle-snake plantain orchids, one-flowered wintergreen, twinflower, and big leaf aster, and enjoy them while you can. They're just about the last flowers of the season in the woodlands.

Bladderworts:
The Fastest-Moving Plant in the World

Marsh flowers bloom in a showy profusion in late July. Pickerel-weed, arrowhead, blue vervain, swamp milkweed, white and yellow water lilies, water shield, yellow loosestrife, boneset, and several blad-derworts make a canoe trip down one of our meandering northern rivers or shallow lakes quite a spectacle.

One late July, I paddled Frog Lake in the Manitowish River Wil-derness Area. Thousands of purple bladderworts had blossomed in the shallow waters rimming the lake. Bladderworts are carnivorous plants that use tiny bladders to suck in and trap tiny animals and in-sects. Their trapping action takes only 1/460 of a second, making them the fastest-moving plant in the world. Their speed is so great that we can't see them move. According to our senses, in fact, they don't move. Most folks unfortunately don't notice them, instead simply cat-egorizing them as another aquatic weed.

The bladders were once thought to be flotation devices that kept the plants afloat, kind of like little life preservers. However, Darwin put the matter to rest by proving that this unrooted marvel is a floating trapline with up to 600 bladders per plant.

The Great Pickerelweed Caper

Mary and I look forward to seeing pickerelweeds in flower every July, but the colonies that bloom below our house assumed an unusual role in our lives during the summer of 1995. Many thousands of pick-erelweeds were stolen from our Manitowish River property. We were told the thief was a man who sells them through a mail order catalog in southern Wisconsin. His customers are landowners who wish to landscape newly built ponds, as well as public and private agencies like the DNR and Trout Unlimited, which purchase them in order to provide better wetland habitat.

We were astonished when the plants were stolen, because we had no idea that pickerelweeds were valuable. They are apparently sold for $1 or more apiece. Our thief must have turned a many-thousand-dollar profit on his pilfering. I mention this only to warn those of you who purchase wetland plants to be sure to ask where your plants were obtained. This sort of activity may be more common than we realize, and I hate to see northern waterways diminished for the profit of a handful of individuals. Most of us have read about the thieves who dig up cactus out west, and some still dig up orchids and sell them. The great Manitowish pickerelweed heist has underscored the fact that wetland plants have value beyond their ecological roles and their aesthetic beauty.

191

If you're not familiar with pickerelweed, beds of their violet-blue flower spikes are in continuous bloom from July through mid-August in river, pond, and lake shallows. Their large, glossy leaves are three inches wide or more; to me, they look like a colony of aces of spades. They should not be confused with arrowhead leaves—check an identification guide to understand the difference. Look for pickerelweed on the inside curves of many rivers, areas where the most sediment is deposited.

Fruits

Along stream banks, dogwoods have set their white berries. In the woods, the blue/black fruits of sarsaparilla and the red berries of false Solomon's seal and bunchberry are formed as well.

The forest table is laden with berries. By mid- to late July, Juneberries (they should be called Julyberries up here) and blueberries are often profuse; raspberries are still good but going-by; and blackberries will soon be ripening.

One late July I visited the Moquah Barrens area, just west and a bit north of Ashland in the Chequamegon National Forest, to look for berries. The landscape is managed with fire to maintain its barrens characteristics, and one of the results is a blueberry paradise. If you are a blueberry picker, you'll find enough berries up there to satisfy an army. But you needn't drive so far. Blueberries like full sun and acidic, sandy soils, as well as acidic boggy edges—habitats we are more than blessed with in the northwoods. Look for recent forest cuts in pine stands with a good supply of sweet fern. Blueberries are often mixed among the ferns.

Humans, of course, are not the only blueberry foragers. Ruffed and spruce grouse eat large quantities, as do songbirds like robins, brown thrashers, catbirds, red-eyed vireos, scarlet tanagers, and veeries. Black bears are less discriminating in their "picking," usually eating leaves, twigs, and anything else in close proximity.

Cattails

Cattail seed heads are usually bursting by late July, shedding thousands of silky seeds. Cattails can easily dominate marshes and become a monotype. One seedhead may contain hundreds of thousands of seeds, which can remain viable for five years. Cattails also reproduce vegetatively through their extensive rhizomes, or underground stems, which start new plants from the mother plant. In fact, cattails are so productive that their dry weight per acre can be as much as 20 tons. An acre of potatoes may weigh only 10 tons, and wheat seldom reaches three tons.

If you have too many cattails in your local shallow lake bed, import a muskrat or two. They eat the rhizomes and the base of the cattail, and thus are the best means of cattail control available. Add a mink family if you wish to control the muskrats, and you should be able to maintain a natural balance between plants and open water.

Rattlesnake Plantain

Rattlesnake plantain is a native orchid whose name originated with the American Indian belief that the plant could be used as an antidote for snake bite. To me, the checkered, low-lying leaves look like the pattern on a snake's back. Thoreau said the leaves "look like art." Search in pine woods for this demure orchid.

Wintergreen

One of the last woodland wildflowers to bloom is wintergreen. Wintergreens usually grow in nutrient-poor, dry, and acid soils; thus they're rather common in our area. Look for their beautiful white, waxy flowers, which hang in little bells beneath their leaves. The leaves, flowers, and red fruits all offer a tasty, wintergreen-flavored snack. Choose the new, light-green leaves over the older, darker ones for the best taste, or steep the dried leaves to make a fine tea once considered a good headache remedy.

193

Pipsissewa

Pipsissewa (*Chimaphila umbellata*), one of the fragile, deep woods flowers, also blooms in late July in the sandy pine soils of the northwoods. The name apparently originated from the Cree Indian word *pipisisikweu*, meaning "it breaks it into small pieces." The name comes from the Cree practice of using a decoction from the leaves to break down gallstones and kidney stones.

The flowers are a soft cream color with a pink center ring. They nod shyly toward the earth from a long, slender, reddish-brown stalk. Five petals with violet anthers (the pollen-bearing ends of the stamens) encircle a large, green ovary and broad style that is sticky on its end. In its center, the flower is waxy and dainty, with a gentle scent. Use a hand lens to examine this beautiful little flower more closely.

Like many conservative northwoods wildflowers, the pipsissewa retains its evergreen leaves all winter. It also hedges its reproductive bets by vegetatively reproducing through horizontal rootstalks just under the surface.

Canoeing

Mary and I often canoe the Manitowish River in late July. One typical paddle yielded the following sightings and discoveries: two families of hooded mergansers; a kingbird nest projecting over the water with five young fledglings hanging around the nest tree; a flicker nest hole in a black ash snag; black-winged damselflies by the bushelful; and the wonderful smell of sloughs filled with white water lilies. There are two species of white water lilies that look quite similar. One has no odor, while the other smells of sweet oranges, so don't be discouraged if you come upon a few that have no smell.

194

Archaeology in the Northwoods

In the 1990s, archaeologists working for the Nicolet National Forest have been surveying the Manitowish Waters area for historic sites. During the last two weeks of July, 1992, they found 10 such sites. Unfortunately, most were inundated by water, due to the artificially high river level created by the Rest Lake dam. The chain of lakes and the Manitowish River are about 20 feet higher than their natural water levels; because most American Indian sites were located next to water, the excavation of these sites is virtually impossible.

Mark Bruhy, archaeologist for the Nicolet National Forest, has listed 1,200 sites within the Nicolet to date. Some of the sites date back 10,000 years, to the time of the retreat of the glaciers. Many of the sites have been used many times by different historic peoples, and they include recent logging camps and current recreational areas.

One summer I took a group of 28 adults to one of these sites, the Hemlock Cathedral archaeological site. Volunteer crews had just found a copper knife blade in one of the excavations that morning, a blade dating back to between 1000 and 4000 B.C. The volunteer diggers were having a great experience as they painstakingly worked their sites. They volunteer through a program called Passport in Time, which amounts to a college class, field work experience, and vacation wrapped into one. A number of the volunteers guided us through the process and shared their discoveries. While nothing spectacular had been found—sorry, no mastodons—shards of pottery, flakes of stone from tool making, charcoal from fire pits, and other ancient debris had been revealed.

Listening to an archaeologist explain how he or she tries to "read" the soil in order to decipher what was once there, I was left with that wonderful philosophical contradiction, realizing that the more I learn, the less I know. It's like initially watching the stars with your naked eye, then acquiring a telescope and gradually increasing the size of the lens. New horizons continually open. With each lens, you know so much more than you did before, yet you begin to suspect the enormity of all there is to learn. I think that's the joy of trying to be a naturalist. My ignorance is continually exposed, but what a pleasure it is to overcome it, if only for a moment.

195

As an aside, the copper knife was found about four inches down in the soil. Four inches of soil holds 2,000 or more years of history in the northwoods. Our soils build so slowly here that the remains of former cultures are barely covered after a thousand years have passed. The general rule of thumb for northern soils is that an inch of soil builds up for every 500 years. It's little wonder that farmers found the soil wanting in the early part of this century, ultimately giving the land back to the trees.

Standing on a spot where another human stood 3,500 years ago is an odd feeling. Reverence mixes freely with wonder. The wooded shoreline assumes an integrity that prompts me to walk lightly, and to consider what may lie beneath each step.

I met several volunteer couples at the site who were using a week's vacation to help explore it. They were bent over one by two meter rectangles, painstakingly brushing soil away. All of them said they wouldn't trade the experience for the world. Contact the Nicolet National Forest Headquarters in Rhinelander, or another national forest near you, for more information about the Passport in Time program.

Sightings

Just about every animal you can imagine eats berries in July and August. Cedar waxwings, ravens, robins, flickers, thrushes, squirrels, bears, chipmunks, raccoons—you name them, they all feast on summer berries. A failure in any of these crops is a disappointment for us, but it can be serious for these animals.

Beaked hazelnuts are formed by late July, though they are not ripe. Beating the squirrels to these nuts is usually a difficult chore.

Goldfinches, one of the last birds to nest in this area, will begin building as soon as the thistles go to seed, providing down for lining the bottoms of their nests.

196

Late July Musings

The invariable mark of wisdom is to see the miraculous in the common . . . To the wise, therefore, a fact is true poetry.

-Ralph Waldo Emerson

AUGUST

The Ojibwe word for August is manomin, meaning simply "rice." Along with maple sugar, wild rice was the main vegetative food staple for the American Indians of our region. The wild rice district of Wisconsin and Minnesota supported nearly 30,000 people, possibly the highest concentration of American Indians in what became the central U.S. Wild rice is the only cereal grain native to North America, demonstrating how little of our current 20th-century diet is native to our area.

Northwoods weather is often cool in August. We seldom have "dog days" like most of the United States. Cool, sometimes frosty August nights create a beautiful fog tunnel over the Manitowish River. If the moon is full, it ethereally illuminates the tunnel; only the tops of the big white pines across the river can be seen above the fog.

The temperature differential between the cold air and the warm water produces the fog. From mid-August until about mid-September, the lakes, rivers, and bogs of our area are bathed nightly in these localized fog pockets. I've experienced many pretty sightings of deer standing along the edge of the fogs late at night. Unfortunately, the frost and fog are also signs that summer is waning.

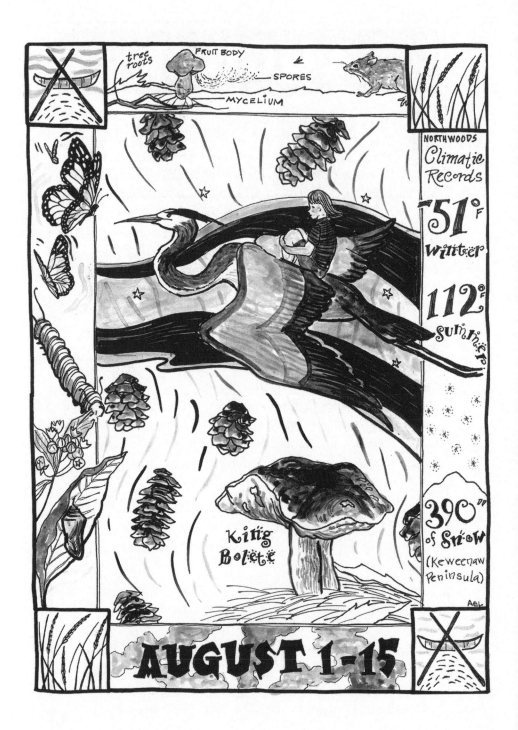

tree roots

FRUIT BODY

SPORES

MYCELIUM

NORTHWOODS Climatic Records

-51°F Winter

112°F Summer

390" of Snow (Keweenaw Peninsula)

King Bolete

AUGUST 1-15

August 1 to August 15

The Manitowish: "Spirit" River

One early August my oldest daughter Eowyn, a friend, and I paddled a section of the Manitowish River from Highway 47 to Murray's Landing on the Turtle-Flambeau Flowage. In 5-1/2 hours we met just one small fishing boat, otherwise sharing the river only with those creatures that belong there. Sightings of eagles, ospreys, bitterns, and black terns punctuated the quiet. I slowed the group down several times, back-paddling to check the identity of blooming flowers like blue vervain, arrowhead, turtlehead, water parsnip, and Joe-pye weed. I

August Musings

Wood is a renewable resource. Forests, in their pristine form, are not. A stand of trees is not a forest . . . [and the] regrowth of trees is not the same thing as the renewal of a forest.
-E.C. Pielou

even managed to impale myself briefly on a branch, turn sideways, and watch as the gentle Manitowish current swept my solo canoe out from under me. I never knew that cameras and binoculars could hold so much water.

I've paddled the Manitowish many, many times, and I feel a kinship with it. I feel at home on it. I've thought about its source, its flow, and its destination, and I've come to some conclusions.

The Manitowish River is in no hurry to become the Flambeau. Content to idle along in looping curiosity, the river acts more interested in exploring its watershed than dashing to its convergence with the Bear River. Perhaps it wishes to stay awhile, like most of us who canoe upon it.

The Manitowish suffers, according to some, because it has no rapids worth rating. The speed chasers sniff at its power and hurtle elsewhere. But this river is not about an exhilarating rush of whitewater adrenaline. An "I beat the river" competitive strut would look silly here. The Manitowish lets you settle in and think your thoughts through. There are no battles here to be fought. The sounds of the river and the life in and around the water scour the blood clean of contaminants. Reflection and heightened perception are the river's menu, and for those who need it, a warm sleep in a slough drowsing in white water lilies.

Reduction in haste, complexity, conflict, and unease are the products of simple time spent on a simple river. The river has its own complexity and conflict, of course, presenting questions galore: Why? What was that? How much? To what extent? These questions are meditative, requiring you to observe more and think less. They are not questions steeped in anger, or in matters of power or territorial turfdom. The discovery of answers offers no competitive edge or material gain, but it provides understanding of the picture we are painted into, and pieces to the puzzle of why we are painted at all.

Every moment, the Manitowish brings the past into the present, then pushes with understated resolve into an uncertain future. Voyageurs portaged to a spot just downstream from my home and paddled for Lac du Flambeau—or they cursed their luck during the upstream struggle through the Manitowish chain toward the Wisconsin River. Before them came Ojibwe canoes, and before them thousands of years of native people living close to the lifeblood of a river rich in the gifts of the wild.

But the past can be measured in more contemporary terms, too. Yesterday's rain deposited the leaves and branches that drift downriver past my house today. All rivers, like long freight trains, carry terrestrial freight. Trains were emblazoned with names like the Chattanooga Choo Choo, but this river's alliterative name might best be "Duff Deluxe."

When I put my canoe onto the river, I drift along too, suddenly buoyant and mobile. I can sit still and yet move silently, using only a slight ruddering effort to effect directional change. In a canoe I have a sense of being a part of the natural world, traveling in the same vehicle at the same speed as the water, with the opportunity to sense the same thing a muskrat or an otter senses.

The river contradicts itself every moment, leading a dual life. Expressing both power and gentleness, the Manitowish flows much like I assume it always has, with pines leaning riverward from its banks, groves of alder and willow in sedgy byways, pickerelweed and lilies emerging from the shallows. Its flow has all the imperfections of a nonengineered channel wrought by snowmelt and vagaries unknown. The Manitowish winds back upon itself in oxbow after oxbow, as if knowing that everyone likes surprises. As the canoe slides around another horseshoe curve, who knows what present the bend will unwrap? The tall marsh grasses between the loops allow privacy for the blue wing teal, even when it's right next door to the great blue heron.

<u>201</u>

The river speaks in a voice contextually clear. It says, "This is the way I was, and the way I will be." No arrogance of pollution distorts the voice, no disinterest of shoreline sprawl. In a world of artifice that breeds further artifice, this is "the real thing," displacing Coke and its imitators, exposing them as laughable aberrations of what was once good water.

The Manitowish burbles along in its shallow windings, impervious to big engines, high-tech materials, and high-speed egos. A wooden canoe suits the river, as old clothes do. The commercials that scream for your attendance at yet another motorized rodeo—be it speedboat, snowmobile, or big wheel trucks—scream to deaf ears along the Manitowish. And the neon, nylon "NOTICE ME" clothing accessories look as out of place on this quiet river as slinky French models might in a country cafe. Overkill versus understatement is a choice presented all rivers. The Manitowish chose to offer itself in the way of all wisdom, with humility and reserve.

Some nights, when my daughter Callie has trouble finding sleep, I speak to her imagination and tell her to "lay on Grandma and Grandpa's dock on the Manitowish, and let the sun begin to warm you. Feel your body start to relax under the sun's touch. Now listen to the river lap against the rocks and the dock. Think of how the water lifts away the weight of your body, so you can float in its warm hands. Hear the loon softly hooting to its chicks, 'I'm here, I'm here.' See the otter dip through the water as if it were a wave. And watch the heron in flight on wings so big you could sit on them like a magic carpet." I go on with other sounds and smells and sights. Most often it works, and she sleeps softly before I am done.

Justin Isherwood writes: "I am reluctant to leave the old river and its buoyancy. I come to the river to be alone, to be quiet, to be a better farmer, father, and friend. I come to talk; and be talked to. I don't use the term God, neither will I quibble."

I, too, come for many purposes, all of which amount to this: I ask the river for guidance in how to travel with wisdom and care along the channels I follow, and for the courage to try to carve a few, too.

Aging

About half the people who join me on hikes and trips afield during the summer are retired. I've been thinking a lot about the spirit, goodwill, and energy they display. Doc, a retired doctor and one of the main characters in Volume II of George Vukelich's *North Country Notebook,* says of old age, "You know, Joe, that's the funny part of growing old. Inside this ancient shell is that 21-year-old kid just rattling around in there like a beagle pup." My hat's off to those "beagle pups" who rattle around with me so often.

Nighthawks

A group of intrepid paddlers and I took a full-moon canoe paddle on Allequash Lake one early August. The moon taunted us from behind the clouds until the last 10 minutes of our trip, when it finally broke clear and lit up the lake. One of the highlights of the night for me was seeing a number of nighthawks feeding near the lake surface as it was getting dark. While nighthawks are considered common, I seldom see them in the northwoods. I was initially slow to identify them, because they weren't listed in my mental files as a possibility.

Nighthawks feed on insects at night, darting through the air with their mouths wide open like fishing trawlers, simply sweeping insects in. At their normal flight speed of 20 miles per hour, the insects they encounter slide right down their throats without the effort of swallowing. This doesn't take a great deal of intelligence; instead, it requires exceptional eyesight, and in fact the eyes of a nighthawk weigh more than its brain. The dissected stomach of one nighthawk in Maine held 2,175 ants; another nighthawk stomach in Massachusetts contained more than 500 mosquitoes.

We didn't hear the nighthawks calling, but they utter a "peent" or "beer" call similar to the call of a woodcock. This clears up a mystery of a bird I heard that summer. It flew over our house as night fell, calling peent constantly. I thought I had an oversexed woodcock seeking excessive female companionship, but now I know better.

Nighthawks migrate in large fall flocks, beginning in mid-August; one flight over Crex Meadows Wildlife Area in 1963 included an estimated 10,000 individuals.

<u>203</u>

Veery Beautiful

During one Turtle River canoe trip we pulled into the shallows, where the pickerelweed and arrowhead blossoms emerged in profusion. We listened to the haunting, downward-spiraling song of the veery. The flutelike notes have a ventriloquial quality that makes the veery difficult to locate; in addition, the song is actually sung on two different pitches at the same time. You can hear the two simultaneous pitches if you slow down a recording of the song to one-half speed. The veery adds to the ethereal quality of its song by singing primarily at dusk and dawn, calling from a dark hemlock grove or a wooded swamp.

How can birds produce two different pitches simultaneously? Humans and other mammals utilize a larynx with vocal cords in the upper part of the windpipe, which is resonated by exhaling. Birds, on the other hand, produce their voices in the lower part of their windpipes through a syrinx—an organ unique to birds. Birds do have a larynx, but it has no vocal cords, so it has little to do with their voices. The muscles of the syrinx control elastic, vibrating membranes within the organ by changing position and tension, much as a violinist alters a violin's pitch by changing the amount of tension on its strings. As a general rule, birds with the greatest number of syringeal muscles produce the most complex songs. Thus the turkey vulture, not exactly known for its heavenly singing, has no syrinx; pigeons have a single pair of muscles; most songbirds have five to nine pairs, and a versatile songster like the catbird has seven to nine pairs.

The veery winters in South America and, like most insect-eaters, starts its migration in late August. Veeries outnumber all other thrushes in northern Wisconsin except the robin, and their lack of distinctive coloration places them in my "LBB" (Little Brown Bird) category, so the best way to identify them is to learn their song.

Merlin Nests

Ron Eckstein, DNR wildlife manager in Rhinelander, reported two nests of young merlins in July of 1993—the first merlin nests ever recorded in Vilas County. Ron banded four merlin chicks on Trout Lake and three chicks on Rest Lake. As rare as these nests are, merlins are like peregrine falcons, in that they sometimes nest in urban areas. In 1994 a merlin pair nested in a tree near the Ashland County Courthouse, right in the middle of Ashland.

The Wandering Egret

I saw a great egret flying low, slowly, and directly over my head on August 7 at the Powell Marsh. The summer range of great egrets generally carries them only as far as southern Wisconsin, so I'm not sure what this one was doing in Vilas County. They do engage in a "wandering period" from July 20 to September 15, according to Sam Robbins' *Wisconsin Birdlife*, but they are truly a rarity in our north country.

Shorebird Migration

I'm always a bit hesitant to bring this up. People get touchy about the subject of summer coming to a close, but some bird species have already begun migrating south. On August 4 at the Powell Marsh, I saw and heard several greater yellowlegs, along with numerous smaller shorebirds that were too far out on the mud flats to identify. Typically, shorebirds like adult lesser and greater yellowlegs, semi-palmated sandpipers, least sandpipers, and short-billed dowitchers leave their tundra nesting grounds between late June and early July. The adult males migrate first, actually leaving during the breeding season, when food is still readily available in the tundra. The young of the year won't leave until late July or early August.

Cedar Waxwings

205

In August, cedar waxwings are often the most visible songbirds along rivers, hawking for insects from perches over the water and moving about in small flocks. Their song, a thin, high "seee-seee," wins few Grammies, but it offers a nearly constant auditory complement to the dipping of one's paddle. We usually think of cedar waxwings as fruit eaters, because fruit comprises 70 percent of their diet over the course of a year. But in July and August, when insects abound, waxwings sally forth from tree limbs in short, quick flights, snatching meals from the air. When they're not in flight, waxwings glean insects from the foliage. One source reported that a flock of 30 waxwings may destroy 90,000 canker worms in a month. Their usefulness in catching and gleaning insects offsets their destructiveness in commercial cherry orchards, where they can eat to the point of gluttony.

Waxwings come by their name due to the red, waxy tips of their secondary feathers, which once reminded people of sealing wax. The function of the red color is uncertain, but two-year-old birds lack the waxy tips entirely or may have just a few feathers tipped, so perhaps the coloration serves as a sign of age and social status. The "cedar" part of the name derives from their preference for nesting in white cedar trees.

We have watched waxwings perch at length near us on several canoe trips, confirming their reputation for tameness. The year's young have been known to land on a trout rod while waiting to be fed by parents. Waxwings don't begin nesting until late in June, and the young may not take wing until late August, so many of the insects caught by adults are still being taken back to the nest to feed the young.

Northwoods Cuckoos

On an early August walk alongside a wetland area, I heard a series of loud, fast calls that consistently featured a series of three notes at the same pitch—"cu-cu-cu, cu-cu-cu." The next day, Mary looked out our back window onto the wetlands below our house, then called me over to see a large bird that was perched on a low branch of a shrub. The bird sat tight for several minutes, giving us ample opportunity to be certain of its identity. It was clearly a black-billed cuckoo, easily distinguished by its long tail, its brown coloration above and white below, its black bill, and its length of about a foot long.

Cuckoos are secretive birds, generally nesting in dense shrubs two to 10 feet above the ground and remaining concealed within the shrubbery during the day. They're quite beneficial, eating hairy tent caterpillars, beetles, and crickets. The stomach of one yellow-billed cuckoo was found to contain 325 caterpillars. A stomach analysis of 46 black-billed cuckoos yielded 906 caterpillars, 44 beetles, 96 grasshoppers, 100 sawflies, 30 miscellaneous bugs, and 15 spiders.

European cuckoos lay their eggs in the nests of other birds, parasitizing the nests, but American cuckoos very rarely do this. The promiscuity of European cuckoos led to the coining of the term "cuckold," which refers to the husband of an unfaithful wife.

Cuckoo clocks emulate the call of European cuckoos, not the American variety. European cuckoos apparently repeat their calls monotonously, which led to the use of the word "cuckoo" to signify being crazy or foolish.

Black-billed cuckoos winter in South America, from Colombia to Peru. They're rarely seen in the north after September 15, due to the lack of insects after our first frosts.

Scat and Blackberries

In a good year, there are more blackberries here than a blackberry lover could ever hope to pick. One upside to a summer like the one in 1993, marked by rain, mosquitoes, and constant cool weather, was the resultant crop of berries. Our husky Keena and I took a walk in

August of that year, along a deserted railbed running from Manitowish to Minocqua. I looked up at one point while I was picking blackberries. Keena was eating blackberries just as I was, though with considerably less concern about their ripeness and about rules of etiquette. I was reminded by her foraging that members of the wild dog family (coyote, fox, wolf) eat berries in the summer. I saw a number of animal droppings along the railbed, so I picked a few apart to see if they contained berry seeds. They were filled with the seeds of fruits; many of the droppings were also "loose," almost certainly indicating a diet comprised of too much fruit for stomachs unaccustomed to such gorging. About one-fourth of the summer and fall diet of a red fox is said to consist of fleshy fruits and seeds like blackberries and blueberries, so finding loose scat is not unusual.

207

Wild choke, pin, and black cherries are also usually heavy with fruit by August. Ninety percent of the diet of cedar waxwings consists of fleshy fruits, so these birds must have been fat and sassy in 1993. Grouse, catbirds, grosbeaks, robins, brown thrashers, various thrushes, and even pileated woodpeckers relish cherries. For black bears, cherries are a four-star meal.

More Berries

Bunchberries, highbush cranberries, and mountain ash are all vivid red berries that come ripe in August. I've eaten them all raw, and none hold much appeal for me. Sharp-tailed grouse, veeries, sparrows, and several vireos enjoy bunchberries. As for the highbush cranberries on my land, I'm not sure what eats them. The shrubby trees in the marsh below my house retain their fruits all winter. The books say highbush cranberries are favored by bears, foxes, squirrels, chipmunks, grouse, thrashers, thrushes, starlings, and cedar waxwings, but perhaps the critters around my place are illiterate. Mountain ash berries attract bears, grouse, cedar waxwings, grosbeaks, and thrushes, while the twigs and foliage are favorites of moose.

Baneberries, commonly called doll's eyes, come ripe now too, but they're poisonous. Elderberries ripen by mid-August. The large, blue beadlike berries of Clintonia reveal the reason behind their common name, bluebead lily (also poisonous). Beaked hazelnuts are ripening, but if you want to beat the squirrels and chipmunks to them, you had best move fast.

Blooming Flowers

In early August, look for Joe-pye weed in bloom along wetland edges. Snowberries come ripe in the bogs, offering a delightful, wintergreen-flavored treat. Other flowers that come into bloom in August include silvery cinquefoil, bugleweed, nightshade, purple loosestrife, broad-leaved arrowhead, swamp smartweed, turtlehead, lady's thumb (redleg), and closed gentian.

Bur Reed

If a hard frost has not occurred, sunny wetlands may remain profusely flowered with colonies of tall emergents like pickerelweed, arrowhead, Joe-pye weed, turtlehead, swamp milkweed, cattail, and bur reed. While not a well-known plant, bur reed produces a flower worth noting, because anyone who has spent time along rivers or "weedy" shorelines has seen it. The male staminate flowers bloom in little green balls. Thin stamens are situated above the female flowers, which have hard, burlike heads. To me the burs look like a mace, a club with a spiked metal head that was used as a weapon of war in the Middle Ages.

Bur reed leaves look exactly like a cattail's, but they aren't as long and they have a distinct keel or ridge, like the bottom of many aluminum canoes. By contrast, cattail leaves in cross section are slightly rounded in a "D" shape. The seeds from the bur reed are eaten by many waterfowl species, including mallards, wood ducks, and tundra swans, while muskrats eat the entire plant.

Wetland plants usually grow in extensive colonies that serve to protect them from being uprooted by river currents and waves. Underground, horizontal rhizomes clone the parent plant again and again, until all members of a colony may in effect share the same first name, but they are so interlaced in the substrate that little can faze them.

Cattails may produce 10 feet of rhizomes in a year, all of which send up new vertical stems along the underground runner. It's little wonder that a shallow lake or river can be so rapidly "choked" by aquatic vegetation. But please remember that those "weeds" provide cover, food, and breeding habitat for a large contingent of fish, waterfowl, and mammals. The words "weed" and "choking" are value-laden terms. A "clean" shoreline serves few purposes beyond providing comfortable swimming.

Fireweed Seeds

209

Fireweed seeds have been drifting on the wind since late July, much as aspen seeds do in the spring—or cottonwood, if you live to the south. If you open a ripe seed pod, the seeds will burst out onto the wind currents and may drift for miles.

Some folks who confuse fireweed with purple loosestrife end up pulling out fireweed in the belief that they are performing a civic duty. By all means, pull out purple loosestrife, but realize that its habitat is wetlands. Fireweed, on the other hand, is a dry roadside/field invader.

Mushrooms

Sara Steele and Nicole Dyhert from Woodruff wrote to me, describing the font of mushrooms produced in the northwoods one year. They surveyed half an acre of mixed forest (pine, popple, and birch) on August 13, counting all the kinds of mushrooms they could find. They came up with 46 species! I appreciated their letter for two reasons. One, Sara and Nicole are teenagers, and it's safe to say that the average teen has little interest in mushrooms. I appreciate hearing from teenagers who care about the natural world. Second, they went out and surveyed to obtain their own data, then looked up as many of the species as they could. I, on the other hand, continue to wait for a mushroom guru to come along and teach me what I need to know. Sara and Nicole took the initiative, relying on their own efforts to provide their education. That kind of insatiable curiosity and initiative is what distinguishes a true naturalist. Kudos to Sara and Nicole.

Late summer and early autumn offer mushrooms in profusion, most of which seem to poke through the soil in just a day or two. Mushrooms are the fruiting body of the main plant, which most folks never see because it's tiny and underground. A mesh of mostly microscopic white fibers, called a mycelium, forms the "roots" of the mushroom. The fibers grow right on their food source and usually into it, penetrating dead leaves, branches, logs, and carcasses. The individual fibers (called hyphae) secrete digestive enzymes, commencing the work of recycling organic matter.

The mushrooms we see are the fruits of the plants, producing billions of extremely tiny spores—generally from the underside gills or pores. A large puffball mushroom "explodes" when struck (most of us have stomped a few), bursting in a cloud of more than a trillion spores. Thankfully, most of them fail to germinate.

Corpse Plant

Indian pipe is still in flower in early August, blooming in the shade of conifers. "Ghost plant" is its other name, because it's pure white from stem to flower. Without chlorophyll and unable to photosynthesize, Indian pipe has to obtain nutrients in another way. It does so by sharing the mycorrhizal fungi that are attached to the roots of conifers. These fungi get their nutrients from the tree's roots, in exchange helping the tree's root system extend itself farther into the soil. The mycorrhizal fungi also attach to the roots of Indian pipe, creating a kind of triumvirate relationship. All this was discovered by injecting radioactive carbon into the bark of a spruce tree, then observing that nearby Indian pipes became radioactive five days later.

So, while Indian pipe is not a direct parasite on conifer roots, it does indirectly obtain its nutrients through them. To further complicate matters, Indian pipe may also receive some of its nutrients from the decay of dead organisms in the soil. As Indian pipe ages, it turns jet black and the stem of the "pipe bowl" straightens.

Kill This Plant

Purple loosestrife is yet blooming in August. Over the last decade, it has spread rapidly. By the mid-1990s, it had begun to dominate a few wetlands in the north. Wisconsin was first invaded by this northern European immigrant back in the 1920s. Purple loosestrife threatens native vegetation, because it aggressively crowds out cattails, sedges, and other native wetland plants. Without native vegetation for food, nesting, and shelter, wildlife species are also threatened, because birds and mammals generally don't utilize purple loosestrife.

Southeastern Wisconsin has the most serious infestation of loosestrife, but loosestrife also abounds in parts of the north. Loosestrife can spread into a virtual monotype. The Montezuma National Wildlife Refuge in central New York contains over 1,000 acres that are almost completely taken over by purple loosestrife.

211

How can we prevent this? Hand pulling before the plants set seed is most effective. Check your plant identification book to be sure you know what you're looking for, or get the color flyer produced by the DNR. If you see any purple loosestrife, pull them up by the roots. They can still reproduce vegetatively if you just cut them off.

Purple loosestrife has a tall, reddish-purple flower spike that's quite attractive. I rarely encourage folks to pick flowers, but don't hesitate to eliminate these. Show them no mercy.

Asters

Asters are flourishing at this time, and their name captures their structure. Aster is Greek for "star," serving as the root for other celestial words like astronaut, astrology, astronomy, asterisk (the "little star"), and even disaster (to be "ill-starred").

Sprucing Up

We built a deck in our yard in 1996, placing it under two white spruce trees so we could display our canoes. We were consistently startled in August by banging sounds coming from the deck. At first we couldn't figure out the source, but on several occasions the sound became almost a steady rain of thumps. We finally realized that the spruces were dropping their solid cones onto the canoes, which make pretty good drums.

1996 was a banner year for conifer cones, as well as hazelnuts. Abundant seed crops occur just once every four to six years, and they usually happen simultaneously over a large area. This is a process typical of most of our cone- and nut-bearing trees. They've evolved to "understand" that if they were to bear consistently good crops every year, the predator population (squirrels, chipmunks, blue jays, others) would grow proportionately, and would decimate the available cones. The mast-bearing trees evolved a better idea. They became very inconsistent in their seed production, thus suppressing predator populations because high populations couldn't survive the lean years. When a flush seed year does occur, the production is so high that the predators can't possibly collect all the seeds, so the chances for successful germination go way up.

It's a system of checks and balances. Meanwhile, the squirrel population was well-fed in the winter of 1996-97, and will probably produce numerous young in the spring of '97, only to go hungry the next winter.

Milkweeds and Monarchs

Walk or bike past a patch of flowering milkweed in August, and the powerful fragrance will nearly overwhelm you. Note that a host of butterflies, bees, moths, flies, and other insects enjoy milkweed, too.

Milkweed is well-known as the plant upon which monarch butterflies deposit their eggs. When the eggs hatch, the caterpillars eat the milkweed leaves for about two weeks, then attach themselves to the underside of a leaf and form a chrysalis. The adult monarch butterfly emerges in late summer, maturing in time to undertake its extraordinary migration to central Mexico.

Milkweed leaves contain cardiac glycosides which, when eaten by the caterpillars and adult monarchs, make the monarchs toxic to birds and other predators. Most predators have learned to leave monarchs alone.

Lake Study

Since 1946, a compulsory count of all harvested fish (a creel census) has been taken on five lakes within the Northern Highlands State Forest: Escanaba, Pallette, Nebish, Spruce, and Mystery lakes. This is the world's longest continuous study of sport fishing on freshwater lakes, and fishery professionals throughout the world request information from this database. A long-term study like this one can reveal relationships and trends that the typical three- to four-year study can't begin to illuminate. This study should continue to provide invaluable information in the future about the ecology of lake systems.

213

The Damn Dams

A contingent of 22 paddlers and I engineered our way down the Turtle River one early August, managing to cross 10 beaver dams in the process. We may consider petitioning the Winchester town board to rename the Turtle the "Beaver River," in honor of its most populous (or at least its most aggravating) resident. While many of our group members felt a lot better about beaver trapping than they had at the start of the trip, I rather enjoyed the fact that the river was theirs and not ours—no matter our momentary difficulties in navigating their obstacles. Other midsummer stretches of the Turtle are so shallow that dragging canoes often substitutes for paddling. At least our water levels were high enough to float our canoes, and we had good paddling between the dams.

Dorothy Bendrick of Boulder Junction sent me a brief note later in reference to the dams we had to portage. I suspect she was also thinking about the thunderstorm that hit us just five minutes short of the landing. The note began, "MEN WANTED FOR HAZARDOUS JOURNEY. Small wages, bitter cold, long months of complete darkness—constant danger, safe return doubtful—honor and recognition in case of success. Sir Ernest Shackleton, London Times, 1907." Shackleton in fact led several expeditions to the South Pole.

Her inclusion of the "complete darkness" quote may refer to the naturalist interpretation I gave along the way, but the note also triggered my memory of Daniel Greysolon Sieur Du Luth, who was one of the early French explorers of the Upper Midwest and is the namesake of the city of Duluth, Minnesota. When Du Luth first ascended the Brule River, he wrote:

"In June, 1680, not having been satisfied with having made my exploration by land, I took two canoes, with a savage who was my interpreter, and four Frenchmen, to seek a means of making it by water. For this purpose I entered into a river which has its mouth eight leagues from the extremity of Lake Superior on the south side, where after having cut down some trees and broken through about one hundred beaver dams, I went up the said river, and then made a carry of one-half league to reach a lake, which emptied into a fine river, which brought me to the Mississippi."

Du Luth must have been a "just the facts" sort of man. If I had been forced to break through a hundred beaver dams, I might have written a bit more on the topic. But I'm sure the air around those beaver dams in 1680 rang with many a French curse, despite the bare-bones narrative.

Of course, beaver dams do serve a purpose. By raising the water level three feet or more, a beaver accomplishes three major objectives:

1. It gains access to more trees and shrubs to feed on, and it has enough water to float the branches back to its lodge. According to one source, an average beaver family knocks down hundreds of trees in a year. Over a number of years, it may denude the riverbanks. Access to the interior then becomes essential.

2. It ensures that the water is deep enough to permit swimming under the ice in winter. Once the ice is formed, beavers are said to poke holes in the dam to drop the water level a bit. This leaves an air space between the often suspended ice and the flowing water.

3. It creates safer, deeper waters. Beavers are expert swimmers, but they're less than adept if forced to walk on land.

So, from a beaver's viewpoint, building a dam is merely a necessary way of providing for its family, as any self-respecting mammal would do.

214

The beaver's dominance on the Turtle River may soon come to an end. Beaver families eventually eat themselves out of house and home, then must pull up stakes and move to the next river or lake thick with deciduous softwoods that are ripe for the chewing. They leave behind drained meadows that are usually quite fertile, thanks to the sediments that have collected over the years. These grasslands were often chosen as the finest sites for farms by the original settlers. One Canadian researcher estimated that 30 to 50 percent of all the streams he had seen were directly affected by beavers. Within the animal kingdom, only the beaver and man can bring about large-scale topographic changes over time.

215

Freshwater Sponges

Between the dam (spelling may be incorrect) portages, we saw freshwater sponges attached to many rocks in the river. Virtually everyone was surprised to learn that the northwoods has sponges, because we usually associate them with oceans. Freshwater sponges are actually relatively common, if not abundant, in most of our streams and lakes.

For me, identification of sponges as a group is most easily accomplished through my nose. They have a uniquely bitter smell. Visually, they are dark green and very plantlike, although they are in fact multicellular animals. Sponges lack a digestive system, a nervous system, and a circulatory system; they have no organs of any kind, and even their tissues aren't well-defined, so they don't look much like an animal to the average eye. According to one source, they look most like a perforated sac. This description would be a good insult to use on someone who's not in your current favor. You'll need a microscope to do any justice to the sponges' organization, as well as a microbiologist to interpret the view.

Sponges digest food by filtering particles out of water that passes through successively narrower chambers in their bodies. They reproduce sexually as well as asexually, and they have a skeleton composed of mineral matter. Sponges look bright green because of the chlorophyll in the algae that is often symbiotically attached to sponges. This gives sponges the appearance of plants.

Few animals feed on sponges, though snails appear to dine on them at times. Their major effect in the food chain of a lake or stream may involve limiting the availability of other plants and animals that might be present if the sponges weren't.

Caddis Flies

One August night my family and I camped on Crystal Lake. In the early morning, we explored the beach and saw hundreds of tiny "sticks" walking in about an inch or two of water. They were a species of caddis fly—in this case, the aquatic larvae of the adult flying insect.

Caddis flies are absolutely remarkable. They build a tubelike case around themselves out of tiny stones, sticks, or leaves that they cement together. They walk around carrying their "homes" and foraging for food in the water. In a way, they are the hobos of the aquatic insect world, toting their homes along with them wherever they go.

Fish love them, so the caddis flies often attach themselves to the underside of rocks for concealment. Next time you're in a rocky riffle area on a river, turn over a few larger stones and see if you can find caddis fly larvae hanging onto the stones.

Timber Wolf Recovery

A new timber wolf pack was discovered in the summer of 1995, southwest of the Willow Flowage in Oneida County. The pack was believed to contain two adults and possibly two to four pups. It was christened the "Little Rice River Pack," and its range appears to border the range of the Boot Jack Pack, which currently lives northwest of the flowage.

As of 1996, nearly 100 wolves live in Wisconsin. For those who might be concerned about potential depletion of deer herds, an individual wolf takes about 14 deer annually, less than a drop in the bucket considering that Wisconsin's herd population is estimated at 1,500,000.

Saving Animals:
Just More Human Interference?

I attended a talk given by Dave and Jacquie DeBauche from the Northwoods Wildlife Center in Minocqua. The DeBauches described how the NWC goes about rehabilitating injured wildlife. Many of their slides were rather graphic, and appropriately so. The process is not simple, and it represents more guts than glory. Some fishermen and hunters need to see these slides, so they will improve their fishing and hunting standards. Fish hooks impaled in stomachs, fish line wrapped around legs and bills, lead sinkers in digestive tracts, shotgun pellets lodged in wings—all are disturbing to see.

The NWC saves about as many animals as it loses, which is actually a high success rate. Some folks believe we should leave injured animals to fend for themselves as nature intended, but the vast majority of injuries that Jacquie and Dave deal with are human-inflicted. Ma Nature never intended that fishermen would cut their hooks, letting them drift and sink; nor did she expect fish and birds to eat lead sinkers and steel shot. The survival of the fittest perspective, while credible in less human-dominated environs, has its shortcomings here. More power to the NWC for their rehabilitative efforts and their concurrent educational programs.

217

Early Frosts

It was 36°F at our home on August 3, 1994. Our cucumbers were nipped, and I heard reports of frost in the bogs. We had frosts on August 12 and 13, 1993. Our last frost of "spring" occurred on June 21 of that year, so we had a 52-day growing season. Consider that most of those 52 days were below average in temperature and often very cool at night; the end result was a gardener's nightmare on Manitowish Street. Our garden was mercifully laid to rest on August 12, and we were relieved to see it put out of its misery.

In the northwoods, one can expect a hard frost between mid- and late August, and our insect-eating birds know that. Many songbird species begin migration movements in mid-August, such as purple martins, tree and cliff swallows, indigo buntings, chipping sparrows, and warblers including Nashvilles, yellow-rumpeds, redstarts, and ovenbirds. Nevertheless, most of these species will still be represented by hardy individuals into September.

Frost forms on still nights, just as dew does. The cool night air can't hold onto the moisture that evaporated during the day, so the water droplets condense out, much like breathing on a cold windowpane. However, when the temperature dips below 32°F, the dew crystallizes into frost, killing many plants and insects but never enough mosquitoes.

218

The frosts are harbingers of winter. We average 140 days of snow cover in the northwoods, and over half of our Wisconsin winters include one day when the temperature dips below -40°F. We usually experience 90°F+ temperatures at some point during our summers, and this 130-degree seasonal differential is the major limiting factor that determines which flora and fauna can survive here. The record temperatures for the area encompassed by the "northwoods" are -51°F in winter and 112°F in summer. The record snowfall occurred in the Keweenaw Peninsula, where 390 inches fell in one year.

August Musings

I held a blue flower in my hand, probably a wild aster, wondering what its name was, and then thought that human names for natural things are superfluous. Nature does not name them. The important thing is to know this flower, [to] look at its color until the blueness becomes as real as a keynote of music.

-Sally Carrighar

Notes

August 16 to August 31

August Songbirds

"Where have all the birds gone?" Many hikers ask me this in August. The answer is that they're not gone (though many are packing their bags); it's just that the birds don't sing much at this time of the year. Singing serves two major functions—establishing and defending territories, and attracting a mate. These functions virtually end after the mating season, especially during the

> ## August Musings
> *It is not enough to fight for the land; it is even more important to enjoy it.*
> -Edward Abbey

post-nuptial molt, a period when food is plentiful, the energy demands of breeding are over, and the energy demands of migration have not yet begun. Songbirds that defend their territories throughout the year may continue singing, but even they sing less often now than they do during the nesting period.

For you statistic fiends, the record, as far as I know, for the number of songs offered in one day is held by a red-eyed vireo who sang 22,197 songs. For obvious reasons, the red-eyed vireo is also known as the preacher bird.

Migrating Nighthawks

On August 17, 1994, at around 7 p.m., I walked to our car and happened to look up. I saw six nighthawks wheeling low over our house, dipping and darting back and forth, apparently feeding on insects. I watched them work the skies for five minutes—we have a princely trove of insects on any given summer night—then they faded toward the east (upriver) and were gone. Subsequently, Mary Beth

Kolarchek from Manitowish Waters called to say she had just watched 50 or more nighthawks sweeping the air over Little Bohemia's fields along Highway 51. The fields had been mown late that afternoon, which probably stirred up the local insect community. Dave Picard later called to report seeing 80 or so nighthawks that same evening along the shores of Whitefish Lake on the Lac du Flambeau Reservation. A friend of Dave's in Hazelhurst had also seen a flock of falcon-like birds swooping near his home. These, too, were probably night-hawks.

Nighthawks migrate in mid- to late August, gradually working their way down to South America—in fact, all the way to Argentina. There, summer is in progress, the insects are fat, and the living is easy. The birds' seemingly random darting actually imitates rather well the flight patterns of the insects they seek. But the numbers of nighthawks we saw recently are nothing compared to the concentrations that pass through Duluth, Minnesota, during late August. One birder counted 43,690 nighthawks in less than three hours along the shore of Lake Superior!

Some folks wonder why the insect-eating birds have to leave at a time when we still have plenty of insects available for their dining plea-sure. To stay too long is to tempt fate. How close to the edge does one want to go? Nighthawks consume enormous numbers of insects, so staying ahead of insect-killing frosts is only prudent.

Nighthawks are easily identified by their falconlike appearance. Their narrow wings are crooked back at the elbow, and each wing has a broad white band toward its tip.

Hummingbird Migration

Hummingbirds migrate all the way to Central America—one heck of a long distance for a bird that's only three inches long. They have been timed flying at 50 to 60 miles per hour, so they are strong flyers. Hummers can also hover, fly backward, shift sideways, and fly straight up and down, which makes them tough for a predator to catch. Some refer to hummingbirds as "living helicopters."

Because of their small size and all the energy they expend in flight, hummingbirds have the highest metabolism of any warm-blooded vertebrate in the world. Only the shrew comes close to burning up food at an equal rate. The hummingbird's metabolism forces them to refuel—in other words, to eat—almost constantly. When they're migrating, eating is impossible—particularly when they cross the 600 miles of open water over the Gulf of Mexico en route to Central America. So they, like many other migrators, feed heavily before migrating, adding more than 50 percent to their body weight to sustain them in their flight.

How Do Birds Know Where They're Going?

223

Various studies have shed light on how birds navigate so precisely, but the whole process fundamentally remains a mystery. The sun is used as a guide by birds that migrate during the day. But consider the complexity of navigating according to a sun that moves across the sky throughout the day. Consider also that the sun is generally in different places in the sky during the fall migration than it is in spring.

What happens when it's cloudy, and the sun can't be used as a guide? Apparently birds have an internal magnetic compass. One experiment placed magnets on the backs of one group of homing pigeons and nonmagnetic bars on the backs of another group. When released far from home on a cloudy day, five of the seven birds wearing nonmagnetic bars made it home. None of the ones wearing magnets returned, indicating that their navigational abilities were thrown off by the magnets.

Still other birds use major landmarks like rivers, mountains, and lakeshores to guide them. Eagles and hawks use this approach. Specific flyways are well-known; most birds follow obvious landmarks like the Mississippi River or the shorelines of the Great Lakes. If you have never visited Duluth during the fall migration, you owe it to yourself to make the trip. Tens of thousands of raptors fly directly over Duluth, rather than taking the risk of flying over Lake Superior.

Other birds migrate at night, using the stars to guide them. Experiments with songbirds that were brought into a planetarium have demonstrated this. The birds learned to navigate by the planetarium sky. But if the brighter stars were blotted out, they circled randomly or stopped flying altogether. Likewise, birds kept in large outdoor cages retain their sense of migratory direction if the brighter stars are shining, but if a cloud blocks the stars, the birds circle randomly.

Birds also have a fluid-filled organ below their inner ear that senses air pressure, thus functioning like an altimeter. Radar studies have shown that birds maintain a constant altitude at night, when flying through clouds, and over enormous distances.

All in all, birds may be using several of these cues to migrate—perhaps even several at one time. Their extraordinary ability to navigate has been compared to our innate ability to acquire language, each ability serving as a dominant defining trait for the species.

Shrinking Songbird Populations

Forty-four of 62 neotropical bird species, meaning those that summer in northern climates and winter in tropical climates, declined in numbers between 1978 and 1987. Common northwoods birds like northern orioles, scarlet tanagers, wood thrushes, rose-breasted grosbeaks, and ovenbirds are among these species. In fact, 70 percent of the birds in eastern deciduous forests are neotropical migrants. However, the forest nesters are in greatest jeopardy. The primary reasons for their decline are loss of habitat on their wintering and breeding grounds, and the loss of essential staging areas used during migration. Fragmented, patchy forests also make predation from raccoons, skunks, crows, grackles, cowbirds, and house cats an easy matter. Where forests remain intact, these predators don't penetrate into the interior, so the remote nesting sites are protected.

As most people know by now, tropical forests are being cut down at staggering rates, and biologists estimate that clearing one acre of wintering habitat has the same impact as clearing 10 to 15 acres of breeding habitat for certain species.

Many northwoods visitors have commented that there seem to be fewer songbirds present now than in previous summers. I don't know if that is statistically true, but given the data for all North American birds, I wouldn't be surprised.

Gliding South

I watched nighthawks migrating through the Bayfield peninsula one August 21st evening. Their darting, erratic flight certainly represents the flip side of the coin from the large hawks that sail effortlessly on the wind.

How effortless a bird's migration really is can be judged from its "glide performance." Glide performance is the ratio of forward speed to sinking speed, essentially measuring how far forward a bird can go before it enters a crash-and-burn descent. The best ratio would result from an airspeed just above the slowest speed that a bird can maintain without stalling. A monarch butterfly's ratio is 3:1, meaning it goes three feet forward for every one foot it drops. This in turn means it will do a lot of flapping on its way to Mexico. A broad-winged hawk's ratio is around 11:1, allowing it to catch and ride thermals for long distances before it must fly upward on the next thermal. Eagles and vultures have ratios between 14:1 and 18:1, and this can increase to 20:1 in a tailwind. A headwind reduces their efficiency to 5:1, keeping them grounded. For comparison's sake, a modern, high-performance sailplane has a 40:1 ratio, allowing it to glide 40 miles for every one mile of descent.

225

Catching Thermals

In the northern hemisphere, autumn bird migration is tied to the passage of cold fronts out of the west and north. These fronts ensure faster flights, which also create greater energy needs. Birds that fly long distances over water must follow the winds closely. For instance, many shorebirds travel from Nova Scotia over the ocean to the West Indies and South America in one continuous flight—a distance of 2,000 miles or more. This can take them 50 to 80 hours with a tailwind, so they need to know how to locate a tailwind and how to use it.

Birds that fly over land must understand the typical daily cycle of the atmosphere. As the sun heats the earth in the morning, warm air rises. Some areas, like rock faces, absorb heat faster than others. Hot air rises faster from these areas, forming columns of air within which vertical gusts can reach 10 miles per hour. These are called thermal updrafts, and they are strongest from late morning to midafternoon.

Migrating hawks use the thermals to gain altitude, rising and falling at the same rate as the thermals. Most thermals extend no higher than 5,000 to 6,000 feet, and are roughly cylindrical in shape. By late afternoon the heat of the sun has dissipated, and so have the thermals. To locate thermals, look for fluffy cumulus clouds that form at the top of these columns. If you watch the clouds, you'll see that they are in motion.

It's not enough for a bird to master using the wind; it must instinctively understand atmospheric structure, in order to maximize energy savings during its flights. Birds have an acute understanding of winds, and will change their altitude to locate the optimal current. They can gauge wind speed and direction, and they make decisions accordingly.

Wood Ducks and Wild Rice

I canoed into the big marsh above Murray's Landing on the Turtle-Flambeau Flowage in late August of 1994. Inadvertently, I kept flushing dozens of wood ducks hidden in the acres of wild rice. Bruce Bacon, wildlife manager at the Mercer DNR station, tells me that woodies often flock up in large numbers prior to migration. They are also the species of duck most attracted to wild rice, so their presence in the marsh that day makes sense. Large flocks of blackbirds wheeled and settled into the marsh vegetation, too, only to consistently rise up in chorus a few minutes later, then dart like big shadows into other clumps. The way they fly in such a reeling but perfect formation, reacting instantaneously to one another's directional changes, is remarkable. A beaver and I also spent five minutes or so watching one another intently, though it turned its back on me numerous times in the tall grasses along the shoreline, as if to say, "You can go now." When I finally picked up my paddle to move on, two beavers literally leapt from the tall grass into the water. The second beaver had remained invisible to me that whole time. One then surfaced within 15 feet of my canoe, smacking its tail with the concussive force of an iron skillet and making waves that bobbed my canoe. I took the hint and moved on.

Wild Rice

One mid-August Dr. Jim Meeker, a good friend and wild rice expert, led a group of 25 canoeists onto Aurora Lake, a state natural area in Vilas County. The boat landing led down to a dense stand of aquatic plants, which stood lush and tall over the entire lake basin. Many people wondered if the lake was really there, because no open water was evident. The water in Aurora's 94-acre surface area reaches a maximum depth of only four feet, so the lake is actually little more than a broad puddle. However, that puddle supports wild rice from shoreline to shoreline, the rice stems standing well above the level of invading canoes. The only way to get a view of the lake in August is to stand up inside the canoe.

227

Much of the wild rice was in flower that day. Like many plants, wild rice has both male and female flowers on the same plant. The male flowers reside well below the female, and are the first to flower. The female flowers, located at and near the top of the stem, are very subtle. When pollinated, they develop into the rice grains. The flowers blossom over a period of many weeks, so the rice doesn't ripen all at once. Harvesters, from people to ducks, can return repeatedly to gather more rice. Traditionally, wild rice harvest begins the last week of August, though nowadays the start of the harvest season in Wisconsin is determined by the DNR and the tribes. If you wish to harvest wild rice, you must do so from a canoe with nonmechanical tools. Permits must be bought, and are available from the DNR.

Great Blues

Great blue herons impress us with their enormous wingspans and their graceful flights and landings. But why do great blues fly with their necks tucked in, rather than stretching them out like other birds of equal size, such as swans or cranes? Nearly everyone has observed the lightning quickness of a heron when it catches a fish; most have also seen the prelude to these strikes. The bird is a model of patient observation, holding its long beak in a coil not far above the water surface. The speed and strength needed to catch fish in such a manner requires greater neck musculature than is needed by cranes, geese, and swans, which feed slowly and almost entirely on plants and insects. The neck muscles of great blue herons are so substantial that if they flew with their necks stretched out, they would stall, then crash and burn. The aerodynamics just wouldn't work, so they pull their necks in to stabilize their flight mechanics.

Safety in Numbers

Blackbirds are beginning to flock together for their movement south. Red-winged blackbirds, grackles, cowbirds, starlings, and Brewer's blackbirds may be seen together in their roosting areas, or in huge feeding flocks that sometimes number several thousand individuals.

Many species of birds flock together, generally after the nesting season. Why birds are drawn together is little understood, but studies and common sense suggest some potential advantages. Finding new food sources is facilitated when a flock contains many members. Birds in a flock tend to respond quickly to the behavior of their companions, so if one bird dives toward a food source, the others immediately follow.

The ability to sight and avoid predators is enhanced as well. Flocks of starlings close up their ranks ("ball up") when they are pursued by a falcon. The falcon won't dive through the flock, apparently because it fears being injured in the midst of so many birds.

Pileated Woodpeckers

Joanne Reynolds wrote to me describing her observations of two pileated woodpeckers, an adult male and his offspring, that were feeding on suet in her yard. I'll quote her, because I couldn't have written it better. Here's a sample of what she saw: "It's easy to distinguish Father from Son; they both have the red crest and red mustache. Father's crest is slicked back to a swirl on the tip, and his mustache is bright red, looking very clean. Son's crest looks like a 'punker's,' standing up in spikes, and his face looks like a kid's—dirty (but it must be the immature coloration). Father works very hard and very long, eating enormous amounts of suet, with Son by his side, watching. Then Father feeds his Son (who is as big as his Dad), cramming his beak down baby's throat. [It] looks like he's stuffing a sausage as he crams and crams that suet into baby. Son is now so full he can't close his mouth."

Joanne and her husband have lived south of Hazelhurst since 1979. During that time, she has identified 86 species of birds on their three acres of land, which demonstrates that backyard feeding and birdwatching can be an oasis of enjoyment.

Pishing

229

Speaking of birds, this is an excellent time of year to be out "pishing." The young of the year seem particularly curious as to the source of such a noise, and I've had some wonderful experiences in August with chickadees and nuthatches that flew in very close and stayed awhile. I've even had a black-throated blue warbler spend several minutes circling all around me in chest-high branches, curious about the source of all the pishing. Strangest of all may have been the ruby-throated hummingbird that responded to my pishing while I was leading a hike on the Star Lake Trail. A hummer in the midst of a red pine plantation is a bit of an oddity.

One pishes by pursing one's lips and saying "pissshhhh" in a drawn-out manner. Many birds come quite close out of curiosity, because the sound is apparently somewhat similar to the call notes that many of them produce. On the other hand, many birds completely ignore such efforts, and a person can look very strange to a passerby while making these odd noises in the woods for no apparent reason. I speak from experience.

Red-Headed Woodpeckers

Several people told me they had seen red-headed woodpeckers in the area in August of 1995. Red-headeds seem to love acorns. Since oak habitat is not as abundant in this sandy area of the northwoods as it is in central and southern Wisconsin, these birds are uncommon hereabouts. The only tree-sized oak in our area is the northern red oak.

Author and bird expert Sam Robbins notes that red-headeds are often seen foraging along roadsides for insects in July and August, so maybe that explains some of the sightings. Red-headeds apparently prefer open groves of large trees, old fields and pastures, prairies, small towns, and cut-over or burned-over forest slash—in other words, open habitats that are in relatively short supply in northern Wisconsin, except for the forest slash habitat. Starlings also contribute to the red-headed's relative northern rarity by stealing their nest holes.

Few birds are more brightly marked. Their brilliant red heads, necks, and throats contrast strongly with their dark backs and snowy-white underparts. In flight and while perched, their white rumps and white inner wing patches are highly distinctive.

Blooming Flowers

Flowers that are still in bloom at this late date include:

Asters	Tall buttercup
Goldenrod	Bush clover
Woodland sunflower	Tansy
Purple loosestrife	Water lilies
Flowering spurge	Black-eyed Susans
Milkweed	Joe-pye weed
Purple knapweed	Turtle head
Hawkweed	Jewelweed

Many of these flowers have been in bloom for several months now, and it's curious that these plants hold their blossoms while the vast majority of our northern flowers bloom and die back rapidly.

Old-growth

A three-day conference on the management of old-growth ecosystems was held in August of 1993 in Land O'Lakes, sponsored by the Ottawa National Forest, the Upper Great Lakes Biological Committee, and the Sigurd Olson Environmental Institute. The conference brought together over 100 professionals from Michigan, Minnesota, Wisconsin, and Ontario. One of the highlights from the proceedings was the long-term commitment made by the USDA-Forest Service and the Ottawa National Forest to obtaining, maintaining, and restoring a viable old-growth component that encompasses northern hardwood timber types in the Great Lakes Region. The Ottawa has set goals for an increase in the amount of old-growth stands, both by maintaining old-growth remnants and by timber management geared to achieving old-growth conditions in the future from cut-over lands.

The Minnesota DNR developed guidelines in 1990 for defining and managing old-growth forests. Some 24,000 acres have been identified; these tracts will be evaluated and ranked for their ecological significance, and may be earmarked for protection.

Two papers were presented on aspects of hemlock-dominated, old-growth forests in northern Wisconsin and western Upper Michigan. I have often wondered how long it takes certain tree species to decay after they're downed. In one paper, the age of downed "very punky" hemlock logs was found to be 52 to 62 years old, but the total decay was estimated to take 200 years!

The Wisconsin DNR estimates that only 20,000 acres, or 0.17 percent, of northern hemlock-hardwood forests retain old-growth characteristics, out of the original 11.7 million acres. According to estimates, aspen comprised 1 percent of our original forest; it now comprises 26 percent of our forests. Add to this the fact that 97 percent of Wisconsin's forest is within one mile of a maintained road (the remaining 3 percent is nearly all bog or swamp land). As a result, virtually all land in Wisconsin is disturbed, and appears as a patchwork quilt of habitats. These statistics become important when discussing the future of species that require large tracts of undisturbed land. We have dramatically increased the presence of species that enjoy forest edge habitat (deer are an excellent example), while dramatically decreasing the presence of those that require large stands of undisturbed habitat.

Deer and Yew

Deer numbers are so high in Wisconsin that the Canada yew, a once-common ground layer conifer loved by deer, is found primarily in three places in the state: on rocky outcrops that are inaccessible to deer; on the Menominee Indian Reservation, where deer are subject to year-round hunting; and on a few of the Apostle Islands, where no deer live. Scattered individual stands of yew may be found elsewhere, but they are generally browsed to ground level.

Hemlock and northern white cedar have also suffered significant declines. Other species favored by deer are suspected to be in decline, including showy and yellow lady slipper orchids, purple fringed orchid, and large-flowered trillium.

To alleviate the threat that deer may browse hemlocks into near annihilation, large blocks of old growth are required, because deer will travel an average of five miles annually in order to feed, according to a U.S. Forest Service estimate. Given their range, deer can easily access the interior of small patches of old growth.

Oak Galls

You may have noticed rounded, papery growths appearing on oak leaves and stems in August. The growths look much like a ping-pong ball, but are tan in color. The balls are oak-apple galls, caused by one family of wasps that bites the leaves, inducing the oaks to form these tumorlike tissues. Galls protect developing larvae, which are often found inside the galls. But just as frequently, the larvae have been eaten, and the gall stands empty.

Evolution has apparently favored gall-producing insects. Nearly 800 species use oaks alone as their hosts. Over half of all plant families are parasitized by gall-makers. A total of 1,440 species of flies, beetles, butterflies and moths, aphids, and wasps do the damage.

Prescribed Burning

On August 25, our one 90° F. day during the summer of 1993, we were returning from a swim on Crystal Lake when we saw a huge smoke plume in the sky to the west. Our first thought (and hope) was that the DNR was conducting a burnover on Powell Marsh, and a subsequent phone call confirmed it. Chet Botwinski, DNR wildlife manager in Woodruff, was at work with his fire crew, trying to knock back the invading successional vegetation in the marsh. Chet only gets conditions suitable for burning one out of every three years. Late summer is the only time the marsh is dry enough to burn, but sometimes conditions are too dry or too wet, and he's forced to wait until next year. The crew was able to burn about 300 acres in 1993; in that area, the grasses and sedges will increase, providing excellent nesting habitat. In the meantime, the succulent new sprouts will offer migration stopover habitat for an assortment of waterfowl.

233

Canada geese begin returning in late August, and the largest concentrations are usually seen in early October. However, the timing varies every year, depending on weather factors. Between 500 and 5,000 geese may stop over in a given year. Historically, snow geese and blue geese have also used Powell, but they have become increasingly rare in the last decade. The migration route has for some reason moved west. Snows and blues are now common in the Dakotas.

The Powell would be better served biologically if we referred to it as a bog, not a marsh. Its ground layer is dominated by sphagnum moss and leatherleaf, and neither species should be mistaken for a wildlife magnet. The greater the marshlike character, the better the overall waterfowl habitat. Fire is the tool needed to create and maintain that character. The efforts of the Woodruff DNR to manage Powell began back in the mid-1950s, a program that was one of the first attempts in North America to manage an enormous, sedge-leatherleaf bog. The 1,300-acre wildlife refuge (within the 12,800-acre marsh) is closed to foot traffic as of September 1 each year.

Healing Asters

One recent weekend, I hiked along a trail near my home, passing an area where birch and aspen had been clear-cut the previous year. At this time last year, the site was an ugly scar. Now it is carpeted with white and purple asters, which are pioneering and healing the ground layer. Aspen will soon take off again and dominate the stand, shading out these particular asters, but in the meantime the asters are performing a welcome aesthetic and ecological service.

Jewelweed

Jewelweed is abundant in low areas. Its reputation as a cure for poison ivy was confirmed by a gentleman on one of my hikes. He apparently crushed the leaves, applied them to his rash, and watched the rash disappear in a short period of time. It might be worth a try.

234

Leaf Change

Some leaves, like sumac and red maple, are often already beginning to change by late August. Most folks think this is a response to the coming colder weather, but it's really just as much a response to coming drought. Winter is a desert environment for most plants, and our hardwood trees respond to this water crisis by dropping their leaves. Leaves transpire enormous volumes of water back into the air; one very practical way to conserve water is to eliminate whatever "wastes" the precious fluid.

Evergreen trees beat this system because they have evolved needles. Needles are leaves, but their shape ensures that they will lose a minimal amount of water. They are also coated with a waxy material, which acts further to prevent water from escaping. Only our tamarack loses its needles in the fall.

By the way, all conifers lose their needles. They do it gradually over several years, rather than losing their entire foliage cover every fall. If you need evidence, then you've never raked a yard full of conifers in the spring.

Closing Up Shop

Aldo Leopold once wrote: "During every week from April to September there are, on the average, ten wild plants coming into first bloom. No man can heed all of these anniversaries; no man can ignore all of them . . . Tell me of what plant birthday a man takes notice, and

I shall tell you a good deal about his vocation, his hobbies, his hay fever, and the general level of his ecological education."

It's sad to say, but these flower anniversaries have nearly ended at this time of year. Only a few shaded woodland flowers remain, among them rattlesnake plantain, wintergreen, and Indian pipe. However, the roadsides still blaze in a lavish array of flowers. Many of these are foreigners/nonnatives/aliens, stigmatized for their immigrant status. The European immigrants include purple knapweed, yarrow, mullein, Queen Anne's lace, bladder campion, clovers, tansy, hawkweed, and birdfoot trefoil. Asian immigrants include butter-and-eggs and oxeye daisy.

235

Some roadside plants are native, including evening primrose, black-eyed Susan, daisy fleabane, fireweed, goldenrod, wild bergamot, asters, and sunflowers.

It's certainly ironic that most botanists regard floral pilgrims with disdain, even though we celebrate our own pilgrimage to North America. Many nonnative plants, however, earn their scorn. They outcompete our native flora, while providing less food, nesting, and cover habitat for native wildlife.

Hazelnuts

Hazelnuts are usually rather difficult to find, due either to poor fruiting years or aggressive feasting by squirrels, chipmunks, deer, grouse, and others. Two species of hazelnut occur in Wisconsin, though the beaked hazelnut is most common in the northwoods. Each beaked hazelnut is, appropriately enough, fluted with a long beak. It's also covered with spiny hairs that can lodge in your skin and may become irritating, so handle them carefully. The nutrient content of the nuts is high—25 percent protein and 60 percent fat. Hazelnuts belong to the same family as the commercial filberts, so they're good eating.

In our sandy pine woods, hazelnuts are easily the most common shrub in the understory. Look for their characteristic, double-toothed leaves, and a brushy growth from four to twelve feet high. The leaves will turn a buttery yellow in September. The male catkins also form at that time, hanging on over the winter and awaiting the female flowers, which blossom in April—often while the snow is still on the ground.

Mummies and Spruce

While reading a book called *Red Oaks and Black Birches* by Rebecca Rupp, I came across an extraordinary passage relating to spruce trees. You may know that spruce is commonly used today for paper pulp, but in the mid-1800s, prior to the invention of mass-produced paper, we Americans printed our news primarily on paper made of cotton or linen rags. For you trivia hounds, the first *New York Times* ever printed from all-wood paper pulp appeared on August 23, 1873. At any rate, as you might expect, cotton rags were at a premium for quite some time. A national rag collecting program was ongoing, because our hunger for news could never be matched by our stockpile of rags.

Scientists worked for years trying to find an alternative fiber for paper making. One Englishman suggested using asbestos, while others tried using such items as potatoes, cattails, straw, dandelion roots, and caterpillar cocoons. Those options were strange enough, but the solution I found most astonishing was proposed by Dr. Isaiah Deck of New York. In 1840, Dr. Deck suggested that we import Egyptian mummies, each of which contained up to 30 pounds of linen wrapping. Apparently Deck's strong suit was not math, given that some 13,500,000 mummies would have been needed each year to meet the rag requirements of the 800 American paper mills in existence at the time.

One would expect Deck's scheme to be greeted with laughter, but one American paper maker, I. Augustus Stanwood of Gardiner, Maine, actually put Deck's idea into motion in the 1860s, importing shiploads of mummies that were converted into brown wrapping paper. Grocers and butchers wrapped their goods in this paper, meaning that Civil War-era housewives prepared many a meal that came home in ancient Egyptian clothing.

We weren't the only ones who saw money in mummies. The Egyptian railroad used whole mummies as its sole source of fuel, though an abacus was probably not required to calculate the number of trains running through Egypt in the mid-1800s.

In the long run, industrialists gave up the ghost, as it were, turning to wood pulp to convey the news of the day. The first wood-grinder for the making of paper pulp was used near Stockbridge, Massachusetts, by Albrecht Pagenstecher. His paper was considered inferior, but the price and the ease of printing turned the tide. I suspect that the term "page" was coined in Pagenstecher's honor, though I have no proof.

Today we use spruce, among other trees, for producing our paper. To identify spruce, simply take a needle from a conifer. If it's not part of a bundle of needles, as you'll see in pines and tamarack, and if it rolls in your fingers, you have a spruce. The needles are actually four-sided, bristling out from the twig like a dense bottlebrush. Black spruce needles are only about half as long as those that grow on white spruce. The black spruce needles measure two-tenths to six-tenths of an inch, while the white spruce needles are seven-tenths to niné-tenths of an inch long.

237

Purples

Late-summer wildflowers seem to specialize in shades of purple. In bloom now are colonies of exuberant purple flowers like wild bergamot, Joe-pye weed, marsh milkweed, pickerelweed, fireweed, blue vervain, steeplebush, and spotted knapweed—along with some purple asters and cow-vetch.

Be sure to crush and smell the leaves of wild bergamot, a member of the mint family. Steep the leaves and flowerheads in hot water for 10 minutes to make an aromatic tea.

I find blue vervain particularly beautiful. It flowers in a sort of candelabra affair, the tall stems rising just above the wetland grasses and sedges along riverbanks.

Historical Plant Uses

I conducted a hike one August on historical plant uses, and discovered that there was a great deal of interest in the subject. I recommend two historical books on Chippewa plant uses: *Chippewa Customs* and *How Indians Use Wild Plants for Food, Medicine and*

Crafts, both written by Frances Densmore. She wrote 20 books and 200 articles on American Indians that lived from Florida to Alaska, but her longest research took place between 1907 and the late 1920s, when she studied the Chippewas. These two books are indispensable.

A more recently written book, *Plants Used by the Great Lakes Ojibwa* by Jim Meeker, Joan Elias, and John Heim, thoroughly summarizes historical uses of plants by the Chippewa. For a copy, write or call GLIFWC (Great Lakes Indian Fish and Wildlife Commission), PO Box 9, Odanah, WI 54861.

The Goose Lady

Carol Hanneman, who lives in Mercer, has fed ducks and geese on her Echo Lake property for years. Her reputation among waterfowl must be impeccable, given the number of feathered friends that frequent her yard. Her popularity should be at its zenith after a dramatic duckling rescue that occurred one recent August.

In the early morning, Carol heard ducks frantically calling from the shallow end of Echo Lake, off her shoreline. She looked out and saw that one duckling from a family of 12 seemed to be desperately trying to fly, but couldn't get off the water. "Musky" went through her mind as a possible cause. She raced down to her boat in her pajamas and tried to get the motor going. It wouldn't start, so she slipped the oars into the oarlocks and began rowing, always straining to see over her shoulder whether the duck was still above water. The little mallard kept fighting. When Carol pulled up next to it, she looked down into the eyes of a large snapping turtle, which had clamped one of the duckling's feet in its mouth. She grabbed the duckling with one hand and began karate chopping the turtle on its beaked nose with her other hand. Eventually the turtle realized it was outmatched, and let loose.

The duckling was panicked and bleeding rather badly, so Carol held it on her lap with one hand and rowed back with her other hand, trying to keep a straight course. I expect she was quite a sight in her pajamas, blood all over her, a duck flailing in her hand, rowing first with one hand and then the other in order to return to her dock. A just-upon-the-scene observer might well have wondered about the crazy lady in her pj's, but anyone who knows Carol and her love of ducks and geese wouldn't have blinked an eye. She bandaged the duckling up, kept it in her home for a day or two to help the wound heal, then released it back to its family. It's all in a day's work for "the goose lady."

Otters

Few mammals combine beauty and personality in so interesting a package as river otters. I listened one evening to a biologist discuss her Ph.D. dissertation on otters, and I came away with these facts: $\underline{239}$

•Only 22 percent of an otter's diet is comprised of game fish, even if the otter lives on a trout stream. If trout are taken, they are usually in the six- to eight-inch class. So don't blame otters for your lack of success on the local trout stream.

•Females breed soon after giving birth in March or April, but egg development doesn't begin until December or January. This is called "delayed implantation," a strategy used by black bears as well.

•If you're unsure whether you're seeing a beaver or an otter swimming, note the swimming style. Beavers swim right at the surface, while otters tend to dip along under the surface as they swim.

•I used to think the piles of empty clam shells I commonly see along the Manitowish River were the work of otters. Apparently not. Muskrats are the most likely culprits.

•Otters are extremely social, or playful. In fact, play is the most frequent interaction that occurs between river otters.

Flying Squirrels

One August just before dusk, Ada Karow from Lac du Flambeau watched her wren birdhouse start shaking with activity, and eventually a flying squirrel emerged. Since then, she and her husband have watched several more enter, with similar house-shaking consequences. Neither Ada nor I are willing to venture a guess as to what's going on in there.

Orb Weavers

If you drive along wetlands on a late August morning with the sun new to the day, you will see hundreds if not thousands of glistening orb spider webs. If you are an early riser, you could watch the many species that build their webs at dawn, although a few other species build later in the morning or early in the evening. Many orb spinners create a new web almost every morning, keeping the main foundation lines intact but laying down new radii and spirals.

Orb weavers have very poor vision, experiencing the world mainly as a series of web vibrations. However, they're fine-tuned enough to easily distinguish between a human wiggling a stick in the silken threads and the struggles of an insect that's trapped in the lines.

How do spiders produce such remarkably symmetrical webs? They make measurements as they probe along the web with their legs. One naturalist suggests testing this hypothesis by removing one front leg (out of a total of eight) with a tweezers, and observing changes in the ensuing web structure. This seems a bit extreme, so I think I'll just take his word for it.

Here's a tip for photographers. Pat some cornstarch through a cloth to produce a powdery cloud that will settle on the sticky web, highlighting the strands.

Sexy Clams

For years, I have noticed sizable clam populations in the sandy riverbeds of our area. One thought led to another, so it eventually seemed natural and only slightly demented to want to know how clams reproduce. They don't seem to have the right reproductive parts to reproduce like the rest of us. I've since learned that, instead of copulating, male clams release sperm into the water, depending on water currents to deliver their sperm to waiting females, which draw the sperm in as they filter-feed in the water.

The female may produce astounding numbers of eggs. One female of the species known as the fragile scale shell generates about five million fertile eggs each year. The fertilized eggs, known as glochidia, are released into a river or lake in tiny bags containing 50 to 100. The packets are often quite colorful, attracting the attention of fish. When a fish bites into one, the glochidia stick in its gills, parasitizing the fish without harming it. Several weeks later the infant clams, now the size of pinheads, drop off the gills into the current. They are carried away but ultimately rest on the bottom where moving water brings them food to filter, and the process of maturing into an adult begins.

Evil Spirit?

My family and I camped one night in northeastern Minnesota, at a backpackers-only camping area along the Manitou River in the George Crosby Manitou State Forest. The native people called the Manitou River the Manidowish—the same name given to the Manitowish River in northern Wisconsin. We were pleased to see a definition for Manidowish that differed from "evil spirit," which is the definition we've heard in this area. On the Superior North Shore, Manidowish simply meant "spirit," a reference to the heavy mists that often cloak the river at the falls, creating an ethereal, ghostly impression. Mary and I wonder if that imagery applies equally well to the river we live on which, while it offers no cascading drops that form mist, instead has tunnels of fog along it nearly every morning in August and September as nighttime air temperatures drop well below water temperatures. We find nothing but beauty along the Manitowish, and we have never understood how "evil" could apply to this quiet, subtle river.

241

Night Sky Observations

August is a good month for observing the summer triangle, a group of three bright stars that rise high in the eastern sky and have long been used for navigation. Each star is part of a separate constellation, and the formation of such stars into an unofficial but recognizable grouping is called an asterism. The triangle consists of Vega in Lyra, Altair in Aquila, and Deneb in Cygnus, each the brightest star of its respective constellation. Deneb is the highest of the three stars in the southeastern sky; Altair is directly beneath it but much lower; Vega is to the right and a bit down from Deneb. Among the three, Vega is the beacon. Altair is about one-third as bright, while Deneb's relative brightness falls halfway between the two.

Deneb is actually far larger than the other two stars and about 60,000 times more luminous than our sun, but because it is 1,600 light years away, it appears modest to us. Though it's considerably less luminous than Deneb, Vega is situated just 27 light years away, so it achieves the greatest magnitude of the three.

What we perceive as the magnitude of a star is dependent on both its luminosity and its distance from earth. If all stars were located the same distance from us (32.6 light years for the purposes of this comparison), the sun would only be a +4.8 magnitude. Deneb would blaze at -7.2, making it bright enough to be seen during the daytime and 10 times brighter than Venus, which is normally the brightest "star" in our sky.

Stalking Versus Still-Watching

In the natural world, learning to stop, sit still, watch, listen, and learn is something I still struggle with. I tend to stalk the experience, rather than letting it come to me. This approach could be filed in the "not smart" folder. "To carry yourself forward and experience myriad things is delusion," according to the Zen master Dogan. "But myriad things coming forth and experiencing themselves is awakening."

Blue Moon

If two full moons occur in one calendar month, the second is called a blue moon. The most recent occurrence of two full moons within one month happened in June of 1996; the previous blue moon materialized in 1990. If you use the expression "once in a blue moon," be aware that the phenomenon is not as rare as you might think.

An August full moon reminded me of a passage from *Watership Down*, written by Richard Adams: "We take daylight for granted. But moonlight is another matter . . . We need daylight and to that extent it is utilitarian, but moonlight we do not need. When it comes, it serves no necessity. It transforms. It falls upon banks and the grass, separating one long blade from another; turning a drift of brown, frosted leaves from a single heap to innumerable flashing fragments . . . In moonlight, two acres of coarse bent grass, undulant and ankle deep, appear like a bay of waves."

Getting Dark

Every year about this time, I look at my watch one evening and say, "My God! The sun's already down!" The summer is becoming three to four minutes shorter every day. In fact, the sun will rise on September 1 at 6:18 a.m., setting at 7:36 p.m., which gives us little more than 13 hours of sunlight. By September 26, we'll have 12 hours of light and 12 hours of darkness. We're on our way toward December's winter solstice, when the sun will grace us for only eight hours and 40 minutes.

243

Sightings

Look for wild cranberries in the bogs. Most snake and turtle eggs have hatched. The fruits of spotted jewelweed, or touch-me-not, are ripening. If you touch the pods, they often explode, sending seeds flying three or four feet. Horned bladderworts have been in flower since early August on bog lakes, and their smell is rich and strong, almost like a jasmine incense. Crows are flocking, as are blackbirds; fawns have lost their spots; young muskrats and grouse are starting their fall shuffles to new habitats. And if you haven't split your wood yet, you better get moving.

Declining Amphibian Populations

According to a 1996 update in Wisconsin Natural Resources magazine, one of the reasons for the decline of frog populations is habitat fragmentation. When development isolates wetlands from surrounding woodlands and other wetlands, frogs have difficulty migrating from one site to another. One University of Wisconsin study showed that, in wetlands located more than 175 yards from a woods, no spring peepers existed. By contrast, peepers sang at 60 percent of the wetlands that were connected to a woods.

Frogs must breed in wetlands, but many species then migrate to upland forests, where they live out the rest of the summer. If the migration must cover hot, dry areas, the frogs may not survive.

Rivers

For many summers I, my family, visitors, and locals alike have paddled together sections of the five major rivers in this area—the Wisconsin, the Manitowish, the Bear, the Turtle, and the Trout. These rivers formed a spiderwork of trails for the native people to follow, and I believe many of the most remarkable northwoods experiences today can still be found on these rivers. Many writers have tried to capture the essence of traveling with a river. Here are a few:

"Who hears the rippling of rivers will not utterly despair of anything."

—Henry David Thoreau

"If there is magic in the world, it is in rivers."

—Loren Eisely

"The study of rivers is not a matter of rivers, but of the human heart."

—Tanaka Shozo

Soon the rivers of August will become the rivers of September, flowing through the color burst of autumn toward the first ice-skim of November. Join the water on its travels, see what it sees, touch what it touches. Paddle, drift, hike, climb, watch, smell the last smells of this summer. Be a part of as much of the natural world as you can—what better way could you spend your life?

August Musings

The true test of a man is how well he balances drive and restraint. . . That task is much on our minds when we go to the woods. We call it recreation, and the space and solitude at first tempt us to exercise the kinds of power we covet in the city; noise, violence, and speed. But given time, we discover silence and stillness. Those who get the scent of gasoline out of their noses and the sounds of commerce out of their ears find much more in nature than analogues of urban power. In time, we find that we can get along without the baggage of the city. We learn that we can sleep out under stars in comfort, that mosquito bites merely itch, that the dampness of dawn passes, and that we can act knowingly and joyously, independent of the edicts and government or manufactured enthusiasms of advertising. We find strengths.

-Peter Steinhart

245

Selected Bibliography

Bates, J. 1995. *Trailside Botany*. Pfeifer-Hamilton, Duluth, MN.

Benyus, J. 1989. *Northwoods Wildlife*. NorthWord Press Inc., Minocqua, WI.

Berry, W. 1977. *The Unsettling of America*. Avon Books, New York.

Billington, C. 1943. *Shrubs of Michigan*. Cranbrook Institute of Science, Bloomfield Hills, NY.

Curtis, J. 1959. *Vegetation of Wisconsin*. University of Wisconsin Press, Madison, WI.

Daniel, G., and Sullivan, J. 1981. *A Sierra Club Naturalist's Guide to the North Woods of Michigan, Wisconsin, and Minnesota*. Sierra Club Books, San Francisco.

Densmore, F. 1974. *How Indians Use Wild Plants for Food, Medicine and Crafts*. Dover Publishing, New York.

Densmore, F. 1979. *Chippewa Customs*. Minnesota Historical Society Press, St. Paul, MN.

Dickinson, T. 1983. *Night Watch*. Camden House Publishing, Camden East, Ontario.

Dunn, G. 1996. *Insects of the Great Lakes Region*. The University of Michigan Press, Ann Arbor, MI.

Dunne, P., Sibley, D., Sutton, C. 1988. *Hawks in Flight*. Houghton Mifflin Co., Boston.

Durant, M. 1976. *Who Named the Daisy? Who Named the Rose?* Congdon and Weed, New York.

Eastman, J. 1992. *The Book of Forest and Thicket*. Stackpole Books, Harrisburg, PA.

Eastman, J. 1995. *The Book of Swamp and Bog*. Stackpole Books, Harrisburg, PA.

Ehrlich, P., Dobkin, D., Wheye, D. 1988. *The Birder's Handbook*. Simon and Schuster, New York.

Erickson, L. 1994. *For the Birds*. Pfeifer-Hamilton, Duluth, MN.

Fassett, N. 1967. *Spring Flora of Wisconsin*. University of Wisconsin Press, Madison, WI.

Halfpenny, J. 1986. *A Field Guide to Mammal Tracking in North America*. Johnson Books, Boulder, CO.

Halfpenny, J., and Ozanne, R. 1989. *Winter, An Ecological Handbook*. Johnson Books, Boulder, CO.

Hamerstrom, Frances. 1980. *Strictly for the Chickens*. The Iowa State University Press, Ames, IA.

247

Houk, R. 1989. *Eastern Wildflowers*. Chronicle Books, San Francisco.

Hubbell, S. 1993. *Broadsides from the Other Orders*. Random House, New York.

Jackson, H. 1961. *Wisconsin Mammals*. University of Wisconsin Press, Madison, WI.

Kappel-Smith, D. 1979. *Wintering*. Little, Brown and Co., Boston.

Kotar, J., Kovach, J., and Locey, C. 1988. *Field Guide to Forest Habitat Types of Northern Wisconsin*. University of Wisconsin-Madison, Madison, WI.

Kricher, J., and Morrison, G. 1988. *A Field Guide to Eastern Forests*. Houghton Mifflin Co., Boston.

Lanner, R. 1990. *Autumn Leaves*. NorthWord Press, Minocqua, WI.

Leopold, A. 1949. *A Sand County Almanac*. Oxford University Press, New York.

Lawrence, G. 1984. *A Field Guide to the Familiar*. Prentice-Hall, Englewood Cliffs, NJ.

Lyons, J., and Jordan, S. 1989. *Walking the Wetlands*. John Wiley and Sons, New York.

Madson, J. 1993. *Tall Grass Prairie*. Falcon Press, Helena, MT.

Martin, A., Zim, H., and Nelson, A. 1951. *American Wildlife and Plants*. Dover Publications, New York.

Newcomb, L. 1977. *Newcomb's Wildflower Guide*. Little, Brown and Co., Boston.

Oliver, M. 1978. *American Primitive*. Little, Brown and Co., Boston.

Oliver, M. 1992. *New and Selected Poems*. Beacon Press, Boston.

Palmer, E., and Fowler, H. 1949. *Fieldbook of Natural History*. McGraw-Hill Book Co., New York.

Peattie, D. 1948. *A Natural History of Trees*. Houghton Mifflin Co., Boston.

Peterson, L. 1977. *A Field Guide to Edible Wild Plants*. Houghton Mifflin Co., Boston.

Pielou, E. 1988. *The World of Northern Evergreens*. Comstock Publishing Associates, Ithaca, NY.

Robbins, S. 1991. *Wisconsin Birdlife*. University of Wisconsin Press, Madison, WI.

Roth, C. 1984. *The Plant Observer's Handbook*. Prentice-Hall, Englewood Cliffs, NJ.

Rupp, R. 1990. *Red Oaks and Black Birches*. Garden Way Publishing, Pownal, VT.

Seno, W., ed. 1985. *Up Country*. Round River Publishing Co., Madison, WI.

Smith, H. 1961. *Michigan Wildflowers*. Cranbrook Institute of Science, Bloomfield Hills, MI.

Stokes, D. and L. 1981. *The Natural History of Wild Shrubs and Vines*. Harper and Row Publishing, New York.

Stokes, D. and L. 1985. *A Guide to Enjoying Wildflowers*. Little, Brown and Co., Boston.

Verch, D. 1988. *Chequamegon Bay Birds*. Dick Verch, Ashland, WI.

Vogt, R. 1981. *Natural History of Amphibians and Reptiles of Wisconsin.* Milwaukee Public Museum, Milwaukee, WI.

Voss, E. 1972. *Michigan Flora, Vol. 1.* Cranbrook Institute of Science and University of Michigan Herbarium, Ann Arbor, MI.

Voss, E. 1985. *Michigan Flora, Vol. 2.* Cranbrook Institute of Science and University of Michigan Herbarium, Ann Arbor, MI.

Weaver, J. 1968. *Prairie Plants and Their Environment.* University of Nebraska Press, Lincoln, NE.

Index

251

Also by John Bates:

Trailside Botany
© 1995, Pfeifer-Hamilton

"Trailside Botany *is concise and presents that blend of science and history often lacking in other guides."*
                    -Howard Meyerson, Grand Rapids, MI Press

"I found it fascinating. . . Bates crafts his language to reflect the beauty he sees in each plant. . . Trailside Botany *is as lively and diverse as a patch of woods."*
                    -Tom Hastings, The Minnesota Volunteer
                    (Minnesota's DNR magazine)

"Trailside Botany *is a perfect addition to any hiker's backpack . . . a natural for everyone who loves the outdoors."*
                    - The Nature Conservancy, Minnesota Chapter

Seasonal Guide to the Natural Year: Minnesota, Michigan, and Wisconsin
© 1997, Fulcrum Publishing

A Northwoods Companion: Fall and Winter
© 1997, Manitowish River Press

Contributing author to:
Harvest Moon: A Wisconsin Outdoor Anthology
© 1993, Lost River Press

Order Form

Telephone: Call (715) 476-2828. Have your Visa or MasterCard ready.
Fax order: (715) 476-2818
E-mail: manitowish@centurytel.net
Postal order: Manitoish River Press, 4245 N Hwy. 47, Mercer, WI 54547.
Website: manitowish.com

Check the following books that you wish to order. You may return any book for a full refund, no questions asked, as long as it is still in good salable condition (in other words, still like new - thank you).

TITLE (BOOKS BY JOHN BATES)	PRICE	QUANTITY	TOTAL
Trailside Botany	$12.95	_____	_____
River Life	$24.95	_____	_____
A Northwoods Companion: Spring and Summer	$14.95	_____	_____
A Northwoods Companion: Fall and Winter	$14.95	_____	_____
Sales Tax: Please add 5.5% for books shipped to Wisconsin addresses			_____
Shipping: Book Rate: $2.50 for the first book, and $1 for each additional book Priority Mail: $4 for first book, $1 for each additional book			_____

TOTAL _____

Payment:
Check _____ Credit Card: Visa _____ Mastercard _____
Card Number:

_____

Name on Card _____ Exp. Date _____

If you would like to receive a copy of the current schedule for Trails North, John Bates' naturalist guide service, please check here _____.

Your Name _____ Street/P.O Box_____

City _____ State _____ Zip_____

Phone_____ Fax _____

E-mail_____